# TERRORISM AND THE POLITICS OF NAMING

Names are not objective, they accrue subjective associations. For example 'Terrorist' has a very different connotation to 'Freedom-fighter'.

This volume assesses the nature, power, role and function of names in global politics and the international media. It seeks the truth beneath the names assigned in an effort to remove the obscurity created by the power of 'the politics of naming' to the reality of the situation. Taking examples from Al-Qaeda, Russia's demonisation of the Chechens, naming in the Israeli-Palestine conflict and other important contemporary debates, *Terrorism and the Politics of Naming* makes a substantial contribution towards elucidating the power of naming in the discourse of conflict.

This book was previously published as a special issue of *Third World Quarterly*.

**Michael Bhatia** is at the Department of Politics and International Relations at the University of Oxford.

# TERRORISM AND THE POLITICS OF NAMING

Edited by
Michael Bhatia

Routledge
Taylor & Francis Group

LONDON AND NEW YORK

First published 2008 by Routledge
2 Park Square, Milton Park, Abingdon, Oxfordshire, OX14 4RN

Simultaneously published in the USA and Canada
by Routledge
711 Third Avenue, New York, NY 10017

First issued in paperback 2014

*Routledge is an imprint of the Taylor & Francis Group, an informa business*

Typeset in Times by KnowledgeWorks Global Limited, Southampton, UK

*British Library Cataloguing in Publication Data*
A catalogue record for this book is available from the British Library

*Library of Congress Cataloging in Publication Data*
A catalog record for this book has been requested

ISBN 13: 978-1-138-87372-8 (pbk)
ISBN 13: 978-0-415-41372-5 (hbk)

# Contents

# Notes on Contributors

**Michael Bhatia** is a 2001 George C Marshall Scholar and doctoral candidate at St Antony's College and the Department of Politics and International Relations, University of Oxford. He has served as a researcher at the Afghanistan Research and Evaluation Unit in Kabul, Afghanistan; as a Scoville Peace Fellow at the Center for Strategic and Budgetary Assessments in Washington, DC; and as a research assistant at the Watson Institute for International Studies, Brown University. He is the author of *War and Intervention: Issues for Contemporary Peace Operations* (2003), and has also worked and researched in East Timor, Kosovo and the Sahrawi refugee camps in the Algerian Sahara.

**James Der Derian** is Professor of Political Science at the University of Massachusetts at Amherst and Professor of International Relations (Research) at Brown University, where he directs the InfoTechWarPeace Project (www.infopeace.org). He has been a visiting scholar at the Universities of Southern California, MIT, Harvard and Oxford, and at the Institute for Advanced Study at Princeton. He is the author of *Virtuous War: Mapping the Military – Industrial – Media – Entertainment Network* (2001), *On Diplomacy: A Genealogy of Western Estrangement* (1987) and *Antidiplomacy: Spies, Terror, Speed, and War* (1992); editor of *International Theory: Critical Investigations* (1995) and *The Virilio Reader* (1998); and co-editor with Michael Shapiro of *International/Intertextual Relations: Postmodern Readings of World Politics* (1989).

**Christina Hellmich** is a 2003 Leverhulme Scholar and doctoral candidate in Middle East Studies at Oxford University. She holds graduate degrees in international relations and oriental studies from the University of Oxford and University of St Andrews and is currently pursuing medical training at the University of Bochum, Germany. During extended fieldwork in Yemen she analysed the role of Islamic preaching as a medium for the communication of Islamic fundamentalism. Her doctoral thesis examines the impact of Islam and tradition on women's comprehensive health care.

**Robert L Ivie** is Professor of Communication and Culture at Indiana University, Bloomington, and a member of the faculties of American Studies, Cultural Studies and Myth Studies. He is the founding editor of *Communication and Critical/Cultural Studies*. He recently completed a book manuscript on *Democracy and America's War on Terror*, and is co-author of

*Cold War Rhetoric: Strategy, Metaphor, and Ideology* (1997) and *Congress Declares War: Rhetoric, Leadership, and Partisanship in the Early Republic* (1983).

**Michael J Schroeder** is an independent scholar who received his PhD in History at the University of Michigan in 1993. He has taught US and Latin American history at the University of Michigan-Flint and at Eastern Michigan University. He was awarded an Honorable Mention Prize at the 1997 Conference on Latin American History for his article 'Horse thieves to rebels to dogs', (*Journal of Latin American Studies*, October 1996); and is currently completing a book manuscript, *The Sandino Rebellion: Tragedy and Redemption in the Mountains of Northern Nicaragua, 1926–1934*.

**Suthaharan Nadarajah** is a doctoral candidate in the Department of Politics, School of Oriental and African Studies, University of London. His research explores the international system as a socialising and subject producing device, using the conflict in Sri Lanka as a case study. **Dhananjayan Sriskandarajah** is a doctoral student in the School of Geography and the Environment, University of Oxford. His research examines the political economy of ethno-political conflict in several developing countries, including Sri Lanka.

**John Russell** is a Senior Lecturer in Peace Studies at the University of Bradford, where he previously served as the Head of the Department of Languages and European Studies. With expertise in Russian and terrorism studies, he has lectured widely and has had a number of articles published on the Russo-Chechen wars. In 2003 he was called as an expert witness for the defence in the extradition proceedings brought by the Russian government against one of the leaders of the Chechen resistance, Akhmed Zakayev. He is currently working on separate books about this trial and the war in Chechnya.

**James McDougall** is an Assistant Professor in the History Department at Princeton University. Previously he held a Leverhulme Trust research fellowship at the Middle East Centre of St Antony's College, Oxford. His publications include *Nation, Society and Culture in North Africa* (2003), *Colonial Words: History and the Culture of Nationalism in Algeria* (forthcoming 2005) and several articles on contemporary North African history and politics.

**Eyal Ben-Ari** is a Professor in the Department of Sociology and Anthropology of the Hebrew University of Jerusalem. His current research focuses on the field units of the Israeli military in the current conflict with the Palestinians and on the present-day Japanese self-defence forces. He is the author of *Mastering Soldiers: Conflict, Emotions and the Enemy in an Israeli Military Unit* (1998); and the co-editor of *Japan in Singapore: Cultural Presences* (2000), *The Military and Militarism in Israeli Society* (2000), and

*War, Politics and Society in Israel: Theoretical and Comparative Perspectives* (2000). **Neta Bar** is a doctoral student in the Department of Cultural Anthropology at Duke University.

**Julie Peteet** is Chair and Associate Professor of Anthropology at the University of Louisville. She is the author of *Gender in Crisis: Women and the Palestinian Resistance Movement* (1991) and *Landscape of Hope and Despair: Place and Identity in Palestinian Refugee Camps* (forthcoming). She has published articles in *Cultural Anthropology, American Ethnologist, Signs, MERIP, Cultural Survival* and *Social Analysis*. Her work has been funded by Fulbright, the Mellon Foundation, the Social Science Research Council and the Wenner-Gren Foundation for Anthropological Research.

**Mona Harb** is an Assistant Professor in the Department of Architecture and Design at the American University of Beirut (AUB), and is completing a PhD in Political Science from Montpellier University in France. She has worked as a researcher with the Lebanese Center for Policy Studies (LCPS) and with the Institut Français du Proche-Orient (formerly CERMOC). Her research examines political and religious institutions and social networks in polarised societies through the analysis of urban, local and social policies. **Reinoud Leenders** is an analyst with the Middle East Program of the International Crisis Group. He recently submitted his PhD thesis in Political Science at London's School of Oriental and African Studies (SOAS). He previously worked as a research associate with the American University in Beirut and taught at SOAS. His research examines state–economy relations, social networks and the politics of corruption in developing countries, with a focus on Lebanon and other parts of the Middle East.

**Stuart Horsman** works at the Foreign and Commonwealth Office, London. He previously taught in the Department of Politics, University of Sheffield and Department of Peace Studies, University of Bradford and he has published a number of articles and book chapters on Central Asian affairs.

# Fighting words: naming terrorists, bandits, rebels and other violent actors

MICHAEL V BHATIA

On 15 May 2003 a new front opened in the conflict between the Philippine government and the Moro Islamic Liberation Front (MILF). The Mayor of Davao City, located on the southern island of Mindanao, argued that President Arroyo should label the MILF terrorists under the belief that: 'They have taken so many lives of innocent civilians, which is inexcusable. No one knows when or where they will strike. It is about time this group should be branded terrorist before they go beyond the bounds of rebellion.' In response, Eid Kabalu, a MILF spokesman, stated that the use of such a label would indicate that the 'government is closing its door to the peace process and [intends to] pursue a military solution', to result in a 'bloodier war'. The degree of weight, and potential offensive power, of this description is further seen in his comment that: 'We have been threatened that we will be pulverized, bombed out of existence and now they're using this terrorist label. We have been threatened enough and nothing can scare us enough.'[1] Implicitly referring to the USA and reflecting wide internal opposition to this potential discursive shift, Vice-President Teofisto Guingona asserted that a change in the government's characterisation of the MILF was not 'for the foreigner to do'. A week later, during a state visit by Arroyo to Washington, which coincided with an artillery and air assault against the MILF, President Bush said of Arroyo: 'She's tough when it comes to terror; she fully understands that in the face of terror, you've got to be strong, not weak. The only way to deal with these people is to bring them to justice. You can't talk to them. You can't negotiate with them. You must find them.'[2] Almost a century earlier, the US military government in the Philippines' response to the first Moro rebellion, occurring from 1901 to 1913, featured distinctly similar accounts of savagery, fanaticism, disorder and banditry.[3] With regard to the latter, the November 1902 Bandolerismo Statute classified all forms of internal resistance as banditry and labelled any armed group brigands.

For the MILF, as well as for others, words were seen to be of equal power to bombs. While the Philippine government wishes to assign the label terrorist *in anticipation* of the MILF's transformation, the MILF have clearly identified the offensive potential of this description and indicated that the result of such name-calling would be a functional escalation of the conflict. This engagement with the rhetoric continues, both by governments labelled part of the 'axis of evil' and by the Anti-Coalition Forces in Afghanistan (ACF—the new name used by the Coalition/International Security Assistance Force (ISAF) to encompass Al-Qaeda, the Taliban and those members of Hizb-i-Islami still following Gulbuddin Hekmatyar). Indeed, in 2004, a poster or 'night-letter' appeared on the wall of an NFO compound in Jalalabad, Afghanistan, declaring:

> To the brave Afghanistan Mujahid Nation! The USA, the head of unbelievers and the root of crime...attacks the weak Muslim countries to capture them and then creates its own evil government. The supreme leaders, correct Mujahideen, were arrested and titled with different bad names.[4]

A similar complaint was made by Ayatollah Ali Khamene'i, Iran's religious leader, when he argued that the USA and Israel 'are fighting Islam by giving other names to their adversary. For instance, they expand the meaning of terrorism so as to crush liberating movements.'[5] While the MILF has no connection with Al-Qaeda, the Taliban or Iran, all three of these cases reveal that movements attach significance to words, and that names are core areas of dispute in armed conflict. In this competition over the legitimacy of violent acts, these groups seek to refute or even appropriate the words and names used against them in order to win the hearts, minds and support (either tacit or active) of the population. In the case of the statement by the ACF, rhetorical offence at the proposed maligning of their leadership was quickly followed by a rhetorical offensive of their own: 'If Jihad was obligatory against the Russian forces then is it not obligated against US forces terrorist acts?'[6] All these examples strongly contradict the old childhood axiom of 'sticks and stones' for, in contemporary armed conflict, 'names' do matter and are seen to 'hurt'. Discourse is thus a tool for armed movements and a battleground and contested space in contemporary conflicts. The politics of naming is about this contest, examining how names are made, assigned and disputed, and how this contest is affected by a series of global dynamics and events.

'One man's terrorist is another man's freedom fighter'—the phrase clearly vies with Mao's 'the guerrilla must move amongst the people as a fish swims in the sea' and 'political power grows out of the barrel of a gun' as that most commonly associated with insurgencies and civil wars. Thus, for the layperson, the variability of interpretation—the potential that a portrayal is biased—is immediately associated with how groups and acts are described. The purpose of the discursive conflict is to attain a victory of interpretation and ensure that a particular viewpoint triumphs. While the counter-arguments of the MILF and ACF rarely echo outside their immediate locality, it does indicate that there are strong (and richly nuanced) contests over words occurring within these conflict areas. The above accounts reveal that the 'Global War on Terror' has occurred not only on the various battlefields defined by the Bush administration (from Afghanistan to Iraq, Georgia and the Philippines), but on web- and editorial pages, in the halls of the UN General Assembly, and on streets and in cafés around the world. As a result, it appears that the Bush administration is not only engaged in a physical war (involving military interventions, seizures and assassinations, interrogations and surveillance, and financial targeting) but also in a dispute over discourse. The pronouncement of a 'war on terror' has forced many to verbally negotiate and assert who they are, who they are allied with, and who they are against. Moreover, this is the new dominant framework in which both governments and non-state armed movements present their acts. Indeed, a transnational element has again been transplanted onto a series of pre-existing local disputes, as occurred during the Cold War. From Uzbekistan to Colombia, from the Philippines to Algeria, the conflict over 'names' and 'naming' is becoming furious.

The articles in this issue seek to provide insight into the contemporary and historical conflict between movements and governments over names—the labels and descriptions given to actors, motives, events, ideologies and places. In doing so, the involved authors have employed a variety of approaches. Although 9/11 and the language of terrorism (of acts and agents) serves as an immediate introductory core, many have sought to broaden the inquiry, situating each conflict in relation to the previous words used by and against former colonial authorities, and in relation to former descriptions such as bandit, criminal, subversive, rebel and any number of different local euphemisms or dysphemisms. Some contrast external perceptions of a movement with how the group views and understands itself, as occurs in the articles on Al-Qaeda, Hizbullah and the Sandinistas in Nicaragua, while others examine how individual soldiers relate to their opponents and 'targets' on the battlefield, as is the focus of the article on Israeli snipers and the Al-Aqsa intifada. A series of other articles extends the examination to how naming affects attempts at political reconciliation and peace negotiations, as is the case with the contributions on Sri Lanka and Chechnya.

The goal of this introductory article is to serve as a review essay and identify some of the core background themes and theories through which the 'politics of naming' and other forms of discourse conflict can be examined. It is divided into three sections: nature, power, and role; function; and ethics. The central unifying theme is the relationship between the actual nature of a movement and the name applied, particularly in terms of the attempt to identify the essence or true nature of a movement and how this relates to other dissenting or surrounding factors. Once assigned, the power of a name is such that the process by which the name was selected generally disappears and a series of normative associations, motives and characteristics are attached to the named subject. By naming, this subject becomes known in a manner which may permit certain forms of inquiry and engagement, while forbidding or excluding others. No doubt such simplifications allow people to both engage with and understand a complex world. However, the need for simplicity can be rapidly appropriated and taken advantage of by those with their own political agenda. Indeed, the long historical relationship between the naming of opponents, empire and colonialism, as well as the manner in which the current global media frames armed conflict, only provide further reason to doubt the truthfulness of the names assigned. Many governments, both in the West and those subject to internal armed contest, cannot be relied upon responsibly and ethically to name their opponents. Again, in the case of the MILF, both President Arroyo and President Bush have sought to associate, amalgamate and compress the MILF with the Abu Sayyaf group and Jemaah Islamiyah, constantly arguing that the MILF needs to 'reject terror' (although it has yet to accept it) and referring to its bases as 'terrorist lairs' and terrorist training camps.[7]

Most authors in this volume are not confident of the ability of any particularly label or interpretive lens to adequately encompass the purpose, activities, local relevance or ideology of a given movement. Far too often complex local variations, motives, histories and inter-relationships are lost in the application of meta-narratives or dominant academic approaches to understanding and assessing conflict. In the case of the former each conflict is seen through whatever classificatory lens has recently been adopted to categorise, label and aggregate violence in the outside world, whether as evidence of communist expansion or Islamic fundamentalism. In the case of the latter, far too often, names, words and discourse are viewed as objective representations of fact in much policy-oriented research on conflict, with those works examining and challenging vocabulary typically consigned to the realm of critical theory. In contrast, the following introduction, as well as the other articles in this issue, is an attempt to show how naming and discourse is immediately relevant to conflicts and conflict resolution.

## The power of naming: nature, truth and transmission

To name is to identify an object, remove it from the unknown, and then assign to it a set of characteristics, motives, values and behaviours.[8] Names can fulfil a similar role as narratives, images, euphemisms and analogies. All serve as a natural reaction to surplus and abundant information, with the use of these and other 'knowledge structures' to 'order, interpret, and simplify'. For the recipient or audience, names, much like analogies, 'help define the nature of the situation confronting the individual', 'help assess the stakes' and 'provide prescriptions', which are then evaluated in terms of 'their chances of success' and 'their moral rightness'.[9] For Plato, names should be assessed according to their 'quality of showing the nature of the thing named', and it is thus necessary to 'learn from the truth both the truth itself and whether the image is properly made'.[10] However, while determining the basis for assessing names, Plato remains sceptical that any name could meet these criteria, for they are but imitations and partial reflections of a form. In the end the relationship between the name provided and the 'true' character of that described is often tenuous. A name may provide truth to an extent, and perhaps even *a* truth, but it cannot reveal the complete 'truth' of an object by encompassing all aspects and facets of that identified. As Talcott Parsons argues in his examination of selectivity, the assigned name may be selectively true, but may 'not constitute a balanced account of the available truth'.[11] While a name may reflect the core or essential qualities of an object, some aspects of the character will remain outside the descriptive boundaries of the name applied. A search for an essential truth may ultimately divert the analyst, reader or politician away from the truths hidden in a discarded periphery.

The actual ability to name, and to have that name accepted by an audience, holds great power. The authority of the 'name-giver'—the individual seen to have this linguistic power by Plato in his dialogue *Cratylus*—will determine just how natural these names, words and narratives are viewed by an audience or reader. Dale Spender, in her feminist examination of naming, argues that:

> Those who name the world have the privilege of highlighting their own experiences—and thereby identify what they consider important. Thus, groups that have a marginal status are denied the vocabulary to define (and express) their own experiences. . .Naming is the means whereby we attempt to order and structure the chaos and flux of existence which would otherwise be an undifferentiated mass. By assigning names we impose a pattern. . .which allows us to manipulate the world.[12]

A type of 'word magic' results, aligning the 'verbal symbol' not only with the 'non-verbal fact' but also with 'quantities, good and evil, that are believed to inhere in the relevant aspects of the world to which the word refers'.[13] By doing so, these magic words serve 'to conjure away the coding of the narrative situation' and 'naturalize the subsequent narrative by feigning to make it the outcome of some natural circumstance and thus. . .disinaugurating it'.[14] Descriptions, and the argument sequences that support them, will appear to be based on a thorough assessment of the available choices. Each name will come with a surrounding set of associations, natures, motives and intents. This results from the fact that most names are not developed independently, but drawn or 'borrowed' from other areas.[15] A name will place emphasis on certain aspects and characteristics of an object, while neglecting or omitting other key areas. In the end these names can be 'infectious', created to spread quickly or strongly adhere to the group thus created, proving hard to shake off and determining the boundaries and key reference points of future debates and discussions.[16]

Recent studies of the media—both a name-giver and a primary mechanism through which names and narratives are transmitted to the public—provide further grounds for critically engaging with 'naming', particularly when this occurs with reference to or within a broader environment of war and conflict. Shaw argues that 'news media generally take their cue from national governments and international organizations and follow their strategic directions', and that 'only rarely do they contest or modify them'.[17] Frame analysis has revealed how most news organisations typically favour certain interpretations, determining what aspects are 'important and what may be ignored, what is subject to debate and what is beyond question, what is true and false'.[18] Moreover, the way a story is sequenced (or the manner in which authors, journalists or academics 'unfold and order the elements of their accounts') 'influence individual assessments of violence as right, wrong or something in between'.[19] As revealed in a study of media reporting of the conflict in the former Yugoslavia, 'the process of news gathering puts reporters in certain places, gives them access to some sources and not others, predisposes them to certain concepts and certain ways of perceiving the world, and leads them to create a world congruent with their culture'.[20] As a result, journalists will recognise what their editors will and will not print, with the involved correspondents often unaware of the 'forces constraining them...determining not only which stories are covered but how they are framed'.[21] A form of self-censorship occurs at the foreign bureaus or field offices, where dissenting information or contradictory interpretations are removed by harried journalists in order to save themselves either time or exasperation. Most of these observations were previously made by Goebbels, perhaps the Master of All Lies, when he argued that:

> Enemy countries keep on talking as though we had discovered propaganda, or at least made it into the devil's tool which many people consider it to be. [However]...Even *The Times*, the most democratic paper in the world, makes propaganda in that it deliberately gives prominence to certain facts, emphasizes the importance of others by writing leaders or commentaries about them, and only handles others marginally or not at all.[22]

All of these factors reveal the manner in which the names assigned to certain groups are both acquired by media organisations and then transmitted to the public. Dissenting information is filtered out, removed by either conditioned reporters in the field or as a result of narrative frames or sequences. A decision is made to focus (sometimes exclusively) on a proposed essence of a story or group, with event-based reporting (on attacks, protests and other violent incidents) obscuring other aspects of an armed movement. However, as will be proposed in the following section, critical media studies have tended to over-emphasise both the pervasiveness and the hegemonic influence of the trends identified.

Nevertheless, any account of a strict hegemony of naming needs to be conditioned by the following. To the disdain of some conservative writers in the USA, certain segments of the media (namely the BBC) are decidedly reluctant to use the term 'terrorist', referring only to terrorist attacks and instead labelling these perpetrators as 'militants' or 'rebels'.[23] Moreover, the media 'line' or 'frame' is not always static, and is capable of shifting over the course of a crisis and representing the parties in a different manner at different times, again depending 'largely upon the representative activities of Western civil society institutions, including media' and 'on the intersection of their needs and demands with the interests, beliefs and agendas of groups in Western society'.[24]

Finally, examinations of discourse assign almost uncontested 'symbolic power' to the West and to national governments. Indeed, too much of critical theory, particularly in media studies and post-colonial approaches, focuses on the impact of dominant, Western or hegemonic actors, while neglecting both variation as well as the role, power and impact of either opposing or resisting groups. Discourse is surely a tool of government and reflects dominant ideologies, but these are certainly subject to competition, resistance and interpretation, particularly on the internet. Non-state groups—as exemplified by the Zapatista movement in Chiapas—are both capable and actively engaged in this dispute over terms. Indeed, those labelled barbarians, savages, bandits, criminals, subversives and terrorists are increasingly able to 'speak' on the world stage, and many are listening. While many of these counter-arguments may not be passively received by all Western readers, only rarely appearing in truncated form on media programmes, an active search by the curious can quickly produce these results on the web, whether produced locally or by supporters in a diaspora. While the USA may have enormous influence on the global media (even now challenged by the rise of Al-Jazeera, where an alternative news channel is accused of being tied to the acts and movements it broadcasts), deficiencies in its tactical conduct of psychological operations have led some US military observers to conclude that the "DOD is not well-prepared or well-positioned to successfully battle for hearts and minds', with local 'competitors on par with or even arguably more sophisticated than the US'.[25]

As a result, even the most powerful state may find its attempts at 'discourse dominance' undermined at any number of different levels, as even the more remote armed movements are adapting to and utilising the revolution in information technology. From the former Yugoslavia, Somalia and Rwanda to contemporary Afghanistan and Iraq, web pages, newspapers and television and radio broadcasts have been used to spread rumours and facts regarding both local 'others' and international military forces.[26] In internal conflicts images and names are used to depersonalise opponents and create fertile ground for intercommunal violence, ethnic cleansing and genocide. Rumours circulate concerning impending attacks or political conspiracies. Offensive action is taken in the name of defence and centuries of coexistence are erased by memories of past wrongs. These locally dominant actors thus use their information resources to polarise internal discourse, quieting dissenting views and defining parameters, thus ensuring that any local debate or contest occurs on their terms. With regard to information action against international forces, in Somalia, Mohammad Farah Aideed's use of 'radio and vehicle-mounted loudspeakers to accuse UNOSOM of atrocities against women and children sparked the 1993 attack on the Pakistani contingent, and was considered so threatening that the UN Security Council authorised action against those behind the propaganda.[27] It should also be remembered that the revolt in Najaf by the Mahdi army of Moqtada al-Sadr was partly sparked by the Coalition authority's decision to close its newspaper, *al-Hawza*, which was accused of inciting anti-Coalition activity.

### The functions of naming: gathering supporters and justifying acts

In this introduction naming is seen to fulfil two primary functions: to recruit supporters by propagating a discourse of belonging and opposition; and to justify action through labelling. An appeal to an audience is founded on a desire first to affirm an identity and to delineate an in-group from an out-group and second to recruit supporters. The role and function of 'the enemy' and 'the other', as further related to the designation of inside from outside, has been thoroughly examined and entrenched in international relations theory and other areas of the social sciences, perhaps to the point of redundancy.[28] For David Campbell, 'the boundaries of a state's identity are secured by the representation of danger integral to foreign policy', with 'a notion of what "we" are...intrinsic to an understanding of what "we" fear'.[29] Others argue that the key to understanding Europe's colonial period lies in the methods used and discourses developed to separate the coloniser from the colonised, or the agent from the subject of intervention.[30] In the absence of such words, imperialism and intervention lose their moral compass.[31]

Over the past decade in the West portrayals of localised disorder have been seen to play a key role in the constitution of an 'international community' based on a concept of order.[32] With the breakdown of concepts such as East and West after the Cold War, new mental geographical divisions have emerged, dividing a 'tame' from a 'wild' and 'violent' world.[33] According to Michael Ignatieff, media representations of civil conflict fortified a belief that 'they're all crazy', reproducing 'that reassuring imperial dichotomy between the virtue, moderation, and reasonableness held to exist in the West and the fanaticism and unreason of the East'.[34] The naming of peoples, territories and phenomena are all part of this attempt to recruit and indicate allies and opponents, as well as to demarcate similarity from difference. During certain periods difference is immediately equated with opposition. For example, in Greece in the fifth century, 'the idea of the barbarian' (with *barbaros* meaning 'not speaking Greek') helped 'to foster a sense of community between the allied states' of the Delian League against the Persian Empire.[35] Since then, 'the space of the barbarian [has served to delineate]...the limits of the political community', with 'the figure of the barbarian—either alone or in a horde—act[ing] as the "constitutive outside" of the *polis*'..[36]

All this is part of a struggle for the sympathy and support of an audience. Yet, as mentioned before, the audience to which each actor is playing varies, even within the same conflict. While the Bush administration's Manichean rhetoric of good versus evil, of murderers and terrorists, of 'with us' or 'against us,' and of a clash between civilisation and its opponents, may appeal to broad segments of the US public, it has served to alienate many both within the country and in the rest of the world. Another example is provided by Northern Ireland in the early 1980s, where Richard Clutterbuck argued that: 'in presenting a story to local, national or world media, a Provisional Sinn Fein spokesman has always had to bear in mind some nine different audiences [from the actual IRA to rival groups, the British public and the Irish diaspora], each with different perceptions, different reactions and different influences on events'.[37] Different words assume dominance at different times, with the word choice selected according to the power assigned at different levels (local, national, international). Some groups or governments appeal to historical imagery of former rebel and revolutionary movements, harnessing a rich mythology of the ideologies and reasons behind their actions, situating themselves in terms of the past in order to again attain the affinity and support of the population. Others play directly to broader international actors, placing what may be a local conflict in terms of a larger international conflict system, and thereby receiving financial, military and diplomatic support. As previously occurred during the Cold War, and as evident in John Russell's contribution on Chechnya in this issue, certain states have quickly adopted and adapted to US terrorist rhetoric to describe their own internal opponents. It is decidedly in the interest of some quasi-authoritarian governments to over-emphasise the militant Islamist character of their opposition, in the hope of US assistance or a *carte blanche* for repression, as may be the case in Uzbekistan, Egypt and Algeria. The goal here is to make local conflicts and armed movements appear as either one big Al-Qaeda or as a series of small Al-Qaedas united in purpose, and as all part of or directly linked to those who attacked the USA on 9/11. As a result, in its 2002 *Annual Report*, Amnesty International proposed that 'in the name of combating "terrorism", governments [have] stepped up the repression of their political opponents, detained people arbitrarily, and introduced sweeping and often discriminatory laws that undermined the very foundations of international human rights and humanitarian law'.[38] This observation has certainly proven true when viewing President Vladimir Putin's response to the Beslan school massacre, which was soon followed by a decree dictating the further consolidation of presidential powers and the extension of his authority over regional governors and the electoral system.

Beyond the creation of allies through the adoption of a shared rhetoric of belonging, the struggle over representation is directly a struggle over the legitimacy of violent acts. Indeed, a site, territory or people are first

9

colonised by words and names before being physically occupied by soldiers, trading companies and statesmen. This particularly occurs when there is a need to argue for defensive action, justify intervention abroad, or delegitimise internal opponents. From St Augustine to Walzer, self-defence is proposed as one requirement for the pursuit of a just war. As a result, naming plays a role in the following assessments: who is the victim and who is the perpetrator? Who is in the right, who is in the wrong, and who is to be blamed?

The relationship between the names applied and the decision to practice restricted or unrestricted warfare is immediately apparent. For the Romans the designation of a population as *homo sacer* permitted a self-designated 'civilised' society to use 'all necessary means' in the pursuit of conquest, including those viewed as being too brutal for general use.[39] Those preaching wars against others within the Islamic community, by Muslims against other Muslims, have taken inspiration from Ibn Taimiyya's 14th century use of the concept of *takfir* (calling a Muslim a non-Muslim) against the Mongols, which was rejuvenated by Abdel Salam Faraj and the *al-Jihad* group in their designation of Anwar Sadat as 'pharaoh' and their subsequent decision to assassinate him.[40]

From the Romans to the British Empire and the present period of United Nations-sanctioned territorial administration, the construction of a savage, lawless or unordered subject is a noted prerequisite of intervention. Not only is this process of creating a subject necessary for legitimising intervention, but it is also used to further delineate the occupier's identity (and conception of self), to normatively situate the tactics applied and to differentiate these from local methods.[41] Descriptions of an opponent are used to emphasise the benefit that would result from the imposition of an imperial order. Any suffering caused by the newly arrived actor is thus dismissed as incomparable to the disorder previously present. Internally, for a state and the associated media, 'referring to their opponents as "subversive elements", "terrorists", "extremists", and "bandits"' is an attempt at 'denying the legality of their opponents and emphasizing the need to maintain law and order'.[42] As the identification of the 'core purpose' of the violent act 'constitutes the *substance* of violence's legitimacy' (emphasis in original), the desire here is to assert immediately that violence against the state is not legitimate, well founded or justified, but driven by subsidiary and less noble motives.[43] An occupation's or empire's designation of an internal resistance as 'bandits' serves to demonstrate their control over territory and deny their opponent legitimacy, indicating that 'economic' interests and desires (greed and plunder) are the dominant purpose for armed action. This is seen in the Romans' repeated use of the term *latrocinium* during their conquest of Europe, in the French characterisation of Spanish insurgents during the Napoleonic invasion, and again in the above-mentioned Bandolerismo Statute.[44]

In the end the description or 'reduction' of a revolutionary movement to that of an insurgency removes the political or anti-occupation core of its actions, relegating it to a position of lawlessness and proposing it as an agent of disorder.[45] There is no doubt that the contest over naming is only heightened by the believed 'irregularity' of these forms of warfare. However, as Gray points out, 'what can be called "option purity" in style among military choices is rare,' with even by most 'regular' and 'conventional of European state armed forces, engaging in various forms of irregular warfare during World War II.[46] Again, as earlier revealed by Parsons and as echoed by many of the authors in this issue, aspects of the assigned description may be selectively true but, as a whole, the name will not embrace all or even the dominant aspects of a movement. Once an act or an attack is classified as criminal or terrorist in nature, the term has a habit of then being used to describe both the group itself and then all the acts which that group engages in, even when they attack military targets. Moreover, even if certain actors or movements within a conflict do engage in acts of terrorism, the actions of the few are consistently used to characterise the experience, beliefs and intentions of the many.

### The ethics of naming: contests in media and academia

Since 9/11 many have struggled to find the appropriate words and narrative frames to describe the current global crisis. However, the previous two sections have introduced aspects of 'naming' that should induce reservations as to Plato's dilemma of the relationship between the name used and the true nature of that described. As demonstrated by the Greek propagation of the term 'barbarian', an announcement or identification of evil is thus closely intertwined with a political project occurring within a society, as 'these alter-drives...are required for the stabilization of an identity'.[47] Particularly in periods of conflict, one assigns virtue to one's own identity and decisions, and draws on a series of negative traits to describe an opponent, relating to greed, irrationality, demonic nature or the absence of civilisation. History provides little additional succour for those seeking examples of intellectual rigour and moderation in the selection of the words used to describe opposing groups, instead providing numerous cases where the idea of a savage, criminal or fanatic opponent was constructed to legitimate empire or intervention. Even World War II, that pre-eminent example of a just war, involved the racist dehumanisation not just of the Japanese Empire but of the Japanese people, as detailed by Robert Ivie in his contribution on trends in American discourse.

The absence of an international definition of 'terrorism' or 'terrorist', which has been under debate in the UN General Assembly since the 1972 Olympic massacre of Israeli athletes in Munich, only further complicates attempts to provide a foundation in international law for the terms used. During these debates, while there has been some compromise and consensus as to what constitutes a terrorist act (such as hijacking, for example), the overall project has been complicated by tense differences over issues of occupation, liberation movements and state-terrorism.[48] Outside the General Assembly unilateral and bilateral initiatives do not appear to be faring any better, as demonstrated by the attempts of the European Union and the US State Department to create a list of Foreign Terrorist Organizations or

Specially Designated Global Terrorists. As demonstrated by Joanne Mariner, the identification of a group by the State Department as 'terrorist' is often driven by arbitrary political influences, with the inclusion of three Basque groups (Batasuna, Euskal Herritarrok and Herri Batasuna) and of a little known separatist group in Xinjiang province apparently traded for Spain's support for and China's acquiescence in the war in Iraq, respectively.[49] The interaction between political interest and the naming of armed actors, combined with the fact that states tend to overlook the brutal acts of their allies, limits the degree to which governments can be relied on to represent opponents accurately and impartially.

Whether attributable to active deceit or laziness, the majority of 'name-givers' in the media and politics have not restrained their naming practices. The declaration of a 'war on terror'—on an act rather than one specific group—left the enterprise tantalisingly open to any number of interpretations or appropriations, with the terminology used by the Bush administration so polarising that contradictory information was discarded as irrelevant. Strangely, the advent of round-the-clock news has only reduced the depth of news coverage on external conflicts, producing not an informative exposition of conflict dynamics but a constant stream of flash images and simplifications. Actual news programming is interspersed with incendiary political talk shows which, while discussing the 'war on terror', actively silence and dismiss those that disagree with the rhetoric used. This bears a striking resemblance to Balfour's description of propaganda, which he sees as seeking 'to avoid or limit such [critical] discussion and secure instead the acceptance of certain interpretations without exposing them to it, to cajole rather than to convince', and which is particularly successful when 'arousing so emotional an atmosphere [through the use of 'highly-coloured, value-impregnated language'] and investing its favoured interpretations with such prestige that only an insignificant fraction of the public will consider any alternative'.[50] As a consequence, the micro-histories of many of today's conflicts become hidden. Complex local variations, motives, histories and interrelationships are consistently played down in favour of meta-narratives and grand interpretations.[51] Each conflict is seen through whatever classificatory lens has been recently adopted to aggregate violence in the outside world. This aggregation is one of Plato's complaints in the Statesman, where the visitor criticises

> the way that most people carve things up, taking the Greek race away as one, separate from all the rest, and tie all the other races together, which are unlimited in number, which don't mix with one another, and don't share the same language—calling this collection by the single appellation 'barbarian.' Because of this single appellation, they expect it to be a single family or class too.[52]

A different form of the 'politics of naming' also emerged after 9/11. Some commentators (on the web and on talk-shows) focused partly on the identification of 'terrorist-sympathising' academics—those who do not show significant amounts of moral clarity and fail to defend the righteousness of American civilisation. Although much of this initial storm has now largely passed, the post-9/11 landscape featured a number of attacks on the proposed left-leaning nature of American academia. Lynne Cheney, the wife of the Vice-President and the head of the Council of Trustees and Alumni, sponsored a report entitled *Defending Civilization: How Our Universities Are Failing America*, which criticised academics as insufficiently supporting the USA, accusing them of giving 'comfort to its adversaries' by critically examining the history of US involvement in the region or seeking to understand the history, logic and evolution of both local and global Islamic militant groups. Daniel Pipes of the Middle East Forum formed *CampusWatch* to list those academics viewed as under-stating the 'Islamist threat', resisting the characterisation of the majority of Muslims according to the actions of an extreme few, and otherwise situating the growth of Islamic radicalism in relation to the authoritarian political environments from which they emerge.[53] While this dispute can be situated within the current cultural clash occurring between the American right and the left, such disdain reveals a deeper source of disquiet, with both the political and religious right long viewing humanism and moral relativism as ideologies of distaste and disgust, both of which have occasionally assumed a position as the primary sources of the continued degradation of society. By questioning judgement, the academic is seen to be problematically interposing the grey of representation between the black and white of good and evil.

As a consequence, as argued by Der Derian, the current media environment is characterised by 'exceptional ahirosticity', whereby 'explana-tion is identified as exoneration'.[54] This is revealed by David Brooks of the *New York Times*, in a column that followed the Beslan attack, where he argued that:

> Dissertations will be written about the euphemisms the media used to describe these murderers. They were called 'separatists' and 'hostage-takers...Three years after Sept 11, many are still apparently unable to talk about this evil. They still try to rationalize terror. What drives the terrorists to do this? What are they trying to achieve?...This death cult has no reason and is beyond negotiation. This is what makes it so frightening. This is what causes so many to engage in a sort of mental diversion. They don't want to confront this horror.[55]

Here, an attempt to situate an act in terms of the context of specific conflict is denounced as transgressive. Even if driven by a desire to inform, any attempts to move beyond condemnation are proposed as being a result of confusion or betraying an absence of moral clarity. The Beslan massacre can thus not be discussed in relation to the first and second Chechen wars, or in terms of the interplay between Russian policy and the tensions and power-plays between various Chechen factions. Once a terror attack occurs, it is held that all such historiography should be consigned to the proverbial scrap heap. It now becomes a matter of a pure 'evil', with no history or reason. As a result, it would appear that the academic, and particularly the area specialist, is being issued with a stern admonishment. Many would seek to place these conflicts firmly in the realm of the undiscussed and undisputed. In the name of defending democracy, freedom and civilisation, some of these authors would appear to encourage silence and the end of critique or thoughtful examination.

In light of the above and given the current circumstances, as Michel Foucault argued, it may be better to 'conceive discourse as a violence which we do to things'.[56] The question then becomes whether an ethics of naming can be negotiated at this critical period, and how we can minimise the verbal violence done to these situations. Some would stipulate 'honesty' or 'sincerity' as a fundamental prerequisite—whereby those involved agree not to employ rhetoric or deception, but instead to mutually examine the assumptions upon which their arguments are founded. For Termes, the honest use of words is fundamental to the pursuit of a just war. As a consequence, a key component of his criteria for assessing a 'just' war is that 'we must name what we do honestly and press language to its limits of directness and clarity. We cannot fight a Just War if we call our enemies anything other than human; we cannot fight a Just War if we call civilians anything other than civilians.'[57] Similarly, given the historical predisposition towards identifying that which is different as evil, Connolly argues that: 'we must strive to relieve its effects by emphasizing the constructed, contestable, contingent, and relational character of established identities, encouraging negotiations of identity and difference to proceed with a more refined sensibility of the limits of claims to self-sufficiency'.[58] However, it is likely that both Termes and Connolly would be seen as yet another example of academic relativism, with few of the accusatory commentators listed above likely to subscribe to their conditions or proposals. The lines between the moralists—or those seeking to assess a group or act in terms of its immediate objective relation to good/evil—and ethicists— those overwhelmingly concerned with subjective influences on these descriptions and designations—are remarkably fortified. The first group (moralists) does not appear to have any generalisable methods of neutral inquiry, while the second group (ethicists) struggles to develop approaches to moral assessment beyond an ethics of examination. As a result, the potential for developing any consensus on an ethics of naming appears remarkably limited.

## Conclusion

Who are they—those ragtag soldiers in the mountains, enclaves, jungles or urban ghettos? What do they want? What drives them—both individually and as a group? And then, why do they hate 'us'? These questions linger beneath most academic and journalistic debates as to the nature of insurgencies and armed movements. And so both academic, media and policy personalities inscribe the combatant with a series of motives and characteristics, as being driven by greed, grievance or fanaticism. Rarely is the combatant's decision attributed to a complex array of factors and events. A view of the reason for a conflict or insurgency will then shape the policy adapted. In the punitive 'hard' approach, which is driven by a concept of a rational fanatic, if you punish their families enough for an individual's acts, they will stop. In the 'soft' approach, which is based on a concept of economic interest, if you address the underlying grievances and make a positive change in the socioeconomic conditions in an area, the insurgency or armed movement will wither away, losing support from the population. An accusation of terrorism will tend to obfuscate whether occupation or forms of structural violence are present. Quickly the barbarism of the acts themselves is assigned to the character of the actor. For the USA, now in Iraq or Afghanistan, every case of rebellion and kidnapping spurs no further inquiries as to the American approach in the country. Instead, each act is further evidence of the fundamental brutality of the opponent, and is used to further cement their otherness, their savagery. This perception of the opponent further buttresses an image of righteous action, obscuring the violent and less than pure elements of one's own action. A heroic or patriotic mythology is created that covers up examples of war profiteering and brutality. As a result, the sins of a government or its soldiers become excusable thanks both to practical factors (a consequence of extreme conditions, such as insurgency, over-work or distance from home) and in comparison to the greater evil of the opponent.

This introduction and this special issue are less a definitive accounting of the role of discourse in this conflict than an attempt to begin a conversation and exchange. Most importantly, it is necessary to further examine the intents of the agents propagating these names. Are they (whether in the media or in politics) aware of any inconsistencies between the name applied and the nature of the subject? Do they radicalise their own descriptions in order to appeal to and recruit a larger audience, in the belief that simplicity is a stronger pull than context? Second, there is a continued need to develop lines of inquiry that avoid describing a one-way process of government versus insurgent, examining the verbal tools and strategies of both governments and non-state movements as they compete for legitimacy. As mentioned, the global discourse is no longer one where a singular hegemon or state is able to dictate one name, and have this universally followed and used by its intended audience. Finally, in a book version of this issue likely to be released in 2005 or 2006, I would like to broaden the included cases, and encourage any readers involved in research on a related conflict or area to approach the editor. Additional invited contributions would focus on Northern Ireland, Egypt, Colombia, West Africa, Kashmir, post-Saddam Iraq and the *fedayeen*, and the relationship between the naming of internal opponents by the Dutch and the Suharto government in Indonesia. I am also interested in the dimensions of the perception of the USA and Israel in the Muslim world (in terms of interests, conspiracies and the relationship with anti-semitic traditions), and in whether the West's focus on 'why do they hate us?' obscures the existence of nuanced views in the Islamic and Arab world.

## Notes

The author would like to thank Shahid Qadir, Thomas Rath, Stina Torjesen, Anthony McDermott, Nicole Evans and Andrew March for their assistance and advice. Dr Michael Schroeder generously provided the title for this article.

1   'Philippines: Moro spokesman warns terrorist tag will result in "bloodier war"', *BBC Monitoring International Reports*, 15 May 2003.

2   'Text of Bush, Arroyo remarks,' Associated Press, Washington, DC, 19 May 2003.

3   See TM McKenna, *Muslim Rulers and Rebels: Everyday Politics and Armed Separatism in the Southern Philippines*, Berkeley, CA: University of California Press, 1998; and S Miller, *Benevolent Assimilation: The American Conquest of the Philippines, 1899–1903*, New Haven, CT: Yale University Press, 1984.

4   Afghanistan NGO Security Organization (ANSO), 'Incident report: insurgent propaganda', 18 April 2004.

5   'Khamene'i says US uses war against terror as excuse to attack Islam', *BBC Monitoring International Reports*, 24 December 2003.

6   ANSO, 'Incident report'.

7   'Weekender', *BusinessWorld* (Philippines), 4 July 2003; and D Riechmann, 'Philippine president to use state visit to seek aid, military assistance to fight terrorists', Associated Press, 18 May 2003.

8   MK Adler, *Naming and Addressing: A Sociolinguistic Study*, Hamburg: Helmut Buske, 1978, pp 12, 93–94.

9   YF Khong, *Analogies at War: Korea, Munich, Dien Bien Phu and the Vietnam Decisions of 1965*, Princeton, NJ: Princeton University Press, 1992, pp 10, 13.

10  Plato, *Cratylus*, trans HN Fowler, London: William Heinemann, 1953, pp 151, 185 (line 439). For further examination of the 'normative' aspect of *Cratylus*, see R Barney, *Names and Nature in Plato's Cratylus*, London: Routledge, 2001, p 4.

11  T Parsons, 'An approach to the sociology of knowledge', *Transactions of the Fourth World Congress of Sociology*, Milan, 1959, pp 25–49, as cited in C Geertz, *The Interpretation of Cultures: Selected Essays*, New York: Basic Books, 2000, p 195.

12  D Spender, 'The politics of naming', in M Curtis (ed), *The Composition of Ourselves*, Dubuque, IA: Kendall/Hunt, 2000, p 195.

13  J Hertzler, *A Sociology of Language*, New York: Random House, 1965, p 268ff, as cited in Adler, *Naming and Addressing*, p 12.

14  R Barthes, 'Introduction to the structural analysis of narratives', in Barthes, *Image-Music-Text*, trans S Heath, Glasgow: Fontana, 1977, p 116. See also MJ Shapiro, *The Politics of Representation: Writing Practices in Biography, Photography, and Policy Analysis*, Madison, WI: University of Wisconsin Press, 1988, p xii.

15  H Arendt, *The Life of the Mind*, New York: Harcourt, Brace and Jovanovich, 1978, p 102, as quoted in K Hicks, 'Metaphors we kill by: the legacy of US antiterrorist rhetoric', *The Political Chronicle*, Fall/ Winter 1991, pp 21–29.

16  K Allan & K Burridge, *Euphemism and Dysphemism: Language Used as Shield and Weapon*, Oxford: Oxford University Press, 1991, p 3.

17  M Shaw, *Civil Society and Media in Global Crises: Representing Distant Violence*, London: Pinter, 1996, p 179.

18  K Hall-Jamieson & P Waldman, *The Press Effect: Politicians, Journalists and the Stories that Shape the Political World*, Oxford: Oxford University Press, 2003, pp xiii–xiv, 1.

19  KA Cerulo, *Deciphering Violence: The Cognitive Structure of Right and Wrong*, New York: Routledge, 1998, p 3.

20  JJ Sadkovich, *The US Media and Yugoslavia, 1991–1995*, Westport, CT: Praeger, 1998, p 6. See also T Allen & J Seaton (eds), *The Media of Conflict: War Reporting and Representations of Ethnic Violence*, London: Zed Books, 1999.

21  SL Carruthers, *The Media At War: Communication and Conflict in the Twentieth Century*, London: Macmillan, 2000, pp 15, 28.

22  W von Oven, *Mit Goebbels bis zum Ende*, Vol 1, *Finale Furioso*, 1974, pp 285, as cited in M Balfour, *Propaganda in War: Organisation, Policies and Publics in Britain and Germany*, London: Routledge & Kegan Paul, 1979, p 431.

23  For the complaints, see D Pipes, 'They're terrorists—not activists', *New York Sun*, 7 September 2004.

24  Shaw, *Civil Society and Media in Global Crises*, p 12.

25  B Bender, 'Revamp urged for USA's psyops program', *Jane's Defense Weekly*, 11 October 2000.

26  JF Metzl, 'Rwandan genocide and the international law of radio jamming', *American Journal of International Law*, 91 (4), October 1997, p 62.

27  S/RES/837 (6 June 1993); and Report of the Secretary-General on the Implementation of Security Council Resolution 837 (1993).

28  RW Rieber (ed), *The Psychology of War and Peace: The Image of the Enemy*, New York: Plenum Press, 1991, p 7.

29  D Campbell, *Writing Security: United States Foreign Policy and the Politics of Identity*, Manchester University Press, 1998, pp 3, 73.

30  D Scott, 'Colonial governmentality', *Social Text*, 43, 1995; and RL Doty, *Imperial Encounters: The Political Representation in North–South Relations*, Minneapolis, MN: University of Minnesota Press, 1996, p 4.

31  'If cultural and psychological divisions between "us" and the "orientals" do not hold fast, imperialism loses its moral justification as a civilizing mission.' J Ruskin, *The Mythology of Imperialism*, New York: Random House, 1971, as cited in S Layton, *Russian Literature and Empire: Conquest of the Caucasus from Pushkin to Tolstoy*, Cambridge: Cambridge University Press, 1994, p 10.

32  L Malkki, 'National geographic: the rooting of peoples and the territorialization of national identity among scholars and refugees', *Cultural Antrhropology*, 7 (1), 1992, pp 24–44.

33  G Ó Tuathail & TW Luke, 'Present at the (dis)integration: deterritorialization and reterritorialization in the New Wor(l)d Order', *Annals of the Association of American Geographers*, 84 (3), 1994, pp 394–395. See also E Keene, *Beyond the Anarchical Society: Grotius, Colonialism and Order in World Politics*, Cambridge: Cambridge University Press, 2002; and F Debrix, *Re-Envisioning Peacekeeping: The United Nations and the Mobilization of Ideology*, Minneapolis, MN: University of Minnesota Press, 1999.

34  M Ignatieff, *The Warrior's Honor: Ethnic War and the Modern Conscience*, New York: Metropolitan Books, 1997, p 80.

35  'Ethnic stereotypes, ancient and modern, though revealing almost nothing about the groups they are intended to define, say a great deal about the community which produces them.' E Hall, *Inventing the Barbarian: Greek Self-Definition Through Tragedy*, Oxford: Clarendon Press, 1991, pp 2, 9, 10.

36  MB Salter, *Barbarians and Civilization in International Relations*, London: Pluto Press, 2002, p 4. See also C Weber, *Simulating Sovereignty: Intervention, the State, and Symbolic Exchange*, Cambridge University Press, 1995, p 5.

37  R Clutterbuck, *The Media and Political Violence*, London: Macmillan, 1981, p 90.

38  Amnesty International, *Annual Report 2003*, May 2003. See also R Foot, 'Human rights and counter-terrorism in America's Asia policy', *Adelphi Paper*, 363 (1), 2003.

39  S Zizek, 'Are we in a war? Do we have an enemy?', *London Review of Books*, 24 (10), 23 May 2002. See also V Harle, *The Enemy with a Thousand Faces*, London: Praeger, 2000, p 75.

40  R Scott, 'An "official" Islamic response to the Egyptian al-jihad movement', *Journal of Political Ideologies*, 8 (1), 2003, p 44.

41  See MV Bhatia, 'Enlightened interventions? The discourse of tactics in military occupation and contemporary transitional administration' (under revision).

42  J Van Doorn, *The Soldier and Social Change*, London: Sage Publications, 1975, p 103.

43  D Riches, 'The phenomenon of violence', in Riches (ed), *The Anthropology of Violence*, Oxford: Basil Blackwell, 1986, p 7.

44  For Rome, see RB Asprey, *War in the Shadows: The Guerrilla in History*, New York: William Morrow, 1994, p 9; for Spain, see Karma Nabulsi, *Traditions of War: Occupation, Resistance and the Law*, Oxford: Oxford University Press, 1999, pp 29–30.

45  P Schlesinger, *Media, State and Nation: Political Violence and Collective Identities*, London: Sage Publications, 1991.

46  CS Gray, *Modern Strategy*, Oxford: Oxford University Press, 1999, p 285.

47  WE Connolly, 'Preface to the Third Edition', in Connolly, *The Terms of Political Discourse*, Oxford: Blackwell, 1997, p xi.

48  J Friedrichs, 'Defining the international public enemy: the political struggle behind the legal debate on international terrorism', paper presented at the Fifth Pan-European International Relations Conference, The Hague, The Netherlands, 9–11 September 2004. See also Geoffrey Nunberg, 'How much wallop can a single word pack?', *New York Times*, 11 July 2004.

49  J Mariner, 'Trivializing terrorism', *Writ*, 13 May 2004, at http://writ.news.findlaw.com/mariner/. See also Mariner, 'Good and bad terrorism', 7 January 2002; and Mariner, 'Our many and varied wars against terror', 21 January 2002.

50  Balfour, *Propaganda in War*, pp 421–423.

51  G McFarlane, 'Violence in rural Northern Ireland: social scientific models, folk explanations and local variation', in Riches, *The Anthropology of Violence*, p 188; and D Campbell, *National Deconstruction: Violence, Identity and Justice in Bosnia*, Minneapolis, MN: University of Minnesota Press, 1998, p 55.

52  'Statesman', in *Plato: Complete Works*, ed J Cooper, Indianapolis, 1997, 262d1–6, as cited in Barney, *Names and Nature in Plato's Cratylus*, p 9.

53  See D Pipes, 'Jihad and the professors', *Commentary*, November 2002.

17

54 J Der Derian, '*In terrorem*: before and after 9/11', in K Booth & T Dunne (eds), *Worlds in Collision: Terror and the Future of Global Order*, London: Palgrave Macmillan, 2002, p 102, as quoted in M Zehfuss, 'Forget September 11', *Third World Quarterly,* 24 (3), 2003, pp 513–528.
55 D Brooks, 'Cult of death', *New York Times,* 7 September 2004.
56 M Foucault, 'The order of discourse', in M J Shapiro (ed), *Language and Politics*, New York: New York University Press, 1984, p 127.
57 P Termes, *The Just War: An American Reflection on the Morality of War in Our Time*, Chicago, IL: Ivan R Dee, 2003, pp 149, 179.
58 Connolly, 'Preface to the third edition', p xi; and MJ Shapiro, *Violent Cartographies: Mapping Cultures of War*, Minneapolis, MN: University of Minnesota Press, 1997, p 31.

# Imaging terror: logos, pathos and ethos

JAMES DER DERIAN

Imagination is not a gift usually associated with bureaucracies.
(*The 9/11 Commission Report*, p 344)

## The logos of terror

Two framed artefacts of the second Cold War hang on either side of my desk. The first is a simple black and white poster made in 1985, most probably inspired by President Reagan's description of the Afghan *mujahideen* as freedom fighters. Next to a photograph of Reagan is one of a New York City firefighter. The caption underneath says: 'A firefighter fights fires. A freedomfighter fights _____' The second image comes from a 1985 issue of *The Manipulator*, a short-lived, large-format art magazine. On the cover is a Nancy Burston photograph entitled 'Warhead 1', a digitised composite of world leaders proportioned according to their country's nuclear weapons, in which the facial features of Reagan (55% of the world's throw-weight) and Brezhnev (45%) dominate the fuzzier visages of Thatcher, Mitterand, and Deng (less than 1% each) (see Figures 1 and 2).[1]

FIGURE 1.
Warhead 1.

These two images speak volumes, revealing the grammatical logos that underwrites the pathos and ethos of terror. As verb, code and historical method, terrorism has consistently been understood as an act of symbolically intimidating and, if deemed necessary, violently eradicating a personal, political, social, ethnic, religious, ideological or otherwise radically differentiated foe. Yet, as noun, message and catch-all political signifier, the meaning of terrorism has proven more elusive. From Robespierre's endorsement to Burke's condemnation during the French Revolution, from the Jewish Irgun blowing up the King David Hotel to the Palestinian Black September massacre at the Munich Olympics, from Bin Laden the Good fighting the Soviet

FIGURE 2.
Reflections on Terrorism.

occupiers of Afghanistan to Bin Laden the Bad toppling the Twin Towers of
New York, terrorism, terrorists and terror itself have become the political
pornography of modernity: one knows terrorism with certainty only when,
literally, one sees it. But, in the blink of an eye, the terrorist can become the
freedom fighter, and vice versa, for at one time or another nearly everyone,
from righteous statesmen who terror-bomb cities to virtuous *jihadists* who
suicide-bomb women and children, seems to have a taste for terror.

Without engaging in nostalgia, one can recognise that the most powerful
form of terror mutated at the end of the Cold War. With the decline (if not

the total demise) of a logic of deterrence based on a nuclear balance of terror, so too eroded the willingness and capacity to inflict mutually unacceptable harm that had provided a modicum of order, if not peace or justice, to the bipolar system. In its place a new *imbalance of terror* has emerged, based on a mimetic fear and hatred coupled with an asymmetrical willingness and capacity to destroy the other without the formalities of war.[2] This cannot be reduced, as much as leaders on both sides of the conflict have tried, to a post-9/11 phenomenon. It can be traced back doctrinally to the 1990's, when a series of US defense policy guidances (subsequently formalized in the 1997 Quadrennial Defense) shifted US strategy from collectively *deterring* and *dominating* to unilaterally and preemptively *destroying* the enemy, and when Bin Laden issued his pseudo-fatwas which decreed Christian and Jewish civilians legitimate targets of the jihad.

As in the older, tidier balance of terror, the doctrine of taking civilians hostage and if necessary killing them still held for both sides, but it now operated as a contingent factor of an asymmetrical relationship. Regardless of nomenclature—'terror' or 'counter-terror'—high numbers of civilians would (and continue to) be killed in the process. It might be small solace to the victims to know they were primary targets as opposed to 'accidental' or 'collateral' victims, especially since casualty rates have been terribly skewed in both cases. When one takes into account how war-related fatalities have been reversed in modern times, from 100 years ago when one civilian was killed per eight soldiers, to the current ratio of eight civilians per soldier killed, then compares the similarly-skewed combatant-to-non-combatant casualty figures of 9/11, the Afghan War, and the Iraq War, the terror/counter-terror distinction begins to fade even further. Perhaps it is time for a new Burson composite, using the leaders of the three conflicts to proportionally represent the number of civilian casualties from the three conflicts.

With weapons systems, war-fighting doctrine and war games often wagging the dog of civilian policy, the narratives as well as the paladins of the Cold War seem destined to an eternal return in US foreign policy. Having mapped this phenomenon before 9/11, I wish to focus on what (if anything) has changed since then, and to understand the celerity and alacrity by which our age has now been defined by terrorism.[3] Although the fundamentalist religious and political beliefs of the major combatants have attracted the most attention, I think we need to pay more attention to the multiple media, which transmit powerful images as well as help to trigger highly emotional responses to the terrorist event. Thanks to the immediacy of television, the internet and other networked information technology, we *see* terrorism everywhere in real time, all the time. In turn, terrorism has taken on an iconic, fetishised and, most significantly, a highly *optical* character. After witnessing the televised images of kamikaze planes hitting the World Trade Center, the home videos of Bin Laden, the internet beheading of Nicholas Berg, we were all too ready to agree with President Bush: 'Evil now has a face'.

However, somewhere between the Pyrrhic victory of Tora Bora and the disastrous post-war of Iraq, the face of terror began to morph into a new

Post-Bursonian composite. The 'terrorist' can now easily do double-duty as an airport security profile, featuring the checkered *keffiyeh* of Arafat, the aquiline nose of Osama Bin Laden, the hollowed face of John Walker Lindh, the maniacal grin of Saddam Hussein, the piercing eyes of Abu Musab Zarqawi ('He could direct his men simply by moving his eyes', said Basil Abu Sabha, his Jordanian prison doctor). The historicity, specificity and even the comprehensibility of terrorism have been transmogrified by the new holy and media wars into a single physiognomy of global terror.

Of course, our image of terror did not arrive by itself or on its own. Just as every image comes with an explicit or implicit caption—what Roland Barthes, the gifted semiotician, referred to as the 'anchorage' which seeks to fix the 'polysemy' of the sign[4]—so too is the war on terror freighted with the narratives of the Cold War. Moreover, the legacy of the Cold War lives on through popular culture, a 'fact' ably noted by a Hollywood actor who knows a thing or two about the morbidity of comebacks. Playing a 'C-fuckin'-I-A agent' doubling as a Gulf war arms dealer, up against FBI straight man (another constant in national security culture) Willem Dafoe, Mickey Rourke colourfully notes how the dead continue to weigh on the living:

> This isn't about sides. This is about confusion. This is about creating enemies when there aren't any. And, man, the whole Goddamn world's falling apart. Peace reigns, freedom reigns, democracy rules. How are we gonna keep the military – industrial complex chugging forward without clear-cut, pit-faced, scum-sucking evil breathing down our neck? Hmmm? Threatening our very shores. Now my job is to make sure the other side keeps fighting; whatever side—I mean whatever side we're officially not on this year.[5]

Seen in this light, the war on terror is not new but part of a permanent state of war by which the sovereignty of the most powerful state is reconstituted through the naming of terrorist foe and anti-terrorist friend.

There are lessons to be learned from an earlier inter-war—one that is beginning to look too much like our own—in which two media critics, *avant la lettre,* first confronted this new matrix of art, politics and terror. Walter Benjamin took his first measure of film production in his celebrated essay, 'The Work of Art in the Age of Mechanical Reproduction', taking note of how mechanically reproduced art, especially film, could be especially useful to, if not generative of, fascism. Rendering politics into aesthetics had the advantage of mobilising the masses for war without endangering traditional property relations. He quotes the futurist Marinetti to chilling effect:

> War is beautiful because it establishes man's dominion over the subjugated machinery by means of gas masks, terrifying megaphones, flame throwers, and small tanks. War is beautiful because it initiates the dreamt-of metalization of the human body...War is beautiful because it creates new architecture, like that of the big tanks, the geometrical formation flights, the smoke spirals from burning villages, and many others...Poets and artists of Futurism!...remember these principles of an aesthetics of war so that your struggle for a new literature and a new graphic art...may be illumined by them![6]

The aesthetic of the reproducible image overpowered the aura and authenticity of the original. In *The Arcades Project* Walter Benjamin studied the significance of this new development for the Rankean realism that hitherto had underwritten much of geopolitical discourse. 'The history that showed things "as they really were" was the strongest narcotic of the century.' He went on to declare that 'history decays into images, not into stories'. Benjamin defined an image as 'that wherein what has been comes together in a flash with the now to form a constellation'; or, as he more simply put it, images are 'dialectics at a standstill'.[7] I believe his endorsement of a counter-medium, the use of montage as 'the art of citing without quotation', in which 'truth is charged to the bursting point with time', has become just as valid for our own times.

Also writing in Germany in the inter-war period, and trying to understand the immense popularity of Berlin's new picture palaces, Siegfried Kracauer thought the Berliners had become 'addicted to distraction'. He called them 'optical fairylands'—'to call them movie theaters', he said, 'would be disrespectful'—where 'distraction—which is meaningful only as improvisation, as reflection of the uncontrolled anarchy of the world—is festooned with drapes and forced back into a unity that no longer exists'. In Kracauer's view the picture palaces served as a kind of Hegelian asylum from Weimar disorder, ornate spaces where the alienated Berliner could seek reunification through what he called a 'cult of distraction'. Substitute Fox, CNN, MSNBC for the picture palace, and we find another potential guide for leading us through an 'Age of Info-terror'.

## The pathos of terror

We 'moderns' might now recognise the increasing power of images over words, but we have been slower to understand the consequences, as they have increasingly taken on a pathological character, for the war on terror. How might we read, in the spirit of Benjamin and Kracauer, the Bin Laden videos as well as the official response to them?

At first viewing the Bin Laden home videos understandably yielded a fairly uniform and deserved response of outrage in the USA and Europe. However, not just in the Middle East but in parts of America with large Arab populations, like Dearborn, MI and Los Angeles, questions were soon raised about their authenticity. The doubts can be understood in Benjamin's terms, of the loss of aura from the original produced by technical reproducibility, but multiplied many times by the convergence of the Ages of Terror and Adobe Photoshop, or what I have referred to as the Age of Info-terror.[8] It reflects as well an increasingly global view that Hollywood, Silicon Valley and Washington, DC have joined forces in the war on terror.

For those who might detect a whiff of conspiracy in such claims, a short history of events after 9/11 might be instructive. By early October 2001 White House advisers had already begun a series of meetings with directors, producers and executives from the entertainment industry on how Hollywood might best help the war effort. To be sure, an alliance between the military and the entertainment industry was not entirely new. The mixing of spectacle and war goes back to the beginnings of film, when DW Griffith, already famous for his 1915 *Birth of the Nation*, went to work for Lord Beaverbrook's War Office in World War I. However, there was some cause for worry with this new overture. My own concern was first triggered at the opening of the innocuous-sounding Institute for Creative Technologies (ICT), which I covered for *Wired* magazine in 1999. The ICT was set up at the University of Southern California to spearhead a remarkable project: with $43 million provided by the US Army it would combine the virtual reality tools of Silicon Valley and the talent of Hollywood film studios to produce state-of-the-art military simulations for future war. On the day of the opening one speaker after another, from the Secretary of the Army to the Governor of California, spoke of 'making the quantum leap to the Army After Next'; 'creating virtual environments for total immersion of participants'; and, my favourite, 'engrossing stories stocked with emotional characters who may either be simulated or manned', Jack Valenti, head of the Motion Picture Association, opened his remarks by correcting a previous speaker: 'Los Angeles is not the "entertainment capital of the world" [pause], Washington, DC is the entertainment capital of the world [laughter].'

I expressed my concern at the opening ceremony in the form of a question to Steven Sample, President of University of Southern California (USC): might not the linking up of Hollywood and the Pentagon repeat the World War II experience, when training films were mixed with propaganda films, and military simulations became a tool for public dissimulations? Were there any ethical checks and balances to assure that the ICT would not produce something like *Wag the Dog*? President Sample deadpanned a nervous sideways look and said, 'As Jack is coming up to respond to that....' But Sample chose to respond by going back to an earlier observation, that the ICT would develop 'synthetic experiences so compelling that people will react as though they were real—a virtual reality of sensations and sights'. He went on to make a deft analogy to Plato's poor opinion of the poets. Not actually using the word mimesis, he suggested as much was going on at the ICT: by performing the classical function of poetry and theatre—artistically and dramatically mimicking reality for a higher purpose—it could not help but arouse anxieties about whose version of reality was the true one. The allegory of the cave lurked behind the curtains.

Where Sample applied nuance, Jack Valenti chose pugnacity. Responding to my question he said: 'I want to illuminate a central truth to the gentleman—everything leaks, in Hollywood, in Washington. There's no way you can keep a secret. You can't fool the people for very long.' He then informed me that I needed to correct my 'Copernican complex'. He contrasted my view to the decision to drop the atomic bomb on the Japanese. Some might have seen that as a 'heartless and terrible thing to do...but not the 150 000 American boys whose lives would have been lost. This is a lesson in Philosophy 101 that I am giving to you right now.'

I came away with a different lesson. Valenti, like many in power today, are all too ready to drop the bomb on dissident viewpoints. Nonetheless, he was on target in one regard: what separates and elevates war above lesser, 'Copernican' conceits is its intimate relationship to death. The dead body— on the battlefield, in the tomb of the unknown soldier, in the collective memory, even on the movie screen—is what gives war its special status. This fact can be censored, hidden in a body bag, air-brushed away, but it provides, even in its erasure, the corporeal *gravitas* of war. However, everything I witnessed that day at the ICT was dedicated to the disappearance of the body, the aestheticising of violence, the sanitisation of war: in other words, to everything we have seen implemented since 9/11.

Barely a week after the terrorist attack, the ICT began to gather top talent from Hollywood to create possible terrorist scenarios that could then be played out in their Marina del Rey virtual reality facilities. Then Karl Rove, White House special adviser, travelled to Beverly Hills to discuss with the top ceos how Hollywood might provide talent and resources for the battle against terrorism. Among those reported as contributing to the virtual war effort were *Die Hard* screenwriter Steven E De Souza, *Matrix* special effects wizard, Paul Debevec and directors David Fincher (*Fight Club*), Spike Jonze (*Being John Malkovich*) and Randal Kleiser (*Grease*). Fans of Kleiser might wonder why his classic work, *Honey I Blew Up the Kid* (about an amateur physicist who turns his son into a giant) went unmentioned in the press releases. Was it proof that the US government might be embarrassed to have hooked up with B-list directors? Or was it part of an info-war campaign to keep the lid on 'Operation Shrink Bin Laden Back to Size'? When holy war comes to Hollywood, the truth is hard to come by.

As more Bin Laden tapes emerged there were calls for censorship, heightened threat levels, and a cottage industry of media critics. Debates continued to focus on whether the tapes were real or not, was he dead or alive and then, most ominously, on whether he had joined ranks with Saddam Hussein. Gone missing was any attempt to understand why Bin Laden continued to command a global audience.

After Al Jazeera broadcast the first videotape, National Security adviser Condoleeza Rice made personal calls to heads of the television networks, asking them to pre-screen and to consider editing Al-Qaeda videos for possible coded messages. Secretary of State Powell interpreted the February 2002 audiotape as proof positive that Bin Laden had forged an alliance with Saddam Hussein. Yet the most significant and constant message, intended for the aggrieved and dispossessed in Islam, has remained, like Edgar Allan Poe's purloined letter, out in the open, in plain sight, and peculiarly unnoticed. Bin Laden was adeptly using networked technology to disseminate a seductive message of prophecy, reciprocity and ultimate victory.

Shortly after the bombing campaign began in Afghanistan, and Bin Laden delivered his first videotape as a counter air-strike to the USA, he spoke with his guest and camera crew of the many dreams that had preceded 9/11: of playing soccer games against American pilots, in which Al-Qaeda members become pilots themselves in order to defeat the

Americans; of a religious leader who dreamt of carrying a huge plane through the desert; of the wife of a *jihadist* who saw a plane crashing into a building a week before the event. An unidentified man off-camera interrupts bin Laden, saying that 'Abd Al Rahman saw a vision before the operation, a plane crashed into a tall building, he knew nothing about it'. At this point Bin Laden turns to his guest and says: 'I was worried that maybe the secret would be revealed if everyone starts seeing it in their dreams. So I closed the subject'. The koranic view of dreams as prophecy appeared to be taken so seriously that Bin Laden believed operational secrecy was at risk. For Bin Laden prophecy anticipates the inevitable: a violent confrontation with the West. He further states in the video that 'America has been filled with horror from north to south and east to west, and thanks be to God what America is tasting now is only a copy of what we have tasted'.

Prophecy is tied to reciprocity once again in the November audiotape, in which he opens with a florid invocation of 'God, the merciful, the compassionate' who sanctifies Al-Qaeda's violence because 'reciprocal treatment is part of justice...as you kill you will be killed and as you bomb you will be bombed'. With the release of the February 2002 tape, most of the media, following Powell's lead, focused on Bin Laden's invocation to defend Iraq against the 'crusaders' by copying the 'success' of trench warfare in Tora Bora. Left unnoticed was Bin Laden once again calling on religious purity not only to counter Western technological superiority in planes, bombs and soldiers but also by an info-war: 'we realized from our defence and fighting against the American enemy that, in combat, they mainly depend on psychological warfare'. He adds: 'This is in light of the huge media machine they have'. Bin Laden instructs the *jihadists* that they will triumph in a 'just war' by fighting 'in the cause of Allah' and 'against the friends of Satan', and by avoiding 'all grave sins, such as consuming alcohol, committing adultery, disobeying parents, and committing perjury'. 'They should,' adds Bin Laden, 'in particular mention the name of God more before combat'.

Unfortunately, the US intelligence and intellectual communities, bound by rational models of decision making, were slow to comprehend this powerful synergy of prophecy, reciprocity and technology. This mythologically informed terrorism, or 'mytho-terrorism', helps explain not only Bin Laden's own motivations but also why his appeal among the aggrieved will probably outlive him and exceed the impact of his own crimes.

Mytho-terrorism has similar characteristics to other forms of violence like wars or revolutions that bind together the deprived, the weak, the resentful, the repressed or just the temporarily disadvantaged. The difference, however, that gives mytho-terrorism its spectacular power *as* well *as* anticipating its eventual failure, is the targeting of innocent victims in the name of a higher good. Conducted for an imagined collectivity, looking backwards to a supposed Golden Age, or predicting a future paradise, mytho-terrorism undermines a political order through asymmetrical violence but is unable to generate public legitimacy for any earthly alternatives. It relies on a perpetual struggle, a *jihad* or holy war.

The messages of the tapes portray an escalating conflict dating from the medieval Crusades that can only end in a final conflagration of vengeance against the infidel and of redemption for the *jihadist*. Bin Laden's vision depends not only on the idea of an original act of injury against Islam, but also on the persistence of reciprocal injustices. From the start, President Bush was quick to fall into this mimetic trap, responding in kind when he vowed at the Washington National Cathedral shortly after the attack 'to rid the world of evil'. By imitating the evangelical rhetoric and practice of with-us-or-against-us, he ignored the counsel and constraint of sympathetic allies who had prior experience with terrorism at home.

The obvious must be restated: this is not to claim any moral equivalence between Bush and Bin Laden but rather to identify a mutual pathology in operation, the kind of mimetic relationship that often develops in war and terror. People go to war not only out of rational calculation but also because of how they see, perceive, picture, imagine and speak of each other: that is, because of how the construction of difference of other groups, as well as the sameness of their own, takes on irreconcilable conditions of hostility. Neither Bush nor Bin Laden is the first to think that mimesis might be mined for political advantage, only to find themselves caught in its own dynamic. From Greek tragedy and Roman gladiatorial spectacles to futurist art and fascist rallies, mimetic violence has regularly overpowered virtuous intentions as well as democratic practices. The question, then, is how to break this mimetic encounter of mythoterrorism?

Historically, terrorist movements without a mass base quickly weaken and rarely last more than a decade. However, the mimetic struggle between Bush and Bin Laden, magnified by the media, fought by advanced technologies of destruction, and unchecked by the UN or our allies, has developed a patho-logic of its own in which assimilation or extermination become plausible solutions for what appears to be an intractable problem.

As subsequent acts of terror and counter-terror surpassed the immediate effects of the 9/11 attack, as Bin Laden morphed into yet another avatar of evil, Saddam Hussein, we now face a pathological form of mimesis that has been medically defined as 'the appearance, often caused by hysteria, of symptoms of a disease not actually present'. Bin Laden's videotapes inflame the mimetic condition by linking terrorist attacks in Tunisia, Karachi, Yemen, Kuwait, Bali and even Moscow to an age-old crusade of Islam against the West. In response, the White House's new 'National Strategy to Secure Cyberspace' called on all Americans to guard against a 'digital disaster' by becoming 'digital citizen soldiers'. The Pentagon's main research arm, the Defense Advance Research Projects Agency (DARPA), proposes under the rubric of 'Scientia Est Potentia' (knowledge is power) data-mining operations to provide 'Total Information Awareness' on citizens and foreigners alike. Meanwhile a 'Green Scare' of Islam threatens the body politic as severely as the hysteria of past Red Scares.

Dead or alive, prophet or crackpot, symptom or disease, Bin Laden as well as Hussein require a mimetic foe. Without a reciprocal hatred their prophecies lose their self-fulfilling powers. As is often the case with narcissistic psychopaths, the worst thing we could do is to deprive them of their reflections.

As we know from medical pathology, the auto-immune response can kill as well as cure. The response to the most powerful images after the Bin Laden tapes, the Abu Ghraib photos, bears this out. Consider Donald Rumsfeld's first complaint upon the appearance of the Abu Ghraib images:

> In the information age, people are running around with digital cameras and taking these unbelievable photographs and then passing them off, against the law, to the media, to our surprise, when they had not even arrived in the Pentagon.[9]

An escalating war of images ensued. Heinous crimes were revealed, public outrage expressed, official apologies proffered, congressional hearings convened and court martials put into progress. But something went missing in this mass-mediated picture of pictures. In the rush to moral condemnation and for political expiation, the *meaning* of the images became moot. In the case of the Abu Ghraib photos, once established as 'authentic', they took on a singular significance: a crisis for the Bush administration and the USA's reputation in the world. Numerous reports of earlier instances of dissimulations, group-think acts of self-deception, and outright lies by the US government, from claims about Iraqi ties to Al-Qaeda, the presence of weapons of mass destruction, and the likelihood of a swift post-war transition to peace and democracy, all paled in comparative political effect to the digital images of simulated sex, dominatrix bondage, and mock KKK-lynchings (with electrical wires substituting for the hangman's noose).

Roland Barthes identifies the source of this power in the image: 'From a phenomenological viewpoint, in the photograph, the power of authentication exceeds the power of representation'.[10] How does the authenticity of the image come to trump the representation of the word? And in the age of Adobe Photoshop, just what does *authentic* mean? This is not to suggest that the photos taken at the Abu Ghraib prison are fake, as proved to be the case with facsimile images published in the *Daily Mirror* tabloid of British soldiers torturing an Iraqi prisoner and with the images published by Egyptian newspapers of an American soldier sexually abusing a woman (actually downloaded from an unrelated porn website). It is rather to raise critical questions that the press and academics have been slow to consider. These are questions on how not just cultural interpretation, moral judgement and ideological fervor, but also new technical means of reproduction, real-time transmission and global circulation via the internet produce profound and potentially uncontrollable truth-effects through the use of photographic and vidcographic imagery.

As we are exposed to loop-images of prisoner abuse, islamicist hip-hop videos, and a brutal snuff film of hostages, at some point (a point rapidly shrinking in duration) between the initial shock produced by the images (they are just too unbelievable) and the banalisation of evil through replication (they have become too familiar), the reality principle itself begins to disappear with a flick of the channel, click of the mouse. Consider just a few of the 'aberrant' responses to the Abu Ghraib images circulating on the internet. According the Associated Press, the editor of the one of the Egyptian newspapers in question, Mustafa Bakri, justified publication of the pornographic images of American sexual abuse because 'the kind of pictures on CBS made us believe that any other picture is authentic' (5 May 2004). The *Guardian* quoted the British Liberal Democrat leader, Charles Kennedy, as saying that the photos showing British abuse of an Iraqi would lead to renewed violence even if they were fake (7 May 2004). And, as one sample from many blogs, 'SkepticOverlord' likened the fakery to an episode of the CBS-produced television series 'The Agency', in which the CIA staged a porno film to discredit a militant Islamic leader.

It may well be that in the search for authenticity we are witnessing a deeper desire for a lost moral certainty, in which the public representation of reality becomes a function of a collective struggle for ethical superiority, of a kind that initially justified the US intervention in Iraq and that ultimately provides the twisted rationale of the torturer.

## The ethos of terror

US foreign policy has always been a struggle of ethics and power, and when politics escalates into war, the first casualty—as isolationist Senator Hiram Johnson famously remarked in 1917—is the truth. With the casualty list growing every day in the war against terror, a war of images was inevitable. The biggest salvos in this homegrown struggle of morality, truth and power came with Michael Moore's documentary, *Fahrenheit 9/11*.

Promoted in the film trailer as the 'true story that will make your temperature rise', duly attacked by Bill O'Reilly as 'Leni Riefenstahl Third Reich propaganda', and challenged by the right-wing group Citizens United as a violation of federal election laws, *Fahrenheit 9/11*, all about the news, swiftly became the news. Lost in the polarised debate was much of an account of *how* this film succeeds, particularly of Moore's uncanny ability to evince powerful moral and emotional responses from an image-saturated mix of media. Like the Rodney King video (or the Stanley Miller sequel) of black men being beaten up by the police, the looped shot of the twin towers falling, Bin Laden's home movies, the Abu Ghraib digital snapshots, and the Richard Berg snuff film, *Fahrenheit 911* plays to the modern sensibility that our leaders might and often do lie but that images cannot.

In the process irrefutable images damn the guilty by association. Blacked-out names from Bush's National Guard records magically reappear like invisible ink in reverse; the Bush posse morphs into the Cartwright family from the TV series, 'Bonanza'; and shaking the hands of an Arab becomes poof-positive of calumny and conspiracy. It might be better to celebrate *Fahrenheit 9/11* as an imaginary rather than a documentary.

This is not a criticism. We had best remember again the words of Benjamin on realism as the 'the strongest narcotic of the century'. He went on to exhort

30

those in the grip of a *faux* realpolitik that 'in times of terror, when everyone is something of a conspirator, everybody will be in a situation where he has to play detective'.

As proof, numerous print reports of earlier instances of dissimulations, group-think acts of self-deception and outright lies by the Bush administration, from claims about Iraqi ties to Al-Qaeda, the presence of weapons of mass destruction, and the likelihood of a swift post-war transition to peace and democracy, continuously surface, sink and bubble-up from a variety of news holes. Confusion, not freedom, reigns. But in *Fahrenheit 911* the image seized and sustained public attention and demanded a response. Why?

We are back to the power of authentication over representation: what the word can only represent, the picture supposedly proves. The traditional print media have been slow to understand how the internet, with its real-time transmission and global circulation of images, has force-multiplied this effect and transformed the political as well as media game. Indeed, many of the most ludicrous as well as most disturbing images in Moore's film—like Bush goofing in the Oval office before he goes primetime to announce the beginning of the Iraq war, or the gun camera shot of an Apache helicopter crew coolly taking out three Iraqis—have been seen on websites for well over a year.

However, in an Age of Info-terror one begins to wonder just how profound and lasting these image-effects truly are. The King video incited plenty of righteous anger, but notably failed to indict the perpetrators. Regardless of photographs and videos to the contrary, a French *nonfiction* best seller arguing that 9/11 was fabricated found a credulous audience. The Abu Ghraib images shocked us but have yet to cause any heads to roll (or at least not any adorned with stars).

How long before photographic immanence loses its power of authentication and stimulation, we stop believing what we see, and the significance of the image itself is called into question? How many times can the truth take a beating before the public just stops believing *anything* it hears, reads and sees? Not soon enough?

It may well be that the early newspaper ads promoting *Fahrenheit 911*— Moore and Bush frolicking hand-in-hand in front of the White House, with 'Controversy…What Controversy?' underneath—contain a hidden answer to these questions. Bush, Bin Laden *and* Moore have tapped into a great insecurity in which the search for authenticity becomes inseparable from the desire for moral superiority. In their projection (dare I say simulation) of exclusive truths, they have each found their mirror other.

In *Twilight of the Idols*, Nietzsche exhorts us in our search for meaning to eschew quick moral judgements in favour of a more arduous semiotic investigation:

> Morality is only an interpretation of certain phenomena, more precisely a
> *mis*interpretation. Moral judgement belongs, as does religious judgement, to a
> level of ignorance at which even the concept of the real, the distinction between

the real and the imaginary, is lacking: so that at such a level 'truth' denotes nothing but things which we today call 'imaginings'. To this extent moral judgment is never to be taken literally: as such it never contains anything but nonsense. But as *semiotics* it remains of incalculable value: it reveals, to the informed man at least, the most precious realities of cultures and inner worlds which did not *know* enough to 'understand' themselves. Morality is merely 'sign' language, merely symptomatology; one must already know *what* it is about to derive profit from it.[11]

So what is it about? Here's an historical clue: 'semiotics', or the study of signs, emerged in the 16th century in the arts of war and medicine. It referred to new methods of military manoeuvre based on visual signals, as well as new medical techniques for identifying pathological symptoms in humans. From day one signs had the power to kill as well as to cure. In the 21st century we need to develop a new semiotics for the images of the war against terror. Otherwise we will continue treating its most morbid symptoms with morality plays rather than finding a cure for the all-too-real disease of imperial politics.

## Epilogue

The war of images continues. Osama Bin Laden, who knocked the balance of terror askew, saw fit in an October-surprise election video to give the USA notice that this particular insurgent was resurgent. Ostensibly directing his remarks to US citizens rather than to the presidential candidates, he provided a civics lessons on the meaning of freedom and security. In case they had found the attacks on the World Trade Center and the Pentagon too subtle, he offered a more explicit explanation for his actions:

> Security is an important pillar of human life. Free people do not relinquish their security. This is contrary to Bush's claim that we hate freedom…We fought you because we are free and do not accept injustice. We want to restore freedom to our nation. Just as you waste our security, we will waste your security.

After a short digression on the strategic advantage al-Qaeda gained by President Bush 'being preoccupied with the little child's talk about her goat and its butting' (prompting former New York Mayor Guliani to remark that Bin Laden was 'taking his lines from Michael Moore's film'), he ends the video by returning to the security dilemma:

> Your security does not lie in the hands of Kerry, Bush, or al-Qaeda. Your security is in your own hands. Each and every state that does not tamper with our security will have automatically assured its own security.

It took *Saturday Night Live* just two days to subvert not only the medium and the message of Bin Laden's videotape, but also the self-image upon which global democracy is supposed to be modelled. In the skit, a news anchor (bearing some resemblance to Tom Brokaw) introduces a clip of an Osama bin Laden impersonator speaking in Arabic with English subtitles:

Hello. I am Osama Bin Laden. And Allah be praised, this is my message to the American people. In a few days, you will hold your election to choose between the ignorant cowboy Bush and the gigolo Kerry. Over the last several months, I have been approached repeatedly by representatives of both candidates, who have asked me if I would please endorse their opponents. But I have refused to do this. First, because frankly, I find this request sort of insulting, which it really is, if you think about it. Especially coming from Bush, who has not shown the least bit of interest in me since he invaded Iraq. And also, because to me, voting is a private matter, and one which I take very seriously. For a time, I feared that I would not be eligible to vote in this election. But recently, praise Allah, I was tracked down by two volunteers from the Kerry campaign. They signed me up, and apparently, I am now registered in Cincinnati.

Facing the logos, pathos and ethos of terror, the weapon of mass whimsy might still be the best way to counter the mimetic war of images.

## Notes

[1]   Based on techniques first developed in the 1870s by the founder of eugenics, Francis Galton, in which photographs of criminals were superimposed into a 'natural kind', Burson's digitalised images of the 1980s subverted the notion of ideal types, for example in 'Warhead' and 'Beauty' (a composite of Hollywood actresses Jane Fonda, Brooke Shields, Meryl Streep, Diane Keaton and Jacqueline Bisset).

[2]   'The art of deterrence, prohibiting political war, favors the upsurge, not of conflicts, but of acts of war without war.' See P Virilio, *Pure War*, trans M Polizotti, New York: Semiotext(e), 1983, p 27.

[3]   See J Der Derian, *Virtuous War: Mapping the Miltiary – Industrial – Media – Entertainment Network*, Boulder, CO: Westview Press, 2001. It is also worth remembering the Pentagon's secret effort to model seven post-cold war 'war scenarios', including the rise of a Resurgent/Emergent Global Threat (REGT) by 2001, which was authored by Paul Wolfowitz. See P Tyler, *New York Times*, 17 February 1992, p A8.

[4]   See R Barthes, 'Rhetoric of the image', in Barthes, *Image-Music-Text*, trans S Heath, New York: Hill and Wang, 1977, pp 32–51.

[5]   *White Sands* (1992) starring Willem Dafoe, Mary Elizabeth Mastrantonio and Mickey Rourke.

[6]   W Benjamin, 'The work of art in the Age of Mechanical Reproduction', in H Arendt (ed), Illuminations, New York: Schocken, 1969, pp 241–242.

[7]   W Benjamin, *The Arcades Project*, trans. H Eiland and K McLaughlin, Cambridge, MA: Harvard University Press, 1999, pp 462–464.

[8]   I would like to thank Tom Levin for the gift of the phrase, 'Age of Adobe Photoshop'.

[9]   M Dowd, 'A world of hurt', *New York Times*, 9 May 2004.

[10]   R Barthes, *Camera Lucida: Reflections on Photography*, New York: Vintage, 1982.

[11]   F Nietzsche, *Twilight of the Idols*, trans RJ Hollingdale, London: Penguin, 1968, p 55.

# Al-Qaeda—terrorists, hypocrites, fundamentalists? The view from within

CHRISTINA HELLMICH

Al Qaeda not driven by ideology[1]

Ideology of Al-Qaeda to be traced back to the origins of Wahhabism[2]

Al-Qaeda corrupts, misrepresents and misinterprets the Koranic text[3]

Al Qaeda, the first multinational terrorist group of the 21st century, embodies the new enigmatic face of terrorism. By organising and perpetrating the world's greatest terrorist outrage on 11 September 2001, the organisation demonstrated the sophistication of its methods and the magnitude of its threat. In the weeks and months that followed, few other issues—if any—have received more public attention than Al-Qaeda and Osama bin Ladin. Yet, despite the ongoing discussion in the media, academic and policy circles, few contributions have usefully explained the phenomenon. An initial search of the term 'Al-Qaeda' on Google generates over 12 900 links to articles, interviews, books and commentaries in multiple languages. However, speculation about the strength and extent of Al-Qaeda, bewildering descriptions of a shadowy network, undercover terrorist cells, new arrests and imminent dangers create alarm but not much clarity. Adding the term 'ideology' to the search does not produce more satisfying results: 'Al-Qaeda not driven by ideology' is the conclusion reached by a Pentagon intelligence team,[4] while, according to Stephen Schwartz, among others, 'Osama bin Ladin and his followers belong to a puritanical variant of Islam known as Wahhabism, an extreme and intolerant Islamo-Fascist sect that became the official cult of Saudi Arabia'.[5]

The voices heard most loudly are those presenting Al-Qaeda as a group of religious fanatics, lunatics mad mullahs or even fascists—embodiments of 'pure evil'. In the words of terrorism expert Rohan Gunaratna, 'aiming to galvanise the spirit of its supporters, Al-Qaeda corrupts, misrepresents or misinterprets the Koranic text'. The deliberate use of such terminology generates the widespread image of bin Ladin and his followers as a group of extremists who intentionally utilise Islam as a tool to rally popular support and legitimise terrorism in the pursuit of their purely political goals. However, in direct contrast to this popular perception, anthropological research shows that religious fundamentalists throughout the world, including the followers of Al-Qaeda, act and consider themselves as the true believers.[6]

A more pertinent line of inquiry into the ideology behind bin Ladin's and Al-Qaeda's politics of violence would be to focus on questions about its inner logic, those related to ideology as seen from within. What is the connection between religious and political parameters blurred by the rhetoric of bin Ladin? What lies behind the espousal of Islam, anti-Americanism and the resort to violence? Is bin Ladin, as the existing literature suggests, abusing Islam to pursue his purely political goals and legitimise terror? How do the followers and supporters of bin Ladin's and Al-Qaeda's ideology perceive themselves? The answers to these questions may shed a new light on the rationale of Al-Qaeda. They will also help clarify existing, or rather non-existing, limits to potential attacks in the future, which is critical in defining an effective counter-terrorism strategy.

## The linking of religion and politics

An inquiry into the inner logic of Al-Qaeda and the connection between Islam and politics should begin with an analysis of the nature of religious fundamentalism. The term, which originally applied to an early 20th century American Protestant movement, has entered the vocabulary of the social sciences as a designation for conservative, revivalist religious orthodoxy. Yet it is the more recent rise of fundamentalist movements, specifically in a range of Islamic societies, calling for a literal reading of the holy text and characterised by the aim of intervening in the political system and mobilising the population that has generated a wide-ranging response.[7] The result of this increased attention is an often arbitrary use of terms such as 'Islam', 'Islamic fundamentalism', 'Islamism', and more recently 'Islamic extremism' or 'Islamic terrorism'.

In this paper the understanding of Islamic fundamentalism is based on a combination of two ways of looking at religion, namely as a source of meaning and as incorporated into reality.[8] The underlying hypothesis is that religion consists of sociocultural symbols that convey a conception of reality and construe a plan for it. These symbols are related to reality, but not a reflection of it, as understood in the cultural anthropology of Clifford Geertz.[9] Important to note here is the distinction between 'models of reality' and 'models for reality'. The former relate to the representation of objects. They are both concrete, by displaying structural congruence with the depicted object, and abstract, as they are views, religious dogmas or doctrines prescribed to effect conditions with which they are not congruent.[10] On the other hand, whether metaphysically or rationally, models for reality relate to human perceptions of how reality ought to be designed. As such, they are normative and consequently can only be penetrated interpretatively.[11]

In Islam human conceptions of reality are not based on knowledge, but on the belief in the divine authority of Allah and the revelation of the Quran as the ultimate truth, immutable and universally valid for all people regardless of time and space.[12] Most discussions—and this holds for both Western and, to a significant extent, Muslim scholarship—of Islam and politics assume that Islam makes no distinction between the religious and political realms.[13] This view of inseparability finds support in over 40 references in the Quran, and the example of the Prophet, at once a spiritual leader and the head of a political community.[14] It is further shown in the creation of the 'Islamicate' as the creation of the Islamic *umma* and the caliphate, the political order of the Islamicate.[15] Yet a careful reading of the historical record indicates that politics and religion became separable not long after the death of the Prophet and the establishment of dynastic rule.[16]

This early historical background is strikingly different from the modern fundamentalist claim for an Islamic state and a corresponding *sharia*-bound (Islamic legal system) Islamic government. The call for a *dawla Islamiya* (Islamic state) made by all contemporary Islamic fundamentalists is based on the belief that a *nizam Islami* (Islamic system) forms the centre of Islam. Yet this assumption is held exclusively by Islamic fundamentalists, not the religion of Islam as revealed in the Quran and the *hadith* (collection of the traditions of the Prophet). These neo-Arabic terms used by contemporary Islamic fundamentalists do not exist in any classical Islamic source, which leads to the conclusion that the notion of an Islamic system exemplified by an Islamic state is an 'invention of tradition'.[17] In theoretical terms Islamic fundamentalism is the result of adapting Islamic concepts to social–political advocacy. In the words of Bassam Tibi, Islamic fundamentalism is an 'ideology, which stands in the context of the oscillation in Islam between culture and politics, and is related to the politicisation of Islamic cultural concepts and symbols'.[18]

Despite the fundamentalists' claim to recognise the universality of the revelation and their declared intention to retrieve its fundamental basics (*usul*)—the original foundations of Islam—the reality of what is taking place is remarkably different. The simultaneous denial of cognitive adaptation to reality, while effectively doing the exact same thing, is striking. This is obvious, for example, in Sayyid Qutb's well known political interpretation of the Quran.[19] In reading Qutb's Quran commentary, one is continually struck by the interplay between his own ideas and the Quranic text, which shows that he did not find the truth in the script itself, but rather found truth in what he believed to be its meaning.[20] The same process is evident when Bin Ladin calls upon his fellow Muslims to fight the enemies of Islam, primarily Americans and Jews. Rather than, in the words of Al-Qaeda expert Rohan Gunaratna, 'aiming to galvanise the spirit of his supporters by corrupting, misrepresenting or misinterpreting the Quranic text',[21] he has transferred the words of the holy text into the current political context and interpreted their meaning in the light of the new situation.

This brief investigation into the relationship of religion and politics contradicts the popular perception of Islamic fundamentalists as a limited number of religious extremists who intentionally abuse Islam to legitimise their political aspirations. Although it is not the aim of this paper to judge the underlying intentions of the individual, the paper does suggest that it would be misleading to assume that the role of religion in political conflicts is merely instrumental. It contests the popular view that in the case of Islamic fundamentalism religion serves as a mechanism for obtaining political legitimisation and is being abused for purely political ends. In contrast, fundamentalists throughout the world act and perceive themselves to be the true believers.[22] Although it may contradict an exclusively spiritual understanding of religion, to comprehend the inner logic of Al-Qaeda it is crucial to acknowledge that Islamic fundamentalists advance a concept of Islam that sees no contradiction between belief and political action. As a direct consequence, many Muslims see those believers who equate their political interpretation of Islamic sources with Islamic religious belief as particularly keen and devout Muslims, persecuted by unjust bureaucracies. It is for this reason that many Muslims support Al-Qaeda and see a hero in Bin Ladin. In the words of a young Pakistani interviewed on Al-Jazeera, 'Bin Ladin is not a terrorist. That is American rhetoric. He is a good Muslim fighting for Islam. I named my son Osama—I want him to become a believer just like him.'

## Al-Qaeda's ideology: influences, sources and appeal

While the process of adapting Islamic concepts to structural changes explains the origins of Al-Qaeda's ideology in theory, questions related to its appeal and impact on the audience, as well as to its ideological influences and sources, necessitate a closer look at the sociopolitical context, the intellectual leadership of Al-Qaeda and the nature of its recruits. In general the Muslim world has not been isolated from the processes of modernisation and the advent of mass education that, among other factors, have influenced the development of modern political societies and produced new identities, opportunities and inequalities. Two results of these social and political changes are particularly important for the advancement of Islamic fundamentalism. The first is the fragmentation of religious authority 'whereby the meaning of scripture no longer needs to be interpreted by a religious establishment but, rather, lies in the eyes of the beholder'.[23] The second one is a process by which basic questions such as the actual meaning of Islam and how it affects—or rather should affect—the conduct of life come to the fore in the consciousness of believers. In other words, what does it mean to be a Muslim in a world that bears no resemblance to the glorious past of Islam? This development is also referred to as the objectification of Muslim consciousness.[24]

As it is becoming more and more difficult to say with reassuring finality what is Islamic and what is not, the issue of precisely who establishes the guidelines for 'proper' Islamic behaviour is of vital importance. The *imam*, for example, who traditionally occupied a position of religious authority, is no longer the only figure to whom believers can turn in their search for religious guidance. As individual Muslims take it upon themselves to interpret the classical sources of Islam, a broad spectrum of interpretations emerges. In the words of the Sorbonne-educated leader of the Muslim Brothers in Sudan: 'Because all knowledge is divine and religious, a chemist, and engineer, an economist or a jurist are all *'ulama"*.[25] Hence it is perfectly feasible that someone without religious training in the traditional sense, like Osama bin Ladin, may obtain the status of a religious authority in the eyes of his followers. By addressing timely issues of grave concern in the Muslim world and by formalising the return to the golden age tradition as a straightforward solution, he provides both a powerful indictment of the waywardness of Muslim societies and a blueprint for action. Thus, the turning towards the Islamic tradition and its interpretation becomes a way of legitimately criticising the existing status quo, providing religious guidance and facilitating revolutionary and incremental changes.[26]

Ideologically bin Ladin started off as a member of the Muslim Brotherhood—which, one might note, is not a Wahhabi-oriented organisation—joining forces with Abdullah Azzam, a legendary Arab fighter against the USSR in Afghanistan.[27] Upon setting up Al-Qaeda in the mid-1980s, the Muslim Brotherhood broke off its links with bin Ladin, who had gone his own way politically. As the name of the newly founded organisation suggests, the idea behind al-Qaeda was the establishment of a 'base' that would bring together different Islamic fundamentalist groups and co-ordinate their activities. Yet the organisation failed to attract the mainstream of the radical Islamic fundamentalist movement in Arab countries. When the Egyptian Islamic Jihad and the Jama'a al-Islamiyya refused to join Al-Qaeda in a meeting in Afghanistan in 1988, it became apparent that, while there were issues over relinquishing leadership to bin Ladin, the key disagreement lay in the scope of Islamist action. With few exceptions the view was maintained that action should be confined to each groups' nation-state. However, some of the key Islamist figures, including the leader of the Jihad movement Ayyman al-Zawahri, began to change their outlook to that of a more internationalist revolutionary movement. Al-Zawahri's decision to join Al-Qaeda was based on the belief that the Islamic fundamentalist groups within their individual states were prevented from achieving any significant change on the domestic front because of a common external enemy. Hence, at the leadership level, Al-Qaeda brings together individuals with both strong religious sentiments and previous terrorist records who regard their actions as a much-needed act of defiance against the 'real enemy'—that enemy being the source of all the ills affecting the Muslim world—primarily the USA, because of its support for Israel and for the corrupt dictatorships of the Middle East.

Thus the key to the ideology of Al-Qaeda, as indicated above, lies in the political view of the situation in Muslim societies in general, and the Middle East in particular. The basis for its ideology of violence that has become the political world-view of Al-Qaeda can be found in al-Zawahri's treatise published in 1996, entitled *Shifa' Sudur al-Muminin* (The Cure for Believers' Hearts). The way he adapts Islamic principles to the present political situation and derives therefrom implications for proper Islamic conduct becomes evident in his analysis of three interrelated issues. The first is primarily of a political nature: By ranking Palestine as the primary problem, al-Zawahri concludes that all Arab and Muslim regimes have lost their credibility by the mere fact that they have accepted the authority of the UN and the legitimacy of Israel. Invoking the Palestinian issue allows him to declare these governments, especially Saudi Arabia, with its close ties to the USA, the main supporter of Israel, to be outside the fold of Islam. Furthermore, Saudi and US support for the *Mujahideen* movement in Afghanistan is seen as a ploy to divert attention from the real goal of change in the Muslim world. Boldly, he declares that the *Mujahideen* saw through this plot right from the beginning and established 'Al-Qaeda—the base' in Afghanistan to carry out their world-wide struggle against the outside enemy.

The second issue is that of personal consequences that arise in this particular political context for the individual believer, expressed in al-Zawahri's interpretations of personal responsibility in Islamic law. In essence, every Muslim who in any way supports these 'un-islamic' regimes places himself outside the fold of Islam. It is not possible to take refuge in the claim of merely following orders, as only God's orders are to be followed, and these include the acceptance of taking personal responsibility. For Al-Qaeda's internationalist struggle, this argument is expanded to Western governments. The inherent logic could be expressed as follows: as citizens of these countries, Muslims vote, and even if they don't vote, they pay taxes, and therefore support these governments. As such, they loose their status of innocent non-combatants in Islamic law, making themselves legitimate targets in the case of an attack.

A frequently encountered point of criticism to this logic is, for example, the mentioning of children, who are specifically exempted from being combatants in Islamic law. In response to the main corpus of Islamic theology, which clearly rejects the concept of collateral damage, Al-Zawahri propounds the ideas of the greater good and the need to react to exceptional circumstances. Clearly expressing his point of view, he states that an overpowering enemy and limited resources allow for a more lax interpretation of the law. It is precisely this logic that also allows him to handle the clear and absolute prohibition of suicide under Islamic law. Drawing on the idea of martyrdom in the Christian sense, he takes the examples of captured Muslims who were asked to recant on pain of death, and refused. Viewing this refusal as suicide for the glory of God that was not condemned by Islamic theologians, he concludes that committing suicide for the greater good is legal.

Another example of the interpretation of the political context and the concepts of the greater good and personal responsibility can be found in the *fatwa* (a legal opinion usually issued by trusted legal scholars about questions that arise in the Muslim community) issued by five leaders of Al-Qaida on 23 January 1998.

> The Arabian Peninsula has never—since God made it flat, created its desert, and encircled it with seas—been stormed by any forces like the crusader armies spreading in it like locusts ... for over seven years the United States has been occupying the lands of Islam, the holiest of places, the Arabian Peninsula, plundering its riches, dictating to its rulers, humiliating its people, terrorizing its neighbors.

Following this assessment of the political interpretation, the *fatwa* calls on

> every Muslim who believes in God and hopes for reward to obey God's command to kill the Americans and plunder their possessions wherever he finds them and wherever he can.[28]

The essence of this adaptation of Islamic principles to the political situation is the complete separation between the 'true believers', ie the Islamic fundamentalists, and the 'enemy', now including all Muslims who are in anyway connected to non-Islamic regimes, rendering them legitimate targets in the fight for the glory of Islam. It is a theory that is not based on the main schools of Islamic theology, but a new ideological starting point that provides Al-Qaeda with a theoretical legitimisation for non-discriminatory, violent action.

Finally, a brief look at the nature of Al-Qaeda's recruits might offer a first insight into the appeal of the ideology. With an array of different nationalities, some of those who joined the network came as committed Muslims, while others needed basic instruction in Islamic dogma and practice. Thus, an essential component in the recruitment and training of new members of Al-Qaeda is the familiarisation—or maybe more appropriately— indoctrination with knowledge of Islamic law and practice as understood by bin Ladin and al-Zawahri. To understand how this ideology is perceived by the recruits and members of Al-Qaeda, in other words to gain an insight into the view from within, the overriding question for the following analysis of an Al-Qaeda training video clearly focuses on the potential impact of the presentation on the audience.

### Communicating the ideology—paving the way for taking action

The following will analyse the ideology communicated by Osama bin Ladin in a recently discovered training manual.[29] The video chosen for this case study exemplifies the kind of address that legitimises the culturally constituted duty of *jihad* or 'struggle' by presenting religion and morality in a symbolic idiom and through the projection of the cultural archetype of the *mujahid* or 'fighter'. By establishing a religious base, interpreting its meaning in the present sociopolitical context and leading the audience into a moral endeavour—in other words, communicating the concept of personal responsibility, it motivates the audience into taking violent action against the declared enemy. Hence, what is communicated here represents the key aspects of Al-Qaeda's ideology discussed in the previous section, but also goes beyond that by providing a straightforward plan of action. To evaluate its potential effect on the audience, close attention will be paid to both the content and style of the address.

The video begins with a citation from the Quran addressing the Muslims' favoured position in the eyes of Allah and their obligation to follow his will at all times, placed against the background of a scenic, quiet mountain view. After a brief but meaningful pause, the scene switches to bin Ladin: standing in front of a blue world map and presenting himself to the audience in the traditional clothing of an Islamic preacher, he creates the image of a religious authority. Very diligently and in very low tone of voice, he speaks, repeating the same Quranic verses (shown below in italics).

> *You are the best community ever brought forth to mankind. The goodness is in you, it comes forth from your hands and from under your feet. You are the best nation ever brought forth to men, biding to honour and forbidding dishonour, and believing in Allah.* (3: 110)[30]

> Thus, forever, let there be one nation, calling for good, enjoining honour and fighting dishonour, those are the prosperous.

By complementing the quotation with his personal interpretation he establishes in embryo both the form and the content of all that is to follow. In terms of form the citations constitute a duality or complementarity, a stylistic device, which can be observed throughout his speech, in which the main points are advanced by means of categorical juxtapositions and mutual oppositions.[31] Furthermore, it should be noticed that from the very beginning citations from the Quran, establishing the religious facts, are immediately followed by bin Ladin's own interpretations of 'what reality ought to be'.

In terms of content, the pairing of the Quranic citation and bin Ladin's practical application firmly establishes two fundamental principles of Islam, as well as their direct consequences for the present, which can be summarised as follows. First, the *umma*—which includes all Muslims regardless of ethnic origin—is the community most favoured by God, which implies (at least according to bin Ladin) the need to act as one nation, as well as the pursuit of what is honourable, ie allowed, or rather expected, under Islamic law, and the prevention of that which is sinful. Second, it reinforces what might be regarded as the cardinal principle of Islam, the duty of every sincere Muslim to 'obey God and his Messenger'.

*And obey Allah and the Messenger that you may obtain mercy. And march forth in the way (which leads to) forgiveness from your Lord, and for Paradise as wide as the heavens and the earth, prepared for the pious. (3: 132)*

We testify that there is no God but Allah, He alone, and no associate with Him.

Having clearly established divine imperatives and the ideal model for reality, the audience is presented with the fact that the actual reality of the present situation is nothing like it ought to be. Pronounced in a highly dramatic tone which is hardly reflected in the following translation, bin Ladin declares that it is the duty of every sincere Muslim—note here the concept of personal responsibility—to correct a situation in which members of the *umma* are subjected to unacceptable levels of pain and corruption by an outside force. Interestingly, bin Ladin's observation of reality is now followed by a quotation from the Quran. Structuring his argument in this manner, he not only makes it impossible to question the Islamic integrity of his solution to the problem—not to ask for peace from the enemies of Islam (who are responsible for the absolutely outrageous abuse of the *umma*)—but also increases the credibility of the invoked threat of eternal hell and the promise of heavenly rewards if this path is followed.

> But what is happening to us? The world is on fire. Endless suffering, increasing corruption, horrendous abuse. Just look at Iraq. Look at Palestine. Look at Kashmir. Atrocities are committed against our brothers and sisters. Yet they are part of our community, and they deserve our sympathy and our support.

> *Oh you who believe. Obey Allah and obey the Messenger and render not vain your deeds. Verily, those who disbelieve and hinder from the path of Allah, they will die as disbelievers and Allah will not forgive them. So be not weak and ask not for peace from the enemies of Islam while you are having the upper hand. Allah is with you and will never decrease the reward of your good deed. (47: 33–34)*

It should not go unnoticed that what has happened here is the direct application of the Quranic message, carrying over its dictates to the present. The fact that the quotation from the Quran is taken out of its original context and used to legitimise a clearly action-oriented strategy indicates that bin Ladin, much like other fundamentalists before him, has found the meaning of this particular verse through applying it to the reality he experiences around him. In other words, the meaning is not actually derived from the source itself, but from its relevance to the surrounding political situation. However, it should be noted that neither the ideology bin Ladin proclaims nor the tropes he employs are by any means original to him. The issue of protecting the *umma* has been addressed in the classic polemical essays of such authors as Sayyid Qutb and Muhammad al-Ghazzali among others.[32] In other words, the arguments are old, and are being recycled in this new context.

Having established a core principle of Islam in a highly emotive manner, the video presents scenes of the current political situation, specifically showing suffering Muslims. In line with the image of a world on fire, headlines in the form of enflamed letters appear on the screen, indicating the localities to be shown—Palestine, Chechnya, Iraq and Kashmir. What follows are frequently repeated images of Israeli soldiers beating up Muslim women, Palestinian children throwing rocks at tanks and the destruction of Palestinian homes, to name but a few. Then the fiery headline changes the scene to Chechnya, presenting images of more destruction as well as scenes of freezing Muslims, dying outside in the snow at night. Turning to Iraq, the audience is confronted with the sight of severely disabled infants. Images of American soldiers and the 'ungodly' ruler Saddam Hussein complete the picture of a Muslim country suffering at the hands of the unbelievers. Finally, bloody images from Kashmir, such as beheaded toddlers and wounded teenagers conclude this display of world-wide Muslim suffering at the hands of 'unbelievers'.

Throughout this part of the video Islamic music of different styles is played, adding to the powerful emotional force of the images presented. The accusations are legitimised by the showing of a series of images that were previously shown on Arabic news broadcasts such as Al-Jazeera and LBC. Thus what is shown in the video is a selection of the most brutal scenes, creating a powerful and emotional image of the truly miserable state of the *umma*. A state that—according to the interpretations and message constructed by bin Ladin—urgently needs to be rectified by all members of the community both in support of their Muslim brothers and sisters and, maybe even more importantly, in defence of Islam itself. Following this highly emotional presentation of human suffering, bin Ladin makes it unambiguously clear what has to be done to change the situation:

> And the world is on fire. Our Muslim brothers and sisters in Palestine and Iraq are suffering under a Zionist–Crusader invasion. The crusader forces control the holy land, eating its riches and controlling its people. And this is happening while Muslims all over the world are attacked like people fighting over a piece of bread.
>
> *Oh you who believe! What is the matter with you, that when you are asked to march forth in the Cause of Allah/Jihad, you cling heavily to the earth? Are you pleased with the life of this world rather than the Hereafter? But little is in the enjoyment of the life of this world as compared to the hereafter.* (9: 38)

Backed by legitimacy derived from an appropriate Quranic citation, bin Ladin has created a situation that allows him to present a straightforward case. Having reinvoked the miserable state of the *umma*, he refers to the enemy in a symbolic phrase as the 'Zionist–Crusader invasion'. The image of the crusades creates a perception of the enemy as a threat not only to the *umma* but, even more importantly, to Islam itself. Using the familiar rhetorical devices identified in the previous sections, bin Ladin now communicates the need to wage *jihad*—the only acceptable response in the present situation—with characteristic fire and brimstone monitions. Plunging into an outright question—pronounced so empathetically that it might almost be regarded as an accusation, 'why do you cling so heavily to the earth?', he now changes to a new form of communication that directly engages each individual member of the audience. In a calm and empathetic tone of voice he reaffirms the obligation of the individual to obey God in a decisive and all-embracing question:

> Oh Muslims, do you [plural] want to walk along the straight path and please God? Do you [singular] submit to the will of Allah?

The way in which this question is formalised reveals the significance of the moral endeavour that it creates for the individual in the audience. First, in terms of format, the initial part of the question addresses the audience as a homogeneous group, while the second part is directed specifically towards the individual. By changing from speaking to the audience as a whole to addressing the individual, bin Ladin engages every listener in a moral dilemma. Second, in terms of content, the question invokes a line from the opening *sura* of the Quran, which is recited several times during the prayer: 'do you want to walk along the straight path?' (*sirat al-mustaqim*). The answer of every Muslim to this inquiry can only be in the affirmative. The same holds true for the second part of the question, which is the condition for pleasing God and walking along the straight path: to submit to His will. The combination of style and content here is manipulative by virtue of the fact that it is simply not possible for the individual Muslim to answer any of these questions negatively. Thus the likely effect on the audience is at the very least that of an acknowledgement of the moral force of bin Ladin's analysis, and possibly an acceptance of his political interpretation as the true meaning of Islam in the present situation. Assuming the intention to communicate his message in the most effective manner, it is hardly surprising that the subsequent lines carry an almost apocalyptic tone:

> Oh Brothers, we all must fulfil the duties that He has placed upon us. We testify that there is no God but Allah, no associate with Him. He is the all-knowing, the most superior, and the ruler of all mankind. To Him we are held responsible on the day of resurrection. There will be no way to hide from God and His judgement.

The example illustrates an atmosphere of risk, opportunity and decision, which furthers the individual moral dilemma, a device that, as the following discussion will show, is used throughout the address.

Linking the moral obligation of the individual believer to the current political situation, which invites the urgent need for *jihad*, bin Ladin brings up the Palestinian theme in a rather interesting manner. By applying a Quranic citation from a different context directly to the Palestinian situation, he allows for the call for *jihad* to be seen as the only acceptable response.

> Oh believers, and the day will come that the Palestinian children will be resurrected and questioned for what sin they were killed. What will you [singular] say to them?

What is not directly obvious from the translation is that the incident in the Quran originally refers to the burying of female children alive: 'the day the female children will be resurrected and questioned for what sin they were killed'.[33] Again, it is possible to recognise how bin Ladin projects the message of the Quran to the present political situation and interprets its meaning. The way he describes the existing political reality makes it literally impossible for the individual listener not to acknowledge the legitimacy of the subsequent call for *jihad* against those who are responsible for the suffering of the *umma*, and for the Zionist–Crusader invasion.

To support his claim, he leaps from his rhetoric of almost confrontational bravura to stinging assertions of imminent realism:

> Nobody who dies and finds good from Allah in the Hereafter would wish to come back to this world, even if he were given the whole world and whatever is in it, except the martyr who, on seeing the superiority of martyrdom would like to come back to the world and get killed again in the cause of Allah.

But:

> *If you [singular] march not forth, He will punish you with a painful torment and will replace you by another people, and you cannot harm Him at all, and Allah is able to do all things. (9: 39)*

The apocalyptic tone and the use of the singular in 'if you march not forth' clearly places the emphasis on the individual's duty to wage *jihad*, which ultimately implies the need to fight. The seriousness that is communicated through this passage, although not directly obvious from the translation, is inherent in the chosen words that communicate the idea of utmost duty, *fard ayn*.

> Oh Brothers, we all must fulfil the duties that He has placed upon us. We testify that there is no God but Allah, no associate with Him.

Almost as if to remind the audience that they have already committed themselves to submitting to the will of Allah, the call to fulfil the duties that God has placed upon every believer is directly followed by a declaration of faith. Finally, addressing each member of the audience individually, bin Ladin asks the final, all-embracing question of why any member would refrain from submitting to the will of Allah and carrying out what he has prescribed for them. This question can only be regarded as a rhetorical inquiry to which the answer has already been provided. Clearly, there can be no reason to refrain from obeying the orders of Allah once the believer has made a declaration of faith, assuming that Muslims should submit to God in everything without demanding proof.

> *Why would you refrain from fighting, if fighting was prescribed for you? They said 'Why should we not fight in Allah's way while we have been driven out of our homes and our families have been taken as captives?' But when fighting was ordered for them, they turned away, all except a few of them. And Allah is all aware of the Zalimun. (2: 37)*

By now, bin Ladin has effectively established his authority and the legitimacy of his interpretation of some the most integral principles of Islam. As a result, his call on the believers to wage *jihad* appears to be bestowed with divine blessing. Thus, in the final part of the speech, while still furthering the cause of convincing the audience of the divine will to wage *jihad*, the primary objective seems to shift to the provision of an adequate assurance that God will be on the side of those who march forth faithfully, despite the risk of physical harm. The citing of the full story of how a small number of believers managed to overcome an overwhelming enemy with the help of Allah—the Quranic version of the biblical account of David and Goliath—exemplifies this intention. Throughout the early stages of the story it is possible for the individual listener to identify himself with those in the account. The final lines of the story clearly illustrate the overwhelming victory of those who have, against good reason, submitted to the will of Allah:

> *But those who knew with certainty that they were going to meet Allah, said, 'How often a small group overcame a mighty host by Allah's leave!' And Allah is with As-Sabirun. And when they advanced to meet Goliath and his forces, they invoked: 'Our Lord! Pour forth on us patience, and set firm our feet and make us victorious over the disbelieving people.' So they routed them by Allah's leave and David killed Goliath and Allah gave him the kingdom and taught him of that which He willed.* (2: 249–251)

The victory of David over Goliath provides a powerful confirmation that righteousness will triumph over evil, and as such can be seen as an incentive for the audience to have faith in Allah even under the most daunting circumstances. At this point, bin Ladin has delivered a straightforward message: It is the duty of every believer to obey God, which under the present circumstances means protecting his favoured community against the aggression of a foreign enemy. Furthermore, there can be no doubt that those who submit to the will of Allah will be victorious in the end. In other words, transferred into the present political context, a comparatively small number of determined fighters motivated by faith and assured that the hereafter is to be preferred over life in the present, is capable of overcoming even an overwhelming force such as the USA. Having established this, it is made abundantly clear that the call for *jihad* can only be understood as a call to take up arms to fight against the Zionist–Crusader invasion. In the following lines, the audience is told that they are expected to fight, as all of them are indeed soldiers of Allah. This time, the words of the Quran have been altered (see inserted lines in Roman type, added by bin Ladin, which is not part of the original Quranic text) for the purpose of calling on the believers to fight in the cause of Allah, again showing bin Ladin's own interpretation of the meaning of the Quran in the current political context:

> *And if Allah did not check one set of people by means of another, the earth would indeed be full of mischief.* Oh those of you who believe, go and fight in the cause of Allah. *But Allah is full of bounty to the Alamin.* (2: 251) Oh those of you [singular] who believe, you are soldiers of the party of Allah. *These are the Verses of Allah, we recite them to you in truth, and surely, you are one of the Messengers of Allah.* (2: 252)

Finally, bin Ladin's closing sentence expresses the central message of the address:

> *When you fight those who disbelieve, smite their necks till you have killed and wounded many of them.* (47:4) If you give up *jihad*, you give up Islam!

After a significant pause, the video begins to show images from Al-Qaeda training camps with the same music played at the beginning of the film. It finishes with the citation of the opening sura of the Quran, a declaration of faith, against the familiar mountain scene.

> *In the name of Allah, the most gracious, the most merciful. All the praises and thanks be to Allah, the Lord of the 'alamin. The most gracious, the most merciful. The only owner of the day of recompense. You alone we worship and you alone we ask for help. Guide us to the straight way. The way you have bestowed your grace, not the way of those who earned your anger, nor of those who went astray.* (1: 1 – 7)

It is obvious that bin Ladin has made every possible effort to convince the audience of the righteousness of his call to take up arms against the Zionist – Crusader invasion, the ultimate enemy of Islam. Having identified two vital Islamic principles and interpreted their meaning against the background of the larger political situation, he effectively becomes an objectifier for his audience. To his audience his words are an explanation of the meaning of Islam in the present political situation, as well as presenting a simple way to obtain salvation from Allah.

## Conclusion

An attempt to analyse the impact of bin Ladin's address and ideology on the audience is methodologically difficult and arguably requires the tools of social psychology. Nevertheless, insights into the level of motivation that bin Ladin creates in his listeners can be gained by analysing the terminology that is used to communicate the central points, based on the assumption that 'the language of religion...is a symbolic language...a language which expresses meaning through images and symbols, the most excellent and exalted of all the languages men have ever evolved.'[34] In fact, anthropologists frequently remark that in any sociocultural context a number of key phrases and images representing central values have special importance as multivocal symbols. Very often, one of the most difficult tasks is '"to determine the meanings of a few key words, upon an understanding of which the success of the whole investigation depends'.[35]

As already indicated in the previous section, the call for *jihad* is invoked by terminology that is loaded with significant meaning, such as 'crusade', 'Zionist – Crusader invasion', 'duty' or '*jihad*'. Ignoring the symbolic dimension of each of these terms carries the risk of losing an important part of the full meaning and depth of the message.

This aspect is particularly interesting in the context of the ongoing war on terrorism, as both sides of the conflict employ words and symbols that evoke bitter memories of past conflicts and conjure up emotions long suppressed.

For example, when US President George W Bush used the word 'crusade' to describe the US-led campaign against international terrorism, the conservative Muslims in the Middle East and South Asia responded immediately with a call for *jihad,* to the effect that both sides are currently locked in a painful and traumatic recollection of the 200-year-long confrontation between Christians and Muslims. As a result of the unfortunate—or possibly intentional—use of these terms, Muslims in different parts of the world have become agitated. To every metaphor or symbol that one camp has at its disposal, the other can respond immediately in kind. One side may be seen to be preparing for an air war with state-of-the-art aircraft and smart bombs, while the other proclaims its readiness through a bearded man on horseback wielding an assault rifle. This in itself is a compelling image, evoking the Muslim warriors during the Crusades defending Muslim land against the invading hordes from the West. Each word, symbol or concept used as part of the language of war is loaded with historical meaning and emotion that is hard to measure unless the protagonists' culture and history are thoroughly understood.

Carl Gustav Jung, the Swiss psychologist, called the deeply rooted and commonly shared feelings that are evoked as a result of this kind of rhetoric the 'collective consciousness'. 'Utilized towards specific goals, this can serve as a powerful instrument to drive a people to commendable activities or heroism, or move them to destructive behaviour at critical moments of human society or community.'[36] Once unleashed, these collective emotions are very difficult to contain and can possibly be directed along a destructive course. In the light of 11 September 2001 and other terrorist acts that followed it, it is all too evident that bin Ladin's rhetoric, with its appeal to powerful imagery embedded in the collective consciousness of the Muslim community, and its juxtaposition of political goals with the teachings of the Quran, inspires his followers to commit terrible acts of destruction while being fully convinced that they are fulfilling the ordained will of Allah.

## Notes

The author would like to thank the Leverhulme Trust for supporting this research. However, in terms of content, this paper owes its existence to my supervisor, James Piscatori. Somewhere during our extended discussions of the 'big picture', I lost track of where my own thoughts ended and his started.

1   Finding of a Pentagon intelligence team, *Washington Times*, 5 June 2003.
2   S Schwartz, *The Two Faces of Islam*, New York: Random House, 2002.
3   R Gunaratna, *Inside Al-Qaeda*, New York: Columbia University Press, 2002, p 14.
4   'Al-Qaeda not driven by ideology', *Washington Times*, 5 June 2003.
5   Schwartz, *The Two Faces of Islam*, p 1.
6   See, for example, W Beeman, 'Fighting the good fight: fundamentalism and religious revival', in J MacClancy, *Anthropology for the Real World*, Chicago: Chicago University Press, 2001.
7   F Halliday, 'The politics of Islam —a second look', *British Journal of Political Science*, 25 (3), 1995, p 400.
8   N Luhmann, *Funktion der Religon*, Frankfurt: Piper Verlag, 1977, p 16; and B Tibi, *Islam between Culture and Politics*, New York: Palgrave, 2001, p 28.
9   C Geertz, *The Interpretation of Cultures*, New York: Basic Books, 1973, pp 87–95.
10  Tibi , *Islam between Culture and Politics*, p 28.
11  *Ibid*, p 29.
12  *Ibid*, p 29; and J Baumann, *Gott und Mensch im Koran: Eine Strukturform religioeser Anthropologie anhand des Beispiels Allah und Muhammed*, Darmstadt: Piper Verlag, 1977, p 9.

13  D Eickelman & J Piscatori, *Muslim Politics*, Princeton, NJ: Princeton University Press, 1996, p 46.

14  *Ibid.*

15  These are the terms used by MGS Hodgson, *The Venture of Islam: Conscience and History in a World Civilization*, 3 vols, Chicago, IL: University of Chicago Press, 1974.

16  Several authors provide different dates for the separation of functions and institutions from Islam. See, for example, N Coulson, *A History of Islamic Law*, Edinburgh: Edinburgh University Press, 1964, pp 128–129; and B Lewis, 'Politics and war', in J Schacht & C Bosworth (eds), *The Legacy of Islam*, Oxford: Oxford University Press, 1979, pp 156–209.

17  Tibi, *Islam between Culture and Politics*, p 2.

18  *Ibid.*

19  S Qutb, *Fi Zilal al-Quran* (In the Shade of the Quran), trans MA Salahi & AA Shamis, London: MHW Publishers, 1979. An interesting discussion of Qutb's interpretation is R Nettler's 'Guidelines for the Islamic community: Sayyid Qutb's political interpretation', *Journal of Political Ideologies*, 1 (2), 1996, pp 183–196.

20  Nettler, 'Guidelines for the Islamic community', p 196.

21  Gunaratna, *Inside Al-Qaeda*, p 14.

22  Tibi, *Islam between Culture and Politics*, p 17.

23  J Piscatori, 'The turmoil within', *Foreign Affairs*, May/June 2002, p. 2.

24  Eickelmann & Piscatori, *Muslim Politics*, p 38.

25  Turabi, quoted in *ibid*, p 43.

26  Eickelman & Piscatori, *Muslim Politics*, p 35.

27  For an excellent discussion of the misunderstood Wahhabi connection, see M Azzam, 'Al-Qaeda: the misunderstood Wahhabi connection and the ideology of violence, *Royal Institute of International Affairs Briefing Paper No 1*, London, February 2003.

28  'Review of 1998 Reports Concerning Threats by Osama bin Ladin to Conduct Terrorist Operations Against the United States and/or her Allies', available online at danmahony.com, p. 3.

29  Access to this video and other Al-Qaeda propaganda material was provided by the Center for the study of Terrorism and Political Violence at St Andrews University, Scotland.

30  The translations of Quranic citations are based on M Taqi-ud-Din Al-Hilali & M Mushin Khan, *Translation of the Meanings of The Noble Qur'an in the English Language*, Riyadh: King Fahd Complex for the printing of the Holy Quran, 1419 AH.

31  By evoking symbols in a pure and abstract form, everything is graded as black and white without intervening shades. Whatever the basis of authority in any culture, the general tendency in ideology is to draw an absolute antithesis between the prevailing authority and the authority on which the ideology is based, between absolute evil and absolute good. For details, see R Nicholas, 'Social and political movements', in B Siegel (ed), *Annual Review of Anthropology*, Palo Alto, CA: Annual Reviews, 1973, p 80.

32  M al-Ghazzali, *Our Beginning in Wisdom*, trans IR al-Faruqi, Washington, DC: American Counsel of Learned Societies, 1953; and *Worship in Islam: Being a Translation with Commentary and Introduction of al-Ghazzali's Book of the Ihya' on the Worship*, translation, commentary and introduction by Edwin Elliott Calverley, London: Luzac & Co, 1925; and Qutb, *Fi Zilal al-Quran*. See Statement by Osama bin Laden, *International Herald Tribune*, 8 October 2001; and Statement by Abu Gaith (Osama bin Ladin's spokesman), *Financial Times*, 10 October 2001.

33  Quran, 81: 7–8.

34  Ali Shari'ati, quoted in Eickelman & Piscatori, *Muslim Politics*, p 13.

35  E Evans-Pitchard, *Social Anthropology and Other Essays*, New York: Free Press, 1962, p 80. Similarly, see also P Gaffney, *The Prophet's Pulpit: Islamic Preaching in Contemporary Egypt*, LA: University of California Press, 1994, p 124.

36  CG Jung, cited in W Schulz, *Psychologie des Widerstandes*, Frankfurt: Westman Verlag, 2002, p 27. See also Jung, 'The archetypes and the collected unconsciousness', in *Collected Works*, ed H Read, M Fordham & G Adler, Vol 9, Princeton, NJ: Princeton University Press, 1936. For an insightful discussion of the dynamics and contexts of social movement participation, see B Klandermans, *The Social Psychology of Protest*, Oxford: Blackwell, 1997, particularly the chapter on 'The transformation of discontent into action', pp 64–93. On group dynamics and the perception of justice, see, for example, M Wenzel, 'What is social about justice? Inclusive identity and group values as the basis of the justice motive', *Journal of Experimental Social Psychology*, 38, pp 205–208; and T Tyler & M Belliveau, 'Tradeoffs in justice principles: definitions of perceived fairness', in B Bunker & J Rubin (eds), *Conflict, Cooperation and Justice*, San Francisco, CA: Jossey-Bass, 2002, pp 291–314.

# Savagery in democracy's empire

ROBERT L IVIE

The USA's present war on terrorism is a variation on an old theme of defending civilisation against savagery. The image of the enemy as a savage is much older than the USA but is nevertheless intimately linked to the defence of democracy, among other aims and aspirations. The incomprehensible babble on the other side of the defensive walls surrounding democratic Athens was the threatening sound of the barbarian in ancient Greece. The Roman Empire, too, fought barbarians, those hordes of crude Germanic tribes who were enemies of culture and civilisation. Indeed, throughout the ages, the archetype of the barbarian enemy has served to legitimise war and empire—Athenian, Roman, British, Japanese, Soviet, American, and other such exercises in dominion and domination—whether in defence of democracy or, in the case of Nazi Germany, to justify the rule of the Third Reich and the extermination of Jews.[1]

After winning its independence from Great Britain and then taking a continent (or all of the northern part of the continent that it wanted) by decimating indigenous peoples and invading its neighbour to the south, America next set out to christianise and civilise the savages of the Philippines. The mission of an exceptional nation now reached beyond manifest destiny to encompass the rest of the world. The beginning of the American century was soon dramatically announced with an atomic bang over Hiroshima and then extended through four decades of bipolarising cold war. Today, American empire has become a unifying project in globalising the world economy and democratising all nations in order to secure a universal peace and thus the end of history.[2]

Pronouncing itself the world's one essential nation, the post-Soviet era USA shortly thereafter declared war, again in the name of civilisation and under the banner of fighting for a democratic peace. Monarchy, fascism and communism had been conquered, each in its turn, in order to make the world free of barbarous tyranny and thus safe for democracy. After the tragedy of 9/11, however, terrorism was proclaimed the new savagery threatening America's empire of democracy. Civilisation would be rescued this time from an international conspiracy of militant Islamist extremists who wished to destroy freedom and instill the tyranny of theocracy. The discourse of savagery versus civilisation, deeply rooted in the American political lexicon, its culture and collective psyche, was easily pressed into service to rally the nation, quell dissent and effectively inoculate the public against any alternative perspective.[3]

## America's indigenous trope of savagery

Although the trope of savagery is not unique to American war rhetoric, it is indigenous to it and deeply ingrained in the political culture. The USA was born in a new world that European settlers had cleared tribe by tribe, nation after nation, of its native savages. British rule was overthrown in the colonies with a call to arms against English monsters that thirsted for American blood.[4] The War of 1812, considered by many to be America's second war of independence, was justified in Congress and to the nation by increasingly intense cries of British diabolism and decivilising metaphors of force that conveyed the image of a people being trampled, trodden and bullied by an enemy portrayed variously as beast of prey, common criminal, ruthless murderer, haughty pirate and crazed tyrant.[5] Similarly, the expansionist war declared against Mexico in 1846 was portrayed by a partisan President Polk, with a disciplined majority party in Congress, as a reluctant act of national defence in response to an irrational and evil Mexican aggressor, a belligerent foe that was easily inflamed and as unstable as a violent storm.[6] President McKinley's justification of commercial imperialism five decades later, as the USA was about to enter the 20th century, was that America, by God's grace, would 'uplift and civilize and Christianize' those who 'were unfit for self-government'. These savages of the Philippines would be the beneficiaries of America's 'noble generosity' and 'Christian sympathy and charity'.[7]

The savagery of war itself, as well as the rationalisation of slaughter, was marked particularly in the modern age by the trope of the machine. War became 'the mechanical human beast', adding yet another metaphor to the heritage of 'discursive support for military conflict' and to the language of 'common sense' that legitimised its destructive reality. A 'delirium of technology' transformed the machine into a deranged and destructive monster. The national character of the evil enemy was contained in this image of mechanised madness, with expansionist Germany representing the perfectly oiled war machine, its individual citizens reduced to uniform mechanical cogs. The beast became a rampaging automaton, an anarchic machine, an abdication of individuality and human responsibility, an uncontrolled threat to democracy that transformed the savage lust of the masses into the modern menace of civilisation. Indeed, the 'broad distinction between "civilisation" and "barbarism"' that was so central to the language of World War I rested heavily on the pejorative characterisation of Germany as a perversion of progress, a degeneracy of 'over-rapid development', a mechanical mentality that elevated atrocity to 'a science and a technology'. The modern primitive had become a 'murdering machine', stripping its victims of their humanity, reducing them to raw material—its mechanical ethos making war into an inevitability, into 'the Frankenstein's monster of the twentieth century'.[8] Thus Woodrow Wilson called for a war against Germany to make the world safe for democracy, with 'civilization itself seeming to be in the balance' because the menace of 'autocratic governments backed by organized force' had taken control 'of the will of their people'.[9]

The very militarisation of America led next, under this technological shadow of war, into a second world conflagration. Franklin Roosevelt, as Michael Sherry observes, 'did not merely perceive the importance of technology in modern warfare, he seized on it as fitting the nation's strengths and he deepened the American impulse to achieve global power through technological supremacy'. Such was his 'ideological construction' of national security. Europe's war-mad barbarians were the product of a technological determinism that assaulted 'the foundations of civilization' and required the USA to adopt 'strategies of annihilation as the measure of its own security against the danger of new technologies and ideologies.[10] Thus FDR called on America, as the world's arsenal of democracy, to lead a crusade against the evil Axis of fascist power, a diabolical enemy that feigned peaceful intentions even as it ravaged the world in the most shocking, brutal, and criminal acts of treachery. The Japanese aggression at Pearl Harbor on Sunday, 7 December 1941 was a cause for indignation, an affront to a God-fearing nation, and it provided an exigency for defending civilisation by vanquishing rampant evil. Roosevelt's war rhetoric condensed belligerency to its pure form for a technological age and enemy.[11]

War itself became, even for Americans who prided themselves on their individualism, a 'mindless, anonymous' expression of 'machine-age dehumanization and cosmic purposelessness'. The bombing of cities was portrayed 'as a process of surgical destruction administered by cool-headed Americans'. This was an image of war rendered benign and a sense of power inflated into a technological arrogance that culminated in the atomic extermination of Japanese treachery and savagery.[12] The mindset of Hiroshima among the US public was 'a collective form of psychic numbing' that carried forward into a regime of cold-war nuclearism. The atomic bomb, President Truman announced in triumph, was repayment for Pearl Harbor many fold, 'a new and revolutionary increase in destruction', a 'harnessing of the basic power of the universe', which Americans were rightly 'grateful to Providence' that decent people possessed, and with which they had righteously vanquished an evil enemy.[13]

The World War II American image of the enemy, although technologised into a numbing abstraction, retained its more visceral vehicles as well, including the raw emotions of racism captured in visions of atrocity. The Japanese were portrayed as subhuman, as apes and vermin, a primitive, childish and mentally deficient threat to civilisation that required extermination by a nation of reluctant warriors.[14] FDR merged the concrete with the abstract image of a barbaric enemy, blaming the 'mechanized might' of the Axis powers for their 'brutality' and condemning their 'order of concentration camps' as a 'savage and brutal' force 'seeking to subjugate the world'. America's 'unscrupulous' enemies were condemned as 'crafty' gangsters and powerful 'bandits' harbouring the morals of a predator, a lowly beast of prey.[15]

### Savagery and America's cold war culture of fear

The rhetorical texture of the savage enemy evolved in its time without losing touch with its history. Decades of cold war, punctuated by hot encounters with communism in Vietnam and elsewhere, constituted a culture of fear premised on a multidimensional image of the enemy's sheer savagery. Truman conjured a powerful cold war spell by representing the Soviet savage in terms of fire, flood and red fever to convey the threatening image of a communist epidemic and impending disaster for the free world. A compelling metaphor of disease framed the inception, and infused the presentation and reception of the Truman doctrine speech at this formative moment, constituting a heroic expression of democratic America questing after total security by eradicating the communist infestation.[16]

Next in the line of presidential succession, Dwight Eisenhower cultivated an image of himself as the aspiring peacemaker, even as he affirmed Truman's vision of national vulnerability by totalising the communist threat. The world's captive nations, Eisenhower insisted, had been 'terrorized into a uniform, submissive mass'. This 'Red cancer' must 'feed on new conquests— or wither'. America could never rest until 'the tidal mud of aggressive Communism receded'. Civilisation was imperilled by savagery—portrayed as primal, primitive, barbaric, monstrous, diseased and brutal—with its insatiable lust for conquest. A voice of perpetual peril, speaking calmly and reassuringly behind a mask of peace, coaxed the nation down a path of nuclear deterrence, based on an insane logic of mutual assured destruction, and in search of a false security.[17] Elites as well as the public had become invested emotionally and intellectually in a visceral image of the enemy that provoked deeply repressed nuclear nightmares. 'Just as empire did not look imperial to most Americans', Sherry observes, 'the militarized state did not look militaristic'.[18]

It is difficult to see something that is everywhere. War was becoming just that, a perpetual and pervasive condition of US political culture, a habit of thought embedded in a manner of speaking, the cultural motif of an embattled nation. This militarised world-view extended to declaring metaphorical wars on poverty, drugs, disease and crime, engaging in 'trade wars' with foreign competitors, and fighting 'culture wars' with one another. The agonising task of Americanising a lingering French colonial war in Vietnam drove the discourse of savagery ever more deeply into the national psyche in order to rationalise world hegemony as a defence of civilisation.

America would expel the barbarian from the garden of democracy to cultivate perpetual peace.

By this reckoning the savage in democracy's empire was marked with the sign of irrationality, represented as coercive, and configured for aggression. Each of these discursive dimensions was a contrasting feature in an overall image of American civility that featured a quintessentially rational, freedom-loving and reluctant defender of the peace. Thus, the rhetorical *topoi* of savagery against civilisation reduced to naturalised and interconnected articulations of force versus freedom, irrationality opposed to rationality, and aggression contrasted to defence. Americans were reluctant warriors defending the South Vietnamese people from communist aggression against the free world, insisting only on the right of choice and free elections rather than a government imposed by force. The USA fought for tolerance and diversity; the enemy insisted on ideological conformity and refused to negotiate. American military actions were sanitised in a language of protective reaction, pacification, incursion, defoliation; the enemy assassinated, kidnapped, strangled, ravaged and terrorised its innocent victims. The USA would settle disputes by law and reason in order to build an enlightened world order; the enemy was cunning but rash and driven by hate to perpetrate chaos. The enemy's aggression was deliberate, wilful and unprovoked; America's response was defensive, involuntary, and reluctant but necessary.[19]

After the debacle of Vietnam drove the USA into a temporary state of malaise, from which it quickly recovered following the Soviet invasion of Afghanistan, Ronald Reagan ascended to the presidential helm to reinvigorate the discourse of savagery versus civilisation by calling upon Americans to defeat communism's 'evil empire'. The standard three-dimensional image of the barbarian was readily expressed by Reagan deploying a reified cluster of decivilising terms. These vehicles, too, had become the conventional idiom of an increasingly militarised culture of fear. They ranged from terms of natural menace, such as fire, flood, disease, tides and storms, to the language of dangerous animals and predators, such as snakes and wolves, and progressed to figures of primitives and brutes, mindless machines, criminals, lunatics, ideologues and fanatics, culminating in references to the satanic and profane enemies of God. Each effaced the Other, constituting a decivilised enemy by caricature, together conveying an image of savagery by indirection and figuration. Thus Reagan's Soviets were portrayed vividly in the language of light and shadow as a dark force, a grey monument to repression, a gale of intimidation, and as an untamed adversary preying upon its neighbours, barbarously assaulting the human spirit, clubbing its victims into submission, bullying the world to submit to its unhappy fate, employing the machines of war to commit murderous crimes against humanity, cheating, lying, driven by psychotic fears and unbounded ambitions, immune to practical reason, and even denying the existence of God in the fanatical machinations of a menacing evil. This was the totalitarian onslaught against civilised ideas and the defenders of liberty of which Reagan spoke with such urgency in an idiom that expressed the common sense of a nation.[20]

The figurative quality of these tropes and their centrality to the recurrent narrative of war, necessitated each time by yet another savage Other, went unremarked and unrecognised for the most part. They were the thoroughly literalised compositional elements of a long-told and often-repeated tale of American exceptionalism and mission. They were the plain-spoken and matter-of-fact words of a no-nonsense Harry Truman embedded in a language of rationality and a voice of reason handed down from the early republic. They were facts made certain and obvious within a narrow framework of interpretation.[21] Moreover, they were reified in their sheer opposition to everything that made sense about freedom, liberty and democracy—the very terms of identity adopted by a peace-loving people to legitimise their warlike habits. Freedom, in the American political lexicon, was feminised and fragile, a risky experiment in a dangerous world, and always vulnerable to the rape of the barbarian if left unprotected.[22]

## Savagery in an age of terror and American empire

Thus the discourse of savagery informed but transcended the long era of cold war and the eventual demise of the USSR, further draining the nation's political imagination of any alternative to militarising its domestic culture and foreign relations, and thereby constituting a people forever in search of new enemies and more wars to fight. The line between metaphorical and real war, Sherry maintains, had been blurred beyond recognition.[23] War had become the master trope of all things domestic and foreign and all issues economic and social. Everyone and everything was potentially an enemy. Saddam Hussein offered an irresistible temptation, not once but twice, in a simulated return engagement with evil under the symbolic shadow of Hitler and Stalin. But it was the sheer savagery of terrorism that put the USA back on its steady rhetorical course of defending civilisation with all its surplus military might. Whether or not there was a demonstrable connection between Saddam and the terror of 9/11, there would be an open-ended 'war' of terror on the axis of evil, a different kind of war that acknowledged no political or territorial bounds within or between states. Freedom would be sacrificed in the cause of defending it against its foreign and domestic enemies wherever they may lurk.

Savagery, then, depicted the post-cold war era as a perpetual condition of ubiquitous violence, a Hobbesian state of nature and vicious warfare on civilians that would seem to indicate the fall of civilisation or signal the arrival of a modern leviathan of imperial peace.[24] Rhetorical conditions seemed ripe for realising Kant's vision of perpetual peace among a world federation of republican states, now called liberal democracies (or just democracies in shorthand).[25] This so-called 'democratic peace' was a peace that would be achieved through the agency, in Kant's words, of 'a powerful and enlightened people' who had formed a republic that could serve as 'a focal point for a federal association among other nations that will join it in order to guarantee a state of peace among nations that is in accord with the idea of the right of nations, and through several associations of this sort such a federation can extend further and further'.[26] This vision of peace was akin to a biblical prophecy of world salvation by virtue of an American ascendancy; a chosen people would lead the world towards the final realisation of an empire of democracy where savagery was forever vanquished.[27]

Terrorism as the legitimising sign of American empire—the reigning symbol of savagery opposed to a civilising empire of democratic peace—grew out of a long tradition of war discourse deeply embedded in the nation's political culture. The pivotal articulation of danger in the American experience, as David Campbell notes, was always the decivilising representation of the enemy as 'alien, subversive, dirty, or sick'.[28] Even as the cancer of communism was being eradicated, Ronald Reagan began to address the rising threat of terrorism. He talked tough about terrorists being able to run but not hide, while he negotiated a secret arms-for-hostages deal with Iran, a regime his government denounced for supporting international terrorism. That should have been warning enough, but 'combating terrorism', Jeffrey Simon observes, 'would now be a top priority for the United States'. Like fighting the evil of the communist empire, combating terrorism was portrayed by Reagan in strict black-and-white terms and as a matter of war.[29]

George W Bush, the rhetorical and ideological son of Reagan, filled in the blanks after 9/11, drawing on the time-honoured language of savagery to justify his so-called war on international terrorism. It was a unique war in some ways, he said, but in other ways a continuation of the great clashes of the 20th century between tyranny and liberty. Democratic America, victimised again by a 'ruthless surprise attack', was committed to the 'forward march of freedom' against 'murderous ideologies' and in defence of world peace. The terrorist enemy 'chose death over life', 'spreading fear and anarchy' consistent with the 'swagger and demented logic of the fanatic'. The war on terror was 'civilization's fight'. Were it lost to Muslim terrorists, 'thugs', 'assassins', and 'despots', books would be 'burned', women would be 'whipped', and children would be 'schooled in hatred, murder, and suicide'; 'darkness' would be imposed by these 'evil' men all across the oil-rich Middle East. The only true path to peace, progress and prosperity, by the logic of this thoroughly conventionalised discourse of savagery, was the military path to freedom, justice and democracy.[30] No other credible option seemed imaginable.

Indeed, for Bush and his fellow believers, the inability to see matters otherwise was an article of faith. The sign of the barbarian marked the presence of sheer evil. The president's messianic call to arms was a secular sermon delivered in a Biblical cadence. America's holy mission now, as in the beginning, was to make the world right in the eyes of the Christian God. One of Bush's generals, William Boykin, described by the administration as a good soldier, declared that the USA was fighting Satan in Iraq, that the Christian God was real, and that the Muslim god was an idol. Americans affirmed that they voted for a president whom they knew to be a Christian man. Just as the USA's morals and ideals were endowed by the Creator, the Almighty's gift of liberty was meant for His chosen people to spread throughout the world to all of humanity. The USA was the 'greatest force for good in history'. Such was the evangelical arrogance of a reborn president's

Christian humility, uttered in the name of an exceptional people whom he represented to the Lord and sent on their holy mission, strong in their faith, undistracted by doubt, and wielding a mighty sword of destruction. Democracy worked in mysterious ways. The world was either with democratic America or with the dark forces of savagery. Civilisation's Christian soldiers were crusading against the terror of evil, fighting for the greater glory of God, and seeking their own salvation. Thus, a material empire was made holy by casting out the Devil himself.[31]

This is a discourse that rendered criticism almost unsayable within the empire of democracy. It emptied democracy of its meaning as a political practice and reduced it to a rationalisation for world domination. Democracy was little more than an open-ended justification of coercion on a global scale, a warrant for forcing the world to become free on US terms, and a moral imperative to kill those who refused to obey. Dissent was undemocratic, in this sense, and disloyal. As Attorney General John Ashcroft, a militant Christian fundamentalist, observed before the US Senate Judiciary Committee, critics of the administration's war on terrorism provided ammunition to the country's enemies. Those who tried to scare a peace-loving people with phantoms of lost liberty were deploying the tactics of terrorism by using America's freedoms as a weapon against itself.[32] Soldiers, not journalists, poets, or protesters, provide and preserve freedom at home and abroad, proclaimed Democratic Senator Zell Miller before the Republican National Convention as it prepared to nominate George W Bush for a second presidential term. It was time again for patriotic Americans to line up and march behind this straight-shooting, God-fearing leader with a spine of tempered steel.[33]

Silencing the voice of democratic dissent in the name of its own sacred cause stifled public deliberation, even in Congress among the people's elected representatives, and thus blunted the country's collective critical faculties. A people reduced by the dichotomous language of good versus evil to a form of patriotism that is reflexive rather than reflective could not debate the character of terror without sounding supportive of terrorists, could not distinguish between explaining terrorism and siding with terrorists, could not acknowledge even a strategic difference between international and nationalist terrorists, could not contemplate variations within the discourse of Islamism, and could not recognise the terror of their own indiscriminate war on terrorism.[34] Even the gruesome visual evidence of American soldiers torturing prisoners in Abu Ghraib and elsewhere could be dismissed by Secretary of Defense Donald Rumsfeld because it was not as bad as terrorists 'chopping someone's head off on television'.[35] The USA simply could not see that much of the terror in democracy's troubled empire was largely of its own making.

## Critiquing images of savagery

The very idiom of democratic persuasion was once again corrupted and co-opted by the coercive language of savagery, leaving discouraged observers to ponder whether there remained any alternative to reciprocal acts of righteous terror. Does an empire of democracy differ from any other kind of empire? Are there resources within the discourse of democracy for addressing the threatening Other in terms other than savagery? Is it possible to articulate more constructive relations among adversaries than that of sheer antagonism?[36] Can rivals within and between political boundaries enunciate working points of identification from different positions of interest and identity? Can an overly narrow perspective be stretched to accommodate the diversity of a now compressed globe?

These questions of language critique must be addressed thoroughly within the particular context of US political culture, but ultimately they entail coming to terms with dissent as the key to enriching democratic practice and with rhetoric as the trick of articulating dissent.[37] Rhetoric is to dissent as dissent is to democracy. Language makes claims upon us, as James Dawes observes, and 'conceptions of language are a factor in the invention, obfuscation, or realization of particular social practices' from which we 'cannot opt out'.[38] Language is not ideologically neutral, but it is subject to rhetorical critique from within. Otherwise language rigidifies and devolves into violence, spawning self-sustaining rituals of vilification and victimisation. Michel de Certeau recognised that marginalisation is no longer just the condition of minorities but instead has become the norm for nearly everyone and, accordingly, that the practice of everyday life now requires a quotidian operation of tactics for turning the tables on elites. Rhetoric, he notes, offers models of such tactics, which amount to discursive operations for reappropriating cultural capital.[39] By extension, Ronald Bleiker envisions dissent itself as an ongoing quotidian practice of language critique, something more manageable on an everyday basis, an operation more protean and less heroic than single-handedly overthrowing the forces of injustice.[40] The everyday rhetorical trickster makes democratic joints a bit more flexible and keeps alive the possibility of resisting overdrawn images of another's savagery. Here is where we might begin to search in the hope of finding democracy's lost voice.

## Notes

[1] For examples of how various regimes have visually caricatured their enemies as barbarians, see S Keen, *Faces of the Enemy: Reflections on the Hostile Imagination*, San Francisco, CA: Harper and Row, 1986, esp pp 43–47.

[2] A substantial body of scholarship and commentary on American empire has been developing in recent years. Examples include, Anon, *Imperial Hubris: Why the West is Losing the War on Terror*, Washington, DC: Brassey's, 2004; J Garrison, *America as Empire: Global Leader or Rogue Power?*, San Francisco, CA: Berrett-Koehler, 2004; M Mann, *Incoherent Empire*, London: Verso, 2003; AJ Bacevich, *American Empire: The Realities and Consequences of US Diplomacy*, Cambridge, MA: Harvard University Press, 2002; C Johnson, *The Sorrows of Empire: Militarism, Secrecy, and the End of the Republic*, New York: Metropolitan Books, 2004; C Boggs (ed), *Masters of War: Militarism and Blowback in the Era of American Empire*, New York: Routledge, 2003; and J Newhouse, *Imperial America: The Bush Assault on the World Order*, New York: Knopf, 2003.

[3] I discuss these points in RL Ivie, *Democracy and America's War on Terror*, Tuscaloosa, AL: University of Alabama Press, 2005.

[4] KW Ritter & JR Andrews, *The American Ideology: Reflections on the Revolution in American Rhetoric*, Falls Church, VA: Speech Communication Association, 1978, pp 7–10.

5   RL Hatzenbuehler & RL Ivie, *Congress Declares War: Rhetoric, Leadership, and Partisanship in the Early Republic*, Kent, OH: Kent State University Press, 1983; and RL Ivie, 'The metaphor of force in prowar discourse: the case of 1812', *Quarterly Journal of Speech*, 68 (3), 1982, pp 240–253.

6   RL Ivie, 'Progressive form and Mexican culpability in Polk's justification for war', *Central States Speech Journal*, 30 (4), 1979, pp 311–320.

7   McKinley, quoted in RL Ivie, 'William McKinley: advocate of imperialism', *Western Journal of Communication*, 36 (1), 1972, pp 15–23.

8   D Pick, *War Machine: The Rationalization of Slaughter in the Modern Age*, New Haven, CT: Yale University Press, 1993, pp 3, 11, 16, 49, 100–102, 106, 108–114, 153–155, 186–188, 203, 227.

9   W Wilson, 'War message', quoted in RL Ivie, 'Images of savagery in American justifications for war', *Communication Monographs*, 47 (4), 1980, p 287.

10  MS Sherry, *In the Shadow of War: The United States Since the 1930s*, New Haven, CT: Yale University Press, 1995, pp 14, 38, 45, 83–85.

11  RL Ivie, 'Franklin Roosevelt's crusade against evil: rhetorical legacy of a war message', in L Rohler & R Cook (eds), *Great Speeches for Criticism and Analysis*, Greenwood, IN: Alistair Press, 2001, pp 98–105.

12  Sherry, *In the Shadow of War*, pp 96–98, 114–115.

13  RJ Lifton & G Mitchell, *Hiroshima in America: A Half Century of Denial*, New York: Avon Books, 1995, p xiv; and Truman, quoted in *ibid*, pp 4–6.

14  JW Dower, *War Without Mercy: Race and Power in the Pacific War*, New York: Pantheon Books, 1986, pp x, 9.

15  Roosevelt, quoted in Ivie, 'Images of savagery', pp 287, 289.

16  RL Ivie, 'Fire, flood, and Red fever: motivating metaphors of global emergency in the Truman Doctrine speech', *Presidential Studies Quarterly*, 29 (3), 1999, pp 570–591.

17  Eisenhower, quoted in RL Ivie, 'Eisenhower as cold warrior', in MJ Medhurst (ed), *Eisenhower's War of Words: Rhetoric and Leadership*, East Lansing, MI: Michigan State University Press, 1994, pp 14–15.

18  Sherry, *In the Shadow of War*, pp 132–34, 139.

19  See Ivie, 'Images of savagery', for a fuller account of these discursive dimensions.

20  RL Ivie, 'Speaking "common sense" about the Soviet threat: Reagan's rhetorical stance', *Western Journal of Speech Communication*, 48 (1), 1984, pp 39–50.

21  See, for instance, Ivie, 'Metaphor of force', and RL Ivie, 'Literalizing the metaphor of Soviet savagery: President Truman's plain style', *Southern Speech Communication Journal*, 51 (2), 1986, pp 91–105.

22  RL Ivie, 'The ideology of freedom's "fragility" in American foreign policy argument', *Journal of the American Forensic Association*, 24 (1), 1987, pp 27–36.

23  Sherry, *In the Shadow of War*, pp 431–432, 441–442, 445–446, 461, 464, 467, 497.

24  See, for instance, Q Skinner, *Reason and Rhetoric in the Philosophy of Hobbes*, New York: Cambridge University Press, 1996, pp 320–321.

25  I Kant, 'To perpetual peace: a philosophical sketch', in *Immanuel Kant: Perpetual Peace and Other Essays on Politics, History, and Morals*, ed and trans Ted Humphrey, Indianapolis, IN: Hackett Publishing Company, 1983, pp 107–139.

26  *Ibid*, p 117.

27  There is a substantial literature on the current appropriation of the idea of a democratic peace, much of which is critically reviewed in RL Ivie, 'Democratizing for peace', *Rhetoric and Public Affairs*, 4 (2), 2001, pp 309–322.

28  D Campbell, *Writing Security: United States Foreign Policy and the Politics of Identity*, Minneapolis, MN: University of Minnesota Press, 1992, p 2.

29  JD Simon, *The Terrorist Trap: America's Experience with Terrorism*, Bloomington, IN: Indiana University Press, 2001, pp xx, 8, 167, 178–179, 185, 195.

30  GW Bush delivering the commencement address at the US Air Force Academy, 'Transcript: Bush casts war on terrorism in historic terms', *Washingtonpost.com*, 2 June 2004, at http://www.washingtonpost.com/ac2/wp-dyn/A9946-2004Jun2?language = printer, accessed 3 June 2004.

31  RL Ivie, 'The rhetoric of Bush's "war" on evil', *KB Journal*, 1 (1), 2004, online at http://www.kbjournal.org.

32  NA Lewis, 'Ashcroft defends antiterror plan and says criticism may aid foes', *New York Times on the Web*, 7 December 2001, at http://www.nytimes.com, accessed 7 December 2001.

33  'Remarks made by Senator Zell Miller', *New York Times*, 1 September 2004, at http://www.nytimes.com/2004/09/01/politics/campaign/01TEXT-MILLER.html?adxnn-l = adxnnlx = 1094098085-v57iOoSoRBwndE6f9OMrQ, accessed 1 September 2004.

34  See, for example, Mann, *Incoherent Empire*, pp 159–163, 185–190; and S Buck-Morss, *Thinking Past Terror: Islamism and Critical Theory on the Left*, London: Verso, 2003, pp 2–3, 10–12, 15, 27, 42, 65, 106.

[35] 'Rumsfeld says terror outweighs jail abuse', *Washingtonpost.com*, 11 September 2004, at http://www.washingtonpost.com/ac2/wp-dyn/A11930-2004Sep10?language = printer, accessed 11 September 2004.

[36] See, for example, an argument for agonistic pluralism in C Mouffe, *The Democratic Paradox*, London: Verso, 2000.

[37] On this point, see RL Ivie, 'Prologue to democratic dissent in America', *Javnost/The Public*, 11 (2), 2004, pp 19–35.

[38] J Dawes, *The Language of War: Literature and Culture in the US from the Civil War through World War II*, Cambridge, MA: Harvard University Press, 2002, p 21.

[39] M de Certeau, *The Practice of Everyday Life*, trans S Rendall, Berkeley, CA: University of California Press, 1984, pp xvii–xx.

[40] R Bleiker, *Popular Dissent, Human Agency and Global Politics*, Cambridge: Cambridge University Press, 2000.

# Bandits and blanket thieves, communists and terrorists: the politics of naming Sandinistas in Nicaragua, 1927–36 and 1979–90

MICHAEL J SCHROEDER

In July 1985 US President Ronald Reagan denounced Nicaragua as part of a 'confederation of terrorist states' that had committed 'outright acts of war' against the USA. Prefiguring President George W Bush's 'Axis of evil' speech nearly two decades later, as well as Bush's cynical denunciation of Al-Qaeda's fight against the USA as driven by an obsessive abhorrence of the US way of life and a loathing of freedom, Reagan propounded a geopolitical paradigm that closely resonates with the one currently emanating from Washington:

> Iran, Libya, North Korea, Cuba, Nicaragua—continents away, tens of thousands of miles apart, but the same goals and objectives. I submit to you that the growth in terrorism in recent years results from the increasing involvement of these states in terrorism in every region of the world. This is terrorism that is part of a pattern, the work of a confederation of terrorist state...And all of these states are united by one simple criminal phenomenon—their fanatical hatred of the United States, our people, our way of life, our international stature.[1]

At the time of Reagan's remarks, the current US Ambassador to Iraq, career diplomat John Negroponte, served as US Ambassador to Honduras. After the triumph of the Sandinista Revolution in 1979, Honduras had emerged as the principal US support base for the Contra war in neighbouring Nicaragua. From 1981 to 1985—the period of Negroponte's ambassadorial stint in Honduras—US military aid to that country skyrocketed from $3.9 to $77.4 million, while death squads linked to the Honduran military 'disappeared' or killed hundreds of alleged 'subversives'. According to a prize-winning series of investigative articles published in the *Baltimore Sun*, the most infamous of these death squads was Battalion 316, headed by Colonel Gustavo Alvarez Martínez, head of the Honduran military and *de facto* strongman of the country. Despite his close ties to the Honduran military, and despite hundreds of newspaper articles and numerous reports by reputable international agencies documenting human rights abuses, Ambassador Negroponte later denied any knowledge of human rights violations in Honduras.[2]

In 1997 Negroponte reflected on his experience in Honduras and his understanding of the geostrategic dynamics at work at the time:

> I had no doubt that these [Central American] conflicts were being fueled by Cuba, and I think by implication by the Soviet Union ... The experience of the late 1970s was for the United States, I think, a very sobering one. Indeed, as far as the Cold War is concerned, you have in particular two events: the Vietnamese invasion of Cambodia in 1978, and the ensuing Soviet invasion of Afghanistan in 1979. So viewed in that context, what then started to happen in El Salvador and Nicaragua were I think of considerable concern to Washington: 'Well gee, is this all part of a pattern? And if it is, or if that appears to be the case, then we really have to do something about it'.

Harking back to an emotionally charged metaphor created during the Eisenhower presidency to justify what became the tragically misguided intervention in a civil war in Southeast Asia, Negroponte concluded, 'It was a Central American domino theory if you will'.[3]

Thus in the 1970s and 1980s the US government once again used the distorting lens of the Cold War to portray home-grown insurgencies in Central America as direct extensions of the Soviet drive for world communist domination. As the US diplomatic and military establishment painted revolutionaries and dissidents throughout Central America as Soviet puppets, US client states throughout the region eagerly adopted the same cold war rhetoric as a key weapon in the battle against forces that threatened to transform long-standing relations of extreme political and economic inequality. Trade unionists, community organisers, opposition leaders of diverse political stripes, as well as armed insurgents and guerrillas in city and countryside, all were tarred with the same broad brush, as elements in a vast communist conspiracy directed from inside the Kremlin. The human suffering and carnage that resulted from this broad-based offensive against reform and revolution remain incalculable.

Perhaps no case demonstrates this pattern more clearly than that of Nicaragua, for this small Central American nation long had been of special interest to the USA. This article looks first at the politics of naming during the period of Sandinista rule (1979–90), then back at an earlier era of intense political struggle, contrasting the US rhetorical assault against the modern-day Sandinistas with the efforts of the USA and its allies to delegitimise the rebellion (1927–34) of Augusto C Sandino, the nationalist guerrilla leader who inspired their name.

## Soviet puppets versus freedom fighters

In 1970s Nicaragua the Somoza dictatorship, following the lead of their US patrons, portrayed the Sandinista National Liberation Front (FSLN) as a Soviet and Cuban puppet, determined to create a Central American beachhead for their communist masters in Moscow and Havana. Shoe-horning the FSLN's diverse tendencies and ideological strands into the one-size-fits-all 'communist' label, the Somoza regime did what US-supported Central American dictatorships conventionally had done during the cold war era: use a convenient tag to denounce, delegitimise and destroy organised opposition to their rule.

In fact, by the late 1970s the Sandinistas had articulated a coherent political programme which emphasised opposition to the Somoza dictatorship, national self-determination, political non-alignment, social justice for the country's impoverished majority, and which was built upon the foundations of nationalism, Christian liberation theology, and a Nicaragua-nised variant of Marxism. Especially after the December 1972 earthquake that destroyed much of the capital city, Managua—after which Somoza and his cronies pocketed most of the millions of dollars of international aid that poured into the country—the unbridled avarice and corruption of the Somoza dynasty became transparent, effectively alienating a substantial segment of the country's small middle and upper classes. A divided elite, Somocista intransigence and the human rights policies of the Carter administration combined to provide the FSLN with a strategic political opening. In July 1979, with widespread popular support and in the wake of a long and bloody struggle, the Sandinistas ousted Somoza and seized state power.[4]

After the triumph of the Sandinista Revolution, the newly elected Reagan administration dramatically intensified the US anti-communist rhetoric. Portraying Sandinista Nicaragua as a direct extension of the Soviet 'Evil Empire' and an abiding threat to US national security, it matched its words with deeds, initiating a range of policies designed to undermine the Sandinista regime and generate domestic support for its own anti-Sandinista offensive. These policies included funding, organising and training counter-revolutionary, or Contra, forces in Honduras, composed mainly of former Somocista National Guardsmen; mining Nicaraguan harbours; imposing a devastating trade embargo; and implementing a sophisticated 'perception management' programme at home.[5]

The Reagan administration's rhetorical approach to the conflict was epitomised by the president's memorable 1984 portrayal of the Contras as 'freedom fighters' against the evil Sandinista communists, as well as his declaration a year later that the Contras were 'the moral equivalent of our Founding Fathers'.[6] These malicious distortions, pronounced by an actor-turned-politician playing to a world-wide audience, became the conventional wisdom throughout much of the USA, while being rejected by relatively small numbers of mainly left-leaning academics and activists in the peace, justice and human rights communities. Outside the USA, many European and Latin American states and ngos rejected Reagan's rhetoric and advanced a far more realistic assessment of the Sandinistas as a home-grown national liberation movement and political party that, despite its flaws, represented the hopes and aspirations of Nicaragua's impoverished and oppressed majority. International aid from Scandinavia, Holland, Spain and elsewhere in Europe, as well as from Cuba and the USSR, poured into the country in an explicit rejection of the Reagan administration's cold war rhetoric.

The CIA's manual on 'Psychological Operations in Guerrilla Warfare' (1984), distributed to Contra forces, clearly demonstrates the Reagan administration's strategy of creating a negative perception of the Sandinistas within Nicaragua, regardless of the truth. The manual instructed that:

> The basic objective of a preconditioning campaign is to create a negative 'image' of the enemy, eg: Describe the managers of collective government entities as trying to treat the staff the way 'slave foremen' do. The police mistreat the people like the Communist 'Gestapo' does. The government officials of National Reconstruction are puppets of Russian–Cuban imperialism…The foreign advisors…are in reality 'interveners' in our homeland, who direct the exploitation of the nation in accordance with the objectives of Russian and Cuban imperialists, in order to turn our people into slaves of the hammer and sickle.[7]

That these misrepresentations bore no relation to reality was of no concern to the anonymous author(s) of the manual or to the architects of US policy in Washington.

Largely in consequence of the Reagan administration's multi-pronged diplomatic, military, economic and propaganda offensive, civil war and counter-revolution tore Nicaragua apart. The Contras violently attacked Sandinista agricultural co-operatives, schools, health care facilities, bridges, power lines and other infrastructure, while committing thousands of documented human rights abuses against the civilian population, especially in the northern departments along the Honduran border. Judging by their actions in the field, Reagan's 'freedom fighters' were much more aptly described as the 'terrorists' his administration denounced.[8]

Despite its blatant misrepresentation of the truth, the Reagan administration's delegitimising labels of 'communist' and 'terrorist' applied to the Sandinistas were generally potent and effective. They formed the most visible elements in an internally coherent and totalising narrative (or master narrative, or meta-story[9]) that allowed no room for compromise and contained within itself effective responses to every plausible critique. That the Sandinistas were puppets of their Soviet masters and stooges of Castro fit into a world-view that saw all international events in dichotomous terms, as part of the death struggle between two contending superpowers. Yet, if the Cold War provided a convenient pretext for the US anti-Sandinista offensive, it also reflected a real geopolitical contest between two nuclear-armed empires who kept score, in part, by aligning and realigning the would-be 'non-aligned' nations. The same was true of the legitimising labels 'freedom fighters' and 'moral equivalent of our Founding Fathers', as applied to the Contras, which fundamentally distorted reality even as they resonated with the US Revolutionary War and the most revered foundational myths of the republic.

In this case, then, as in others, the politics of naming was integral to a larger struggle between the contending narratives of groups with vastly unequal access to material and cultural power. As so many who have tried to tell their own stories in their own terms have discovered, merely objecting to a particular name or epithet proves insufficient if the offending narrative remains intact. To displace or subvert the delegitimising names deployed by dominant actors requires turning the rhetorical tables: challenging the totalising narrative as a whole, from its underlying assumptions and epistemological underpinnings to its specific manifestations, and doing so from a position of deep historical understanding.

Consequently, effectively displacing the 'communist' label that the Reagan administration applied to the Sandinistas required a wholesale review of Nicaraguan and Central American history, especially the long and tangled history of US interventions; the social injustices generated during the Somoza years; the convoluted history of the Comintern and Soviet policies toward Latin America; and so on. Waging this discursive battle within and outside Nicaragua, the Sandinista government and its supporters developed a multi-layered media strategy intended to illuminate the hypocrisy and mendacity at the root of the Reagan administration's allegations and to promote their own counter-narrative. Telling their story to an international audience, the Sandinista regime garnered the diplomatic support of dozens of countries; arranged and promoted interviews in print, audio and visual media; issued press releases explaining their policies, goals and philosophy; encouraged foreign citizens to travel to Nicaragua; and cultivated alliances with sundry individuals and organisations in solidarity with the Revolution. Promoting their story among its own citizens, the regime and its non-governmental allies used newspapers, radio, television, music and song, wall murals and statuary, sports, popular theatre, museums, as well as government programmes like the Literacy Crusade and educational and health care initiatives. New names displaced the old: the airport became Sandino International Airport; the National Palace became the Museum of the Revolution; 40 square blocks in the heart of old Managua, destroyed in the 1972 earthquake, became the site of a new national recreational facility, the Luis Alfonso Velásquez Flores Park, named after a 10-year-old martyr of the struggle against Somoza.[10] Neighbourhoods, streets, markets, buildings, schools, hospitals, parks, estates, these and other infrastructure were given new names to express and memorialise some part of the new Sandinista narrative. As a result of these and many related efforts, for several years in the early and mid-1980s the Sandinista narrative became hegemonic across most of the country. But the crippling US trade embargo and the devastation wrought in the Contra war combined to make that hegemony short-lived, and by the late 1980s the Sandinista narrative was being eclipsed by competing narratives more aligned with that promoted by the US government.

During the 1980s organisations and individuals in the USA seeking to provide a broader context and challenge their government's totalising narrative typically lacked access to the dominant media and faced impatient and unreceptive audiences unfamiliar with Central America, past or present. Countering the Reagan administration's misrepresentations was, without doubt, an uphill battle. Yet that same 'communist' or 'terrorist' label also offered a wedge that under favourable circumstances could be used to pry open and displace the meta-story as a whole. The USA, after all, began its interventions in Nicaragua nearly a decade before the Bolshevik Revolution (or six decades before, if one considers the William Walker episode of the 1850s). The nation-states of Central America, like those of Southeast Asia, were not like dominoes. The metaphor of small blocks of wood lined up in a row was as misleading here as it had been in Vietnam. To tell a different story and advocate a different set of policies in Central America, church, academic, solidarity and peace and justice organisations sponsored demonstrations, marches, protests, rallies, vigils, speakers, lectures, meetings, discussion groups, film showings and letter-writing campaigns to major media outlets and members of Congress; the alternative and left print media, like *The Nation, The Progressive, Mother Jones* and others provided a robust and cogent counter to the administration's claims, as did a spate of books on the Nicaraguan Revolution and Sandinismo, like Margaret Randall's *Sandino's Daughters*; Thomas W Walker's edited volumes; and many others.[11] Convincing US citizens how and why they needed to understand the specifics of the Nicaraguan situation, rather than merely adopt their government's simplistic anti-communist paradigm, proved daunting, frustrating but also possible.

## To the victors go the stories

This recent cold war era history in the politics of naming in Central America is relatively well known. Less familiar are the battles over names and narratives in the antecedents to this struggle, the first Sandinista revolution of the 1920s and 1930s. From 1927 to 1934 in the mountains of northern Nicaragua, a region known as Las Segovias, the nationalist guerrilla chieftain Augusto Sandino led an armed *campesino* insurgency against the US invasion and occupation of his homeland. The roots of the conflict were complex, but as was the case throughout much of the Caribbean and Central America in the first decades of the 20th century, the USA was seeking to impose its version of 'order' and 'stability' on what it portrayed as a profoundly 'disorderly' and 'unstable' land.[12] For nearly six years the Sandinista rebels fought the Marines and National Guard to a stalemate. In January 1933 the

Marines withdrew from Nicaragua, and a year later, in the midst of peace talks, the founder of the Somoza dynasty, Anastasio Somoza García, ordered the assassination of Sandino and the annihilation of what remained of his rebel organisation. In subsequent years Somoza and his regime systematically distorted and caricatured Sandino's aims and actions, relegating the history of the rebel movement to the margins of its own master narrative. Two years after assassinating Sandino, Somoza published a landmark book denouncing the rebel chieftain as a maniacal sociopath and his followers as motivated only by mayhem, robbery and murder.

Somoza's book, *El verdadero Sandino, o el calvario de las Segovias* (*The True Sandino, or the Calvary of Las Segovias*, 1936), which some still regard as a reliable account of Sandino and his rebellion, represents a fascinating and revealing exercise in the politics of naming. The plot of Somoza's story is eloquently expressed in the iconography of violence on the book's cover: an oversized machete poised over a map of the central part of Central America, its cutting edge dripping torrents of blood across the northern half of Nicaragua. The map is white and blue, Nicaragua's national colours, suggesting normality and tradition, while the blood and Sandino's name appear in bright crimson. Literally from cover to cover, Somoza's book depicts Sandino and his followers as crazed killers whose only goals were to desecrate the national heritage and drown Nicaraguans in their own blood.[13]

A maliciously one-sided and inaccurate text, *El verdadero Sandino* remains a masterpiece in creating and projecting its own authority. Essentially a compendium of carefully selected and often deceptively edited captured Sandinista documents tied together by a one-dimensional and tendentious storyline, it uses a variety of techniques to convince the reader of its veracity. It includes selections from more than 200 captured Sandinista documents; more than two dozen individual and group photographs of Sandinistas; 25 photographs of alleged victims of Sandinista atrocities and their families (most at funerals); and 20 facsimiles of Sandino's correspondence, most of which include Sandino's signature over his Defending Army's official seal. Accompanying each facsimile is the formulaic reminder: 'We insert a photograph of the document just transcribed so that our readers will not doubt their authenticity'. The text reminds the reader no fewer than 15 times that 'the original documents are at the disposal of anyone who still doubts their authenticity, at the Operations Office of the Guardia Nacional'. Relentlessly hammering its single theme, the book only includes evidence buttressing its portrayal of the rebels as bloodthirsty bandits bent on destroying the nation.

In subsequent decades Somoza's story became the anchor of what can be called the Somocista narrative of Sandinismo, which built on and synthesised several storylines circulating within Nicaragua for most of the decade before its publication. One derived from the reports of the Marines and National Guard, which systematically portrayed Sandino and his rebels not as nationalists but as gangs of bandits and cut-throats lacking any motivating ideology beyond robbery and murder. Another can be traced to the newspapers of the traditional power centres of Managua, León and Granada in the Pacific Coast region, which also portrayed the rebels as marauding bandits, their ostensible cause—Nicaraguan independence and expulsion of the Marines—admirable, but their means—organised banditry—deplorable. A third storyline derived from the derogatory labels applied to the rebels by their local enemies at the time—the townsfolk, landowners, coffee growers and political power holders of Las Segovias.[14] The denunciatory stories circulating in each of these spheres both informed and were informed by the others, making efforts to disaggregate their relative potency or the intersecting lines of transmission among and between them difficult. Suffice it to say that their similarities far outweighed their differences and that all contributed to the totalising indictment of the rebel movement that Somoza and his allies fashioned and propagated after the war.

## The leatherneck version

From the beginning of the US invasion of Las Segovias in mid-1927, the US Marines contrived a robustly delegitimising storyline that painted Sandino and his followers as 'bandits' and 'outlaws', 'murderers', 'criminals' and 'marauders' engaged in 'robbery, pillage, rape and murder' against the 'defenceless people' of the Segovian countryside. Their actions, shrouded behind Sandino's 'false standard of patriotism', were inspired by no ideology or 'cause' beyond 'pillage and loot' and fostering 'unrest' and 'disorder' in the 'bandit infested' areas under their control. The 'bandit hordes' were like a 'cancerous growth', a 'disease', a 'virus' that had 'invaded' the Nicaraguan social body. 'Exterminating bandits', as one rids oneself of vermin and pests, thus became the Marines' official *raison d'être* in the Segovian countryside.[15]

The semi-official Marine Corps publication *The Leatherneck* was replete with such imagery. Paradigmatic here was its account of the deaths of Lieutenant Thomas and Sergeant Dowell, whose plane the rebels shot down in October 1927. 'Both were later surrounded by the murdering machete bearing bandits, followers of Sandino', reported a 'Plane Observer', who likened the scene to the 'black' days of his own country's past. 'The English translation of the word Nicaragua is "black water"', he fabricated imaginatively, and 'Black it is indeed to fly over the charred remains of the crash and look away down there in a native banana patch on a little black spot where the skeleton of the battle plane reposes not unlike a covered wagon in the early pages of our country's history possibly burned by some marauding band of Indians and rests there until the transpiration of the ages'. Invoking his country's long history of anti-Black and anti-Indian racism, and the genocidal Indian wars concluded less than half a century before, this 'Plane Observer' made explicit what was more often implicit in the sterile language of official reports: Marine Corps representations of Sandino and his rebellion rested on a foundation of racist ideologies stretching back to the beginnings of US history.[16]

In the 1920s and 1930s the US Marine Corps was comprised exclusively of white males, many from the lower echelons of a society profoundly divided by race and social class. It would be surprising indeed to find that some Marines were not deeply influenced by the racist cultural politics of the era. The private letters of Marine Private Emil Thomas to his fiancée offer a window on the extent to which racist attitudes permeated Marine Corps culture. Writing from the Sick Quarters in Quantico, VA in January 1928, Thomas expressed his desire to go to the Nicaraguan theatre. 'I'll bet I'd bring me back a couple of nigger's toes', he wrote, 'and they wouldn't be the kind that grow on nut trees either'. By March, after having learned from his returned comrades of the 'bad food...mud up to the waist, drunkedness, sickness, filth, and also blood thirstyness [sic]', he had changed his mind: 'All those fine white American boys being killed just so a few less niggers will be killed...what makes me mad is that those perfectly good white men should be sacrificed to save a few ignorant niggers'. Significantly, after some months in Nicaragua, Thomas's favoured racist epithet changed from 'nigger' to 'gook', suggesting that 'gook' was the racist term of choice among his comrade-in-arms; after being stationed in the northern town of Ocotal for a few months, he wrote that 'most of us are only to [sic] glad to have an excuse to bump off a few gooks'.[17]

Partly in consequence of this racism and cultural arrogance, Marine intelligence analysts in Nicaragua in the 1920s and 1930s profoundly misconstrued and misrepresented the nature of the enemy they confronted. Despite mounting evidence that they faced a nationalist insurgency by genuine patriots, the Marine intelligence apparatus systematically dismissed Sandino's oft-expressed motives for rebelling, which by early 1928 were being disseminated across Latin America via pamphlets and newspapers. 'Sandino is out for the money and nothing else', reported Marine Corps Major Floyd, who led the first ground assault against Sandino's forces in late 1927. A few months later Managua-based intelligence analyst Lieutenant Larson speculated on the reasons behind Sandino's organising successes: 'The life promised is one of banditry and looting, which is a means of existence for many persons'. Similar assessments were repeated hundreds of times in the coming months and years. Mid-level officers like Floyd, Larson and others both reproduced and amplified the conceptual and semantic framework formulated by their military and civilian superiors. If no official directive ordering intelligence or field officers to use this language of 'banditry' has been found, the consistency of such language strongly suggests that such a directive was being followed. At the same time, all the evidence indicates that virtually all Marines accepted this 'bandit' label as an accurate description of their adversaries.[18]

Emblematic of these racist cultural politics was Marine Corps Major Julian C Smith's officially commissioned *History of the Guardia Nacional de Nicaragua* (1933), which offered a patronising evaluation of the 'factors entering into and affecting the police mission' of which he was a prominent participant.[19] He began by observing that:

> The American officers of the Guardia Nacional were immediately confronted with the problem of personal adjustment to a situation requiring a sympathetic

understanding of a people who had originated from different racial strains and who had developed under entirely different conditions of environment and who were animated by different ideals...Each strain [Spanish, Indian, African] had its corresponding effect upon the psychology of the people.

Emphasising 'the fundamental differences between Latin and Anglo-Saxon ideals and characteristics', Smith quoted approvingly from 19th-century clergyman Henry Ward Beecher, an early proponent of Social Darwinism:

There are two dominant races in modern history; the Germanic and the Roman races. The Germanic races tend to personal liberty, to a sturdy individualism, to civil and political liberty. The Romanic race tends to absolutism in government; it is clannish; it loves chieftains; it develops a people that crave strong and showy governments to support and plan for them.

Nicaraguans, in this schema, clearly dwelled on the 'Romanic' side of this racial divide. Hence their proclivity for civil war and authoritarianism, and animosity towards liberty as well as the Marine intervention. For Smith, who implicitly construed himself and the Marines as embodying 'Germanic' tendencies, coming to grips with the persistence of 'organised banditry' in Nicaragua despite 'so many tactical defeats and indecisive actions' required understanding the peculiar 'racial psychology' of 'the poorer classes of Nicaraguans':

Densely ignorant...little interested in principles...naturally brave and inured to hardships, of phlegmatic temperament, though capable of being aroused to acts of extreme violence, they have fought for one party or the other without considering causes since time immemorial...a state of war is to them a normal condition.

Like many other imperial ethnographers of his day, Smith naturalised, essentialised and dehistoricised the colonial Other, construing historically produced social and political conditions as natural and immutable realities. His assessments were echoed repeatedly by his superiors and subordinates. '[Sandino] has been routed from his selected region east of Chipote', wrote Captain Reagan in April 1928, 'and will probably drive farther into the wild fastnesses East of the Coco, said to be inhabited by Indians who are little removed from savagery'.[20] The Commandant of the Marine Corps, Major General John Lejeune, writing in early 1928, observed that 'The political situation there is very bitter, and that is really the cause of all the trouble in Nicaragua'. He tried to explain the intense passions driving these political struggles: 'The people in Western Nicaragua have a great deal of Indian blood in them. Some families are pure Spanish descent, but the majority have Indian blood', making them 'a very courageous race of people; nothing cowardly about them'— 'courageous' here a synonym for 'violent'.[21] Imagining Nicaraguans as fundamentally violent and inferior in consequence of their immutable racial heritage, the Marines legitimated their own extreme violence in their prosecution of the war.

After Sandino's return from Mexico in mid-1930, his Defending Army intensified its military and propaganda efforts and expanded its zones of operation. By this time the Marines and Guardia had abundant evidence that the Sandinistas represented not 'organised banditry' but a genuine national liberation movement inspired by nationalist and internationalist ideals. Yet the same language of 'banditry' continued to infuse their intelligence assessments. Such assessments were issued in weekly, bi-weekly, monthly 'Bn-2' (battalion-level), 'R-2' (regiment-level) and 'B-2' (brigade-level) reports—and after October 1930 the monthly 'GN-2' (Guardia Nacional) report—in which Managua-based analysts tried to synthesise all the strands of information coming in from different parts of the country to present a comprehensive portrait of the current state of intelligence on the rebels and the war effort. One requisite section of these reports, 'Enemy Probable Intentions', routinely described the rebels as intent on nothing more than banditry and murder. Typical was the Bn-2 Report of 22 June 1930. After speculating about what would happen if Sandino had indeed returned to Nicaragua, the analyst continued: 'If, on the other hand, Sandino is not in Nicaragua, the various jefes [chieftains] will continue as before, ambushing small patrols, robbing and murdering the defenseless natives in the outlying districts'.[22] In September 1930 the author of the GN-2 report began the 'Enemy Probable Intentions' section as follows: 'From all reports it appears that Sandino is attempting to organize the various bandit forces along some military lines, to be known as the "Army Defending the National Sovereignty of Nicaragua"'. Remarkably, Sandino had founded his Defending Army in September 1927, three years before this report, a fact that the marine–guardia intelligence apparatus should have known, considering all the captured correspondence and published materials at their disposal. The analyst then expressed his view that 'the backbone of banditry is breaking and that Sandino's so-called army is crumbling'.[23] Events proved him wrong, as the Defending Army continued to grow in power. A month later the same analyst reported that 'the bandit prospects are not very bright...Sandino's army is a failure'—this after he noted in an earlier section of the report, entitled 'Enemy Strength', that 'Large groups are reported here and reported there and even if only a reasonable percentage of the numbers reported were considered and totaled, it would be surprising to note how the number of reported bandits increases each month instead of decreasing'.[24] That such contradictory assessments could be combined in the same intelligence report suggests the extent to which the Marines and Guardia had internalised their own disparaging epithets and narrative on the rebels.

This language of 'bandits' and 'banditry' continued unabated for the rest of the war. 'Thus the curtain falls on the attempt of the bandit robbers to gain a foot-hold in the departments of the west', reported Captain Carlson in January 1932 on the first sustained Defending Army movement into the more populated zones of Chinandega and León. A few months later, another Managua-based intelligence analyst acknowledged that, in the same area, 'the country people are practically 100% in sympathy with them'; that 'they have a system of espionage...that is highly efficient'; and that 'reports received from all sources indicate that all people living in [that area] are very friendly to the bandits and helping them in all ways possible and state that they are ready at any time to join forces for whatever operations the bandit jefes may order'.[25] In October 1932, only three months before the final Marine withdrawal, another analyst predicted that 'the various bandit jefes and their groups...will unquestionably continue as per routine, to rob and collect contributions.'[26] Absent the conceptual blinders they insisted on retaining, the Marines–Guardia Nacional probably would have understood from the outset that their adversaries were far more than the 'bandit robbers' they imagined and represented them to be.

## Patriotic plunder and retribution

Dominant groups' denunciatory narratives tend to exhibit a tenuous, distorted, de-contextualised connection to some aspect of the truth. In the case of Sandino's rebellion, the 'bandit' label had such a connection, rooted in the rebels' need to acquire the material resources for waging war, invariably an expensive proposition for any army. This rebellion's survival required food, clothing, medicine, horses, firearms and ammunition. Although the rebels enjoyed widespread support among the *campesinos* of Las Segovias, the crushing poverty of the region meant that most *campesinos* could only extend them food and labour power. Unlike the Sandinistas of the 1970s and 1980s (and unlike the 13 British American colonies two centuries earlier, for example), Sandino's rebels in the 1920s and 1930s garnered virtually no international material support. Without any state supporting them, with only a handful of non-Central Americans in their ranks, and with precious few elite Nicaraguan allies, the rebels had few options except to plunder the wealthy in order to finance their operations. They did so by systematically appropriating the moveable property of landowners, cattle ranchers, coffee growers and other elites and bartering these items, most often in the lucrative Honduran market, for the material necessities of war.[27]

This was the aspect of reality in the 'bandit' epithet that permitted the Marines and Guardia to project this pejorative term as the single most accurate descriptor of the rebels. A similar dynamic was at work with respect to the 'murderer' label. With many civilian collaborators in their midst, and with betrayal a constant threat, the rebels did in fact attack and kill many Nicaraguan civilians. Careful analysis of the evidence indicates that most of their victims had in some way assisted the invading and occupying forces, by acting as informants, guides and in other capacities.[28] It was also true that, with a long history of firearms shortages, cutting weapons like *machetes* and *cutachas* had historically comprised the most important weapons in the Segovian countryside. For these reasons, most of the assaults and murders perpetrated by the rebels against other Nicaraguans were committed with these cutting weapons, in historically determined cultural ways. Thus the 'murderer' and 'cut-throat' labels, like 'bandit', contained elements of truth that in their adversaries' narratives became radically separated from their historical, cultural, political and military contexts.[29]

74

All the while, within and outside the USA and antecedent to the solidarity movement of the 1980s, a small but vocal group of progressive journalists, academics, politicians, activists and others sought to counter this 'bandit' label by situating the Sandino rebellion within a broader anti-imperialist context. In 1928 the radical journalist Carleton Beals became the first foreign reporter to interview Sandino, his series of articles in *The Nation* providing a forum for Sandino and his followers to justify their rebellion as a legitimate nationalist response to years of US imperialist intervention. The All-American Anti-Imperialist League, the National Citizens Committee on Relations with Latin America, the Hands Off Nicaragua Committee and other organisations worked to galvanise international and US opposition to the US invasion and occupation, as did Senator William E Borah of Idaho and his allies in Congress, Sandino's half-brother Sócrates Sandino in his fund-raising efforts in New York, and others. Confronting head-on the lies and misrepresentations of the US military and diplomatic establishment, these and many other individuals and organisations' efforts to turn the rhetorical tables were important elements in the transformation of US policy from the late 1920s, which culminated in President Roosevelt's Good Neighbor Policy after 1934.[30]

### Bandits Rob Merchandise! Demand Contributions!

Within Nicaragua the newspapers of the major urban centres of the Pacific Coast region portrayed the rebels in ways very similar to the representations of the Marines and Guardia. The 'news' these papers deigned to carry from Las Segovias was usually inaccurate, sensationalised and focused on the theme of rebel violence against property and persons. 'Bandits Rob Merchandise' announced the headline of a typical article in mid-1928, which went on to call for 'energetic action to guarantee commerce against those marauding on the roads'. 'They Are Demanding Contributions From the Principal Coffee Growers!' screamed the front page of one of Managua's leading newspapers in January 1931, accompanied by a lengthy article describing recent Sandinista 'outlaw' activities in the coffee districts of Jinotega and Matagalpa. Going to the heart of the politics of naming, a June 1931 headline in León's *El Centroamericano* posed the question: 'Is Sandino a Bandit or Patriot?' The answer was obvious. In the words of 'Professor Paul Lavalle, prominent man of science and French writer', interviewed for the story:

> In more than twenty cities and towns that I have visited in Nicaragua, I have asked people what they thought of Sandino. Everyone invariably answered, 'Sandino is a bandit'...Sandino and his so-called 'Movement for the Defense of National Sovereignty' is not only dedicated to expelling the Marines, but has attacked, sacked, and burned towns and killed their inhabitants, most of them Nicaraguans.[31]

By his own account, 'Professor Lavalle' never ventured into the Segovian countryside, where he would have found widespread support for the rebels.

As the war progressed, the denunciations of Sandino and his followers in the urban press grew ever more vitriolic. Sandino worked tirelessly to counter these denunciations by issuing scores of manifestos and proclamations explaining and justifying his rebellion but, like the Marines and Guardia, the major Pacific Coast newspapers either ignored or ridiculed these efforts at self-legitimation.[32] 'The hordes of Sandino are made up of mercenaries and men without scruples', opined one editorialist of Managua's *La Prensa* on 2 April 1932.

> I civilly reject...the ludicrous patriotism of Sandino and the horde of bandits who follow him...The true patriot attacks the enemy valiantly but he does not attack his brother or his co-patriots. He does not kill in a cowardly or traitorous manner, does not violate women, does not rob strong-boxes, does not burn their homes. To those who proceed in such a fashion I find only these dry and cold-blooded names: thieves, assassins, and incendiaries.

As these excerpts suggest, Sandinista violence against property and persons in Las Segovias provided property owners across the country with the raw materials they could use to fashion a coherent denunciatory narrative. To most such property owners the Sandinistas represented their worst nightmare: the spectre of social revolution from below, an overturning of existing social relations of extreme inequality, an unending spiral of violence, and loss of their lives and fortunes. No wonder the rebels proved unable to cultivate any organic links with middling or large property holders, or with any social class beyond the impoverished *campesinos* of Las Segovias. Brought together in an alliance of convenience by their shared fears of violent social revolution, property owners in Las Segovias and beyond soon came to form a relatively solid if internally heterogeneous anti-Sandinista front, allying with the Marines – Guardia and deploying the same delegitimising labels against their rebel foes.

### They called us cow eaters, chicken eaters, blanket thieves

The extreme class divisions that characterised Nicaraguan and Segovian society meant that this language of 'banditry' also found an organic social basis independent of the Marines – Guardia and the urban press. Soon after the rebellion was launched, requests and petitions for Marine – Guardia protection against 'the hordes of Sandino' began pouring in from across the north. The refrain soon became familiar, epitomised in the following petition from the *municipio* of Mosonte of December 1930:

> We the undersigned, of age, workers and natives of Mosonte...state as follows: That we are threatened by the bandits who remain in several parts of the department and who go around in the valleys and villages where we live, aided by the cover of night when no military unit can pursue them...these groups of bandits are composed of bad men...who continue killing peaceful and honest citizens...these bandits hate us because we are not their sympathisers, on the contrary we condemned their activities and criminal proceedings.[33]

As the petition indicates, these enemies of the rebels had 'condemned their activities' to the military authorities. By the rebels' lights, such 'treasonous' behaviour rendered these 'citizens' neither 'peaceful' nor 'honest' but active allies of the nation's enemies, thereby legitimating the retribution served upon them.

Memories of the denunciatory epithets and narrative that emerged across Las Segovias in response to Sandino's rebellion survived into the 1980s and after, as the Sandinistas themselves documented through oral history interviews. In 1983 70-year-old Cosme Andino, half a century earlier a soldier in Sandino's ranks, began his oral testimony on the period of the rebellion by recalling the violence committed by the Marines and Guardia against his family: 'We were persecuted by the Yankees...they burned my mother's house, my brother's house they burned too, and they shot my sister. Of my family only I remained, by God's will, so I could tell the story, come what may.' This broader context established, he turned to the pejorative labels pinned upon himself and other rebels by his fellow Segovianos: 'And from there, well, the tragedy that we lived, the people, during our journeys, they called us bandits, they called us cow eaters, chicken eaters, blanket thieves'; his pain and bitterness at the injustice of such names were an almost palpable feature of his testimony.[34]

Other ex-soldiers interviewed in the 1980s also framed their recollections around the contours of an implicit counter-narrative that denounced them as bandits and communists. Lizandro Ardón, for instance, denied that Sandino was a communist without ever being prompted to do so, insisting that Sandino fought 'so that no foreign country would come and trample on our homeland; if the Russians had come, he would have fought against them just like he did the Yankees'. In a similar prolepsis, former rebel Francisco Centeno vigorously denied any link between Sandino and communism, despite the interviewer having never broached the topic: 'He said he wanted a free homeland, a free Nicaragua, that there would be no intervention of any kind, that there would be a government put in by the people, this was the struggle. Speeches about communism, he never said anything, nothing, nothing, never did he speak of that. The Russians offered him help and he refused it! He didn't receive anyone's help, he fought all alone.'[35]

Occasionally former rebels acknowledged that they robbed to acquire the material necessities of war. Tiburcio Zelaya was asked in 1983 how the Defending Army obtained medicines. 'This was easy', he replied. 'We robbed the apothecaries in the towns, we'd arrive in the towns, the prescription clerk would pick out the medicines. We robbed because we had to rob.' Sixto Hernández, another former rebel, was asked about the main difficulties the rebel army experienced. 'The hunger!' he responded. 'You should have seen, naked, in rags, we arrived in the towns to rob, we had to rob, to take.'[36]

In short, the rebels systematically plundered the propertied in order to finance their rebellion and committed considerable violence against the invaders' collaborators. Focusing exclusively on these two aspects of the war, their enemies concocted a totalising narrative that framed them and their rebellion as pure and simple banditry, wedded seamlessly to murder, mayhem, and senseless outrage—a meta-story that wholly elided the larger reality that the Sandinista rebels were patriots fighting for national self-determination and social justice. Yet larger truths endured, in the whispered stories and clandestine songs sung in the wake of Somoza's post-rebellion massacres, and re-emerged as a new generation listened to and learned from the stories and songs of the old.

'What else did Sandino tell you about the struggle you were undertaking?' the youthful interviewer asked 72-year-old former rebel soldier Joaquin Fajardo in 1984. 'A great many things', the old man responded.

> like he told us: 'Boys, most of the people of Nicaragua don't want us; they persecute us and call us bandits and they sell us out with whatever words they want to use. Even though they don't want us, in other parts, our name will shine like the stars in the sky.' This he told us...

> I am like a beacon that lights up the world
> Showing its idea of redemption
> And the people will break the filthy yoke
> And will carry on with my idea of redemption

So said Sandino.[37]

## The politics of naming

Just as the Sandinistas of the 1970s and 1980s borrowed from and modified the discursive field that seemed to them the most empowering and emancipatory—the languages and concepts of nationalism, Marxism, liberation theology and non-alignment—so too did their predecessors in the 1920s and 1930s, who appropriated and recast the languages and concepts of national liberation, *campesino* autonomy, and social justice. In both cases more powerful foreign and domestic groups, whose interests were threatened by Sandinista visions of a more just and humane society, articulated coherent narratives that magnified aspects of Sandinista ideology and social practice and wholly effaced others. There were, of course, important differences between the two periods. Public discourse in the earlier era was shot through with explicitly racist, biologised language; public opinion played a less central role in shaping US policy; and the pejorative terms 'bandits' and 'murderers' effectively delimited Sandinismo as an exclusively local problem most effectively resolved by imposing 'law and order'. In the later era, with racist and biologised discourse no longer acceptable in the public sphere, with more rapid and globalised communications networks, and with a local or national delimitation of the struggle no longer suiting their interests, dominant groups located the conflict within an equally convenient framework, ie the broader global context of the Cold War and the fight against rogue 'terrorist' regimes. These differences in world-historical time, public discursive boundaries and rhetorical strategies notwithstanding, in both cases dominant groups and their allies concocted a series of pejorative, delegitimising names and images, strung together into totalising narratives, to legitimate their efforts to destroy emergent collectivities whose agendas ultimately threatened their own superior power.

The politics of naming Sandinistas in Nicaragua was thus embedded within a larger politics of storytelling. Whose story prevailed depended on a host of unpredictable political dynamics. From 1927 to 1934 two contending stories vied for supremacy. After 1934 Somoza's story carried the day, becoming hegemonic for several decades but unable wholly to extinguish its antithesis. In the 1970s the battle over stories reached another crescendo, and after 1979 a revised Sandinista story displaced its rival and itself became hegemonic. The Sandinistas told part of their revolutionary story in their party's battle hymn: 'We fight against the Yankee/ The enemy of humanity'. Turning the rhetorical tables to challenge directly the US projection of itself as the defender of freedom and justice, the fledgling regime deemed the US self-projection a monumental lie, not just for their own small country of three million people but for the entire planet. The USA refused to listen to the accusation, however. In Managua on 19 July1980, the first anniversary of their overthrow of the Somoza regime, the Sandinista leadership led a crowd of thousands in singing their revolutionary battle hymn. Rather than hear their country disparaged as 'the enemy of humanity', the 11-member US delegation, led by the US Ambassador to the United Nations, Donald McHenry, walked out of the commemoration.[38]

A few months after Ambassador McHenry's refusal to hear his country branded by this pejorative epithet, Ronald Reagan was elected president, and within the year Reagan named John Negroponte US Ambassador to Honduras. More than 20 years later George W Bush, the son of Reagan's vice-president, appointed Negroponte to McHenry's former post, as US Ambassador to the UN. In March 2003 Negroponte repeated McHenry's theatrics when he and the US delegation to the UN Security Council walked out of a meeting in which Iraq's Ambassador accused the USA and UK of 'criminal, barbaric' aggression 'that is killing women, children, and the elderly and destroys the life and future of the people of Iraq'.[39] A few months later Bush appointed Negroponte US Ambassador to a 'liberated' Iraq. In July 2004, soon after Honduras had withdrawn its small contingent of troops from Iraq, Negroponte stood before a mass grave near Hillah, Iraq, 'to reaffirm America's commitment to the cause of justice, freedom, and respect for human rights'—a self-portrayal that, coming in the midst of the Abu Ghraib prisoner torture revelations, was received with incredulity by much of the world.[40]

Unlike their more powerful adversaries, subordinate groups struggling for self-determination, social justice and human rights historically have not had the luxury of ignoring or closing their ears to the names and narratives imposed upon them. Instead, these imposed names and narratives have a weight and power of their own, comprising crucial components in the efforts of dominant groups to retain their superior power. In the struggle for human emancipation in this age of global terror, global capitalism and global lies, the meta-stories of the dominant—and of subordinate groups like religious or nationalist extremists struggling not for social justice or human rights but for national – ethnic purity, cataclysmic confrontation, or the destruction of secularism—need to be displaced by relentless chiseling at their very foundations. Academics, human rights activists and others committed to creating a more emancipatory future can most fruitfully contribute to this struggle over narratives and naming by conveying in print, visual and other media their understanding of context and complexity, by showing the sliver of truth in these meta-stories for what it is—a very small part of a much bigger truth. If the partly true stories told by the powerful or demagogic can be enormously persuasive, the stories told by those seeking a more just and humane world must be truer, wiser and more persuasive still.

## Notes

I would like to thank Michael Bhatia, Thomas W Walker, an anonymous reviewer and especially Nora Faires for their incisive comments on drafts of this article. Special thanks are also due to Doug McCabe, Archives and Special Collections, Alden Library, Ohio University, for his very kind assistance

1   President Reagan's Remarks at the Annual Convention of the American Bar Association, 8 July 1985, at www.reagan.utexas.edu/resource/speeches/1985/70885a.htm. It is noteworthy that 'fanatical hatred' of the USA, its people, its way of life, or its international stature—or, for that matter, 'fanatical hatred' of anything when not linked to actual criminal behaviour—was not and is not defined as a crime in either US or international law, and that Reagan's remarks therefore contained smaller and more discrete lies embedded within his larger lies about a 'confederation of terrorist states'.

2   See  http://english.aljazeera.net/NR/exeres/554FAF3A-B267-427A-B9EC-54881BDE0A2E.htm;  and www.baltimoresun.com/news/local/bal-negroponte4,0,2326054.story.

3   See www.cnn.com/SPECIALS/cold.war/episodes/18/interviews/negroponte/.

4   See C Vilas, The Sandinista Revolution, London: Monthly Review Press, 1986; and M Zimmermann, Sandinista: Carlos Fonseca and the Nicaraguan Revolution, Durham, NC: Duke University Press, 2000.

5   T Walker (ed), Nicaragua: The First Five Years, New York: Praeger, 1985; and T Walker (ed), Nicaragua without Illusions, Wilmington, DE: Scholarly Resources, 1997. The secret 'Presidential Finding' of 1 December 1981, whose 'Purpose' was to 'support and conduct paramilitary operations against. . .Nicaragua' and which officially authorized the CIA's Contra war against the Sandinistas, can be found at www.gwu.edu/~nsarchiv/usa/publications/nicaragua/nicadoc2.html.

6   'Notes and comment on the moral equivalent of our Founding Fathers', The New Yorker, 25 March 1985.

7   The full English-language text of the 'Psychological Operations in Guerrilla Warfare' manual can be found at www.webcom.com/pinknoiz/covert/tacayantoc.html. That the Gestapo was a Nazi organization, and that the Nazis were dedicated to the extermination of communists and communism, was evidently of little moment to the manual's author(s).

8   R Brody, Contra Terror in Nicaragua, Boston, MA: South End Press, 1985. See also the resources listed at www.library.utoronto.ca/robarts/microtext/collection/pages/nicaragu.html.

9   The concept of master narrative, totalising narrative or meta-story—terms used interchangeably here—derives mainly from scholarship inspired by the work of Antonio Gramsci and Michel Foucault. See A Gramsci, Selections from the Prison Notebooks, London: Lawrence & Wishart 1971; and M Foucault, The Archaeology of Knowledge, New York: Pantheon, 1972. See also EW Said, Orientalism, New York: Pantheon, 1978; and H White, Metahistory: The Historical Imagination in Nineteenth-Century Europe, Baltimore, MD: 1973.

10  See D Barndt, 'Popular education' and Elizabeth Dore, 'Culture', in Walker, Nicaragua: The First Five Years, pp 317–346 and 413–422. See also V Miller, 'The Nicaraguan literacy crusade' and EA Wagner, 'Sport and revolution in Nicaragua', in TW Walker, Nicaragua in Revolution, New York: Praeger, 1982, pp 241–258 and 291–302.

11  Among the most widely read English-language books on the Sandinist Revolution in the early and mid-1980s were M Randall, Sandino's Daughters: Testimonies of Nicaraguan Women in Struggle, ed L Yanz, Vancouver: New Star Books, 1981; TW Walker's two edited volumes, Nicaragua in Revolution and Nicaragua: The First Five Years, as well as his monograph, Nicaragua: The Land of Sandino, Boulder, CO: Westview, 1981; G Black, Triumph of the People: The Sandinista Revolution in Nicaragua, London: Zed Press, 1981; H Weber, Nicaragua: The Sandinista Revolution, London: Verso, 1981; JA Booth, The End and the Beginning: The Nicaraguan Revolution, Boulder, CO: Westview, 1982; S Christian, Nicaragua: Revolution in the Family, New York: Vintage, 1985; CM Vilas, The Sandinista

*Revolution: National Liberation and Social Transformation in Central America*, New York: Monthly Review Press, 1986; P Rosset & J Vandermeer (eds), *Nicaragua: Unfinished Revolution*, New York: Grove Press, 1986; P Davis, *Where Is Nicaragua?*, New York: Simon and Schuster, 1987; and P Kornbluh, *Nicaragua: The Price of Intervention*, Washington, DC: Institute for Policy Studies, 1987.

[12] From an expansive literature a superior general history of US intervention in Nicaragua remains K Bermann, *Under the Big Stick: Nicaragua and the United States Since 1848*, Boston, MA: South End Press, 1986.

[13] A Somoza G, *El verdadero Sandino o el calvario de las Segovias*, Managua: Robelo, 1936.

[14] For excellent treatments of comparable instances of popular patriotic struggles being rejected and dismissed by native elites as mere 'banditry', see F Mallon, *Peasant and Nation: The Making of Postcolonial Mexico and Peru*, Berkeley, CA: University of California Press, 1995; and GPC Thompson, *Patriotism, Politics, and Popular Liberalism in Nineteenth-Century Mexico: Juan Francisco Lucas and the Pueblo Sierra*, Wilmington, DE: Scholarly Resources, 1999.

[15] The phrase 'robbery, pillage, rape, and murder' is in Lt HR Huff, R-2 Report, 17 December 1929, US National Archives, Record Group 127, Entry 209, Box 1 (hereafter cited as RG127/[entry no.]/[box no.]). The phrase 'false standard of patriotism' is in JC Smith *et al*, 'A review of the organization and operations of the Guardia Nacional de Nicaragua', unpublished manuscript, Personal Papers Collection, Marine Corps Historical Center, Washington, DC; the phrase 'bandit hordes' appears in *The Leatherneck*, January 1928, p 13; 'cancerous growth' is in General McDougal to Francis White, 10 October 1930, US Department of State, M633, reel 1; and 'exterminating bandits' is from Robert L Denig, Northern Area Commander, 'Restriction for certain areas of Nueva Segovia, recommendation for', 10 May 1930, RG127/202/17. Most of these terms are so diffuse throughout the material in RG127 and elsewhere that they require no citation.

[16] *The Leatherneck*, January 1928, p 13.

[17] Emil Thomas Papers, Box 2, Folder 23, 4 January 1928, Box 3, Folder 25, 11 March 1928 and Folder 31, 3 September 1928, Alden Library, Ohio University, Athens, OH. I am indebted to Thomas W Walker, Political Science Department, Ohio University, and especially to Doug McCabe, Archives and Special Collections, Alden Library, for their very kind assistance with this source.

[18] Major O Floyd, Field Message No 11, San Albino, 6 August 1927, RG127/43A/6; and Lt Larson, B-2 Report, 4 March 1928, RG127/43A/3.

[19] Smith *et al*, 'A review', pp 2, 26, 50.

[20] R-2 Report, 15 April 1928, NA127/209/2.

[21] *The Leatherneck*, April 1928, pp 10, 52.

[22] Bn-2 Report, 22 June 1930, NA127/209/1.

[23] GN-2 Report, 1 September 1930, NA127/43A/29.

[24] GN-2 Report, 1 October 1930, NA127/209/1.

[25] GN-2 Reports of 1 January and 1 April 1932, RG127/43A/29.

[26] GN-2 Report, 1 October 1932, NA127/43A/29.

[27] See MJ Schroeder, 'The Sandino rebellion revisited: civil war, imperialism, popular nationalism, and state formation muddied up together in the Segovias of Nicaragua, 1926–1934', in GM Joseph, CC LeGrand & RD Salvatore (eds), *Close Encounters of Empire: Writing the Cultural History of US–Latin American Relations*, Durham, NY: Duke University Press, 1998, pp 229–231.

[28] A comparison of the names of alleged victims of Sandinista attacks, as these appear in Somoza, *El verdadero Sandino*, and in the records of the US Marines and Nicaraguan National Guard, with the names of Nicaraguans who collaborated with the US invasion and occupation, as these appear in RG127—a comparison made possible by the author's database of all names to appear in marine and Guardia intelligence, patrol and combat reports, in captured Sandinista correspondence, and other sources—reveals scores of instances in which the victims of rebel attacks had actively collaborated with the occupying forces. For example, Somoza, *El verdadero Sandino*, p 129, claims that in April 1929 Sandinistas murdered Juan Bautista Rivera of Somoto. In fact Rivera, who survived the attack, had acted as a guide, scout and recruiting agent for the Marines in the Somoto district from early 1928. See R-2 Report, 23 September 1928, NA127/209/1; R-2 Report, 12 February 1929, NA127/209/1 ('Juan Bautista Rivera...is now reported to be...recruiting in the name of the Commanding Officer Somoto.'). See also the personal diary of Gen Robert L Denig, Northern Area Commander, 'Diary of a Guardia Officer', unpublished manuscript, US Marine Corps Historical Center, Personal Papers Collection, Denig Box, Vol I, p 89, which includes a letter from Rivera to Denig, dated 21 March 1930, in which Rivera informs Denig: 'I have been working with the Marines for the last two years'. For another example, Somoza, *El verdadero Sandino*, p 192, claims that in December 1930 Sandinistas burned the farm of Emilio López near Yalí. A marine intelligence report of two years earlier indicates that the same Emilio López, owner of a farm near Yalí, gave the marines and guardia a list of 13 local men active in the rebel ranks. R-2 Report, 16 December 1928, NA127/209/1.

29  On violence making in the Segovian past, see MJ Schroeder, 'Horse thieves to rebels to dogs: political gang violence and the state in the western Segovias, Nicaragua, in the time of Sandino, 1926–1934', *Journal of Latin American Studies*, 28, 1996, pp 383–434.

30  On C Beals, see his series 'With Sandino in Nicaragua', *The Nation*, 22 February–11 April 1928. See also Beals, *Banana Gold*, Philadelphia, PA: Lippincott, 1932; and Beals, *Great Guerrilla Warriors*, Englewood Cliffs, NJ: Prentice Hall, 1970. On the US anti-imperialist movement in the 1920s and 1930s, see RV Salisbury, *Anti-Imperialism and International Competition in Central America, 1920–1929*, Wilmington, DE: Scholarly Resources, 1989; and J Zwick (ed), *Anti-Imperialism in the United States, 1898–1935*, at www.boondocksnet.com/ai/.

31  *El Centroamericano*, 21 June 1930 and 19 July 1928; and *Diaro Moderno* (Managua), 23 January 1931.

32  The most comprehensive collection of Sandino's writings remains AC Sandino, *El pensamiento vivo*, ed Sergio Ramírez, 2 vols, Managua: Nueva Nicaragua, 1984. The best English-language collection is RL Conrad, *Sandino: The Testimony of a Nicaraguan Patriot, 1921–1934*, Princeton, NJ: Princeton University Press, 1990.

33  Petition from 'workers and natives' of Mosonte to Jefe Director GN, 27 December 1930, NA127/202/2/2.3. Similar letters can be found in NA127/220/3 (La Concordia and Jinotega, 14 and 15 May 1929); NA127/43A/15 (Jalapa, 15 November 1928); and NA127/198/1 (Matagalpa, April 1930).

34  Instituto de Estudio del Sandinismo, Managua (hereafter IES; these documents are currently housed in the Instituto de Historia de Nicaragua, Universidad Centroamericana, Managua), Interview No 049, p 1.

35  IES, nos 032, pp 13 and 066, pp 5–6.

36  IES, nos 072, p 7 and 036, p 4.

37  IES, no 100, p 4.

38  Christian, *Nicaragua: Revolution in the Family*, pp 191–194.

39  'US walks out of Iraq's address to UN', at www.cnn.com/2003/US/03/27/sprj.irq.us.un.walkout/.

40  'Negroponte visits mass graves site near Hillah, Iraq', at http://iraq.usembassy.gov/iraq/20040715_mass_graves_hilla.html.

# Liberation struggle or terrorism?
# The politics of naming the LTTE

SUTHAHARAN NADARAJAH &
DHANANJAYAN SRISKANDARAJAH

The conflict in Sri Lanka remains one of the world's most intractable. The ongoing Norwegian-backed effort to peacefully resolve one of South Asia's longest wars is, at the time of writing, bedevilled by fresh acrimony and antagonism between the Sri Lankan state and the Liberation Tigers of Tamil Eelam (LTTE)—sometimes referred to as the 'Tamil Tigers'. Since tensions in the Tamil-dominated areas of the island erupted into open confrontation between several armed groups and the state in 1983 in the wake of the fiercest anti-Tamil rioting since independence from Britain, the fighting has grown in intensity and affected most of the Northeast as well as the capital, Colombo. Inevitably, the origins, nature and character of the conflict are contested by the main protagonists and others. But the two protagonists' rationale for their actions generally falls within two explanatory frameworks. The LTTE says it is spearheading an armed struggle for political independence for the Tamils as a response to institutionalised racism and violence against the Tamil people by a Sinhala-dominated state. In short, it is waging a 'national liberation struggle'.[1] The LTTE describes itself as a 'national liberation movement deeply embedded in [the] people, articulating the wishes and aspirations of the Tamil nation'.[2] On the other hand, describing itself as a democracy, the Sri Lankan state denounces the LTTE's violence as a challenge to its authority, unity and territorial integrity. The state is 'fighting terrorism'. Thus, the state's military response is rationalised as intended to 'destroy the terrorists' and 'break the back' of terrorism.[3]

While the narratives presented by the LTTE and the state in support of their respective positions are complex and range across a number of issues, this paper is primarily concerned with the politics of the terrorist label as applied to the LTTE. To be clear, it does not set out to answer the question of whether the LTTE is a terrorist organisation or not, but instead to demonstrate how the state's characterisation thus has affected the conflict. The article begins by pointing out that the terrorist label has been a central feature of Sri Lankan political discourse for several decades, irrespective of the scale of violent challenge to the state. Second, we outline how the Sri Lankan state has deployed the label of terrorism to further its strategic aims in the domestic and international spheres. Third, we contend that, while the label of terrorism has not necessarily impeded the growth of the LTTE's military capability, it has, by denying the organisation international legitimacy, undermined its political project. Fourth, we outline the contradictions between present international attitudes to terrorism and the conduct of key international actors in regard to the conflict in Sri Lanka. Finally, we argue that, in the context of its armed forces' failure—and perhaps inability—to defeat the LTTE, the state's sustained rhetoric of terrorism has become a serious impediment to reaching a permanent resolution of the conflict. Beginning with a brief outline of the Sri Lankan conflict, the article then turns to each of these issues in turn.

## Context

In early 2002 a long-running but low-key Norwegian initiative to bring about a negotiated solution to the conflict in Sri Lanka began in earnest with the establishment of an internationally monitored ceasefire. The truce brought to an end the most intense phase of the conflict—seven years of pitched battles between the LTTE and the Sri Lankan armed forces. The armed struggle for independence launched by the LTTE and other Tamil armed groups in the late 1970s escalated in 1983 following the widespread anti-Tamil riots in the capital city of Colombo and other parts of the island in July that year. Despite three previous attempts at negotiation—in 1985, 1989–90 and 1994–95—fighting between the LTTE (which emerged on top from a series of internecine battles amongst the Tamil groups in the late 1980s) and the state's armed forces had gradually escalated in both intensity and scope. An estimated 90 000 people, mainly civilians, have been killed and a million others internally displaced or made refugees.

Since its emergence in 1972 as a small group of fighters, the LTTE has expanded into a substantial military organisation, fielding several thousand fighters in set-piece battles supported by heavy artillery and a large naval force.[4] By the time the ceasefire came into effect, the LTTE was claiming control of over 70% of the predominantly Tamil areas of the North and East (though not the five main population centres, which remain under government control). The LTTE has built a civil administration structure in the areas it controls, including a police force, justice system and a humanitarian assistance arm. It operates a taxation system, both in the territory under its control and in government-held areas, and a customs regime at 'borders' on the frontlines.[5] Since the late 1990s this civil administration has developed to the extent that it has been described as a *de facto* state.[6]

The LTTE has expanded its political presence since the advent of the peace process. Even before the truce began, Sri Lanka's four largest Tamil political parties forged a coalition with a manifesto of recognising the LTTE as the 'sole representatives' of the Tamil people.[7] In parliamentary elections held in April 2004 the Tamil National Alliance (TNA), campaigning as self-acknowledged 'proxies' of the LTTE, swept the polls in the Northeast and secured 22 seats. From September 2002 to March 2003 the LTTE engaged in six rounds of high-profile talks with the government. The negotiations were chaired by Norway and held in Thailand (September, October, January), Norway (December), Germany (February) and Japan (March). The LTTE withdrew from the talks in April 2003, protesting at the government's failure to implement agreements already reached. Efforts to restart negotiations have been unsuccessful and, at the time of writing, although the truce is holding, strains are deepening.

## A pivotal device

Even before the advent of Tamil militancy, the term 'terrorism' had entered Sri Lanka's political discourse in the wake of the brief but bloody insurgency launched by the Marxist Janatha Vimukthi Perumana (JVP) against the state in 1971. Notably, the JVP membership was almost entirely made up of Sinhalese youth—an estimated 10 000 of whom perished in the state's response. Despite occurring on a much smaller scale than the JVP insurgency and involving a handful of political killings and relatively small acts of sabotage, Tamil militancy in the 1970s was already being described domestically, and in some cases internationally, as 'terrorism'. The introduction of the Prevention of Terrorism Act (PTA) in 1979 formalised the language of terrorism and, as detailed below, conflated terrorism with the Tamil political project in Sri Lankan political discourse. By the time the Tigers staged a landmark ambush of an army convoy in July 1983, killing 13 soldiers and shocking the state (the 'terrorist' attack was even cited as a cause of the anti-Tamil pogrom days later), the language of terrorism was already well entrenched. For example, President Jayawardene's call in June that year for Sinhalese to 'do their bit' to fight terrorism was typical of the language used to describe Tamil militancy: 'We are in the throes of increasing terrorist activity in the north...The Tigers are getting bolder and bolder. Hence I appeal to the nation not to allow terrorism to take root in other parts of the country.'[8] At the international level, this characterisation of Tamil militancy as terrorism was quickly adopted by some Western states.[9]

How this early language of terrorism developed, and its impact on the conflict, can best be understood by looking at the historical and wider discursive contexts in which it took place. For a start, it is important to note the process by which ethnicity has been essentialised in Sri Lanka, such that major actors within and outside Sri Lanka have come to understand the conflict within a specific framework. The process by which this essentialisation has taken place, eloquently described by Ronald Herring, has had a critical impact on the politics of naming the LTTE and the conflict.[10] Similarly, these politics must also be considered in the context of the LTTE and the Sri Lankan state addressing three separate audiences: Tamils, Sinhalese and the international community (including other governments, international non-governmental organisations, and the media). Although somewhat crude, this typology helps explain how the politics of naming has evolved.

When several Tamil armed groups emerged in the late 1970s and early 1980s to mount a violent challenge to the Sri Lankan state, they did so in a context of acute ethnic polarisation in the island's politics and a sense of victimisation among Tamils. Indeed, the growth of a Tamil *political* community was conditioned by rising concern about Sinhala dominance in the island's governance in the wake of Ceylon's independence from Britain in 1948. Tensions between Tamils and Sinhalese became serious in 1956 after the election victory of the Sri Lanka Freedom Party (SLFP), the implementation of the 'Sinhala Only' policy and the first anti-Tamil riots. An ethnic fault-line at the centre of the island's politics was thus crystallised: '*Tamils* and *Sinhalese* [became] dangerous shorthand devices for politically complex communities' and the essentialising of ethnicity—'to speak of Tamils as a whole and Sinhalese as a whole'—fed into the stereotyping of both sides.[11]

The growth in Tamil militancy in the late 1970s also took place in the context of growing Tamil agitation for self-determination. Indeed, the call for an independent state of 'Tamil Eelam' was a central plank of the newly formed Tamil United Liberation Front (TULF) which swept the parliamentary elections in the Tamil-dominated districts of the North and East in 1977. At this time armed Tamil groups were in the shadows of the Tamil independence movement, which was dominated by the TULF. Apart from being numerically small—which only changed, albeit rapidly, following the anti-Tamil pogrom in 1983—the groups awaited the TULF's progress in pursing the goal of Tamil Eelam.

The state's response to these two developments—the Tamil call for independence, led by the TULF, and the sporadic violence of armed groups—are critical to understanding the trajectory of ethnic relations and the conflict in Sri Lanka. The United National Party (UNP) government of President Jayewardene conflated the two issues through an 'incremental reframing of secessionist protest in Jaffna as terrorism' and, in turn, 'terrorism in the late 1970s and early 1980s became conjoined with Tamil ethnicity'. Most importantly, 'once the political demands of Tamil youth were perceived in terms of terrorist threat, mirror images of ethnic entities hardened'.[12]

The proscription of the LTTE and other armed Tamil groups in May 1978 and the enactment of the PTA in July 1979 underline the emphasis placed on the labelling of Tamil militancy as terrorism by the Sri Lankan government. At that time there was an incongruence between the scale of Tamil militancy and the scale of the government's discursive and military response. The LTTE's own 'diary of combat' lists only a handful of small-scale attacks in the years before 1983 and the LTTE was officially blamed by the state for only one political assassination—in 1974—in the lead-up to its ban and the PTA. In contrast, the ban on the JVP, which had staged a far more spectacular insurgency by then, did not take place until July 1983, and even then only after the JVP performed well in local and presidential elections.

Shortly after the PTA was passed, a substantial military force—made up overwhelmingly of Sinhalese personnel—was dispatched to the North. Ensuing reports of human rights violations were widely publicised by international human rights groups 'and frequently raised with the government by aid donors, particularly the Nordic countries and Canada'. However, simultaneously, 'there was a certain amount of rallying around the state' by international actors and, 'despite harsh international criticism, the regime continued to garner critical external support in the aggregate'. Amid the economic hardships of the late 1970s and early 1980s, 'the [subsequent] escalation of the conflict created scapegoats for mass frustration and at least some perception among the Sinhalese majority that "our government" is besieged by Tamil insurgents and deserves support'. Much of this was in the context of the pro-West regime's enthusiasm for liberalisation and donors' 'holistic' approach in using the nation-state as the primary unit of analysis, thereby masking 'internal differentiation experienced by real people on the ground'.[13]

In short, deploying the rhetoric of terrorism had three distinct benefits for the Sri Lankan state: it de-legitimised (Tamil) agitation for political independence (with which terrorism had been conflated) thereby enabling the 'securitisation' of the issue; it mobilised Sinhala sympathy for the regime and its actions; and, international criticism of rights abuses notwithstanding, accomplished the same abroad. These dynamics were amplified in 1983, a year widely considered a watershed in Sri Lanka's ethnic relations and conflict.

## The road to war

The serious consequences of the conflation of ethnicity and violence ('Tamil terrorism') by the state, particularly in the context of long-standing and now serious communal antagonisms, were inevitable. As noted above, while

Tamils and Sinhalese were politically complex communities, they came to be referred to as monolithic wholes. Crucially, the militants and the state also came to be viewed by the *other* community as genuinely representing, respectively, Tamil and Sinhalese political interests. The state played a crucial role in this by publicly adopting a partisan role as leaders of the Sinhalese in their conflict with the Tamils. President Jayewardene's declaration, weeks before the events of July 1983, is a typical example:

> I am not worried about the opinion of the Tamil people...now we cannot think of them, not about their lives or their opinion...the more you put pressure in the north, the happier the Sinhala people will be here...Really if I starve the Tamils out, the Sinhala people will be happy.[14]

Another important response by the state was to prohibit the espousal of independence. This manifested itself most clearly in an amendment to the Sri Lankan constitution in 1983 that ended the possibility of a debate on the central Tamil political demand and compelled the TULF's MPs to resign their seats. The amendment stated:

> No person shall, directly or indirectly, in or outside Sri Lanka, support, espouse, promote, finance, encourage or advocate the establishment of a separate state within the territory of Sri Lanka.

In the wake of the July 1983 pogrom and this criminalisation of Tamil independence demands, the ethnic conflict escalated sharply. The Tamil militants' call for armed struggle for independence struck a chord among Tamils. Several militant groups expanded rapidly, drawing recruits and financial support from the Tamil community, both in the island and from the diaspora. The scale and frequency of guerrilla attacks on security forces rose rapidly, mainly in the Jaffna peninsula but in other parts of the Northeast as well. The conflict has continued since, apart from a few months in 1990–91 and 1994–95. The guerrilla war of the 1980s gradually changed to one in which both the LTTE and the state controlled different areas of the Northeast and launched full-scale military offensives against each other. Furthermore, by the late 1980s, which saw an Indian intervention to impose a solution, the LTTE had emerged victorious from a series of internecine battles with other Tamil militant groups.

These developments, however, have not been translated into changes to the discursive context, which remains one of 'liberation struggle' versus 'terrorism'. Here, it is useful to turn to the three separate audiences (Tamils, Sinhalese and the international community) that the state and the LTTE have been addressing. Domestically, the label of terrorism, though prevalent, became relatively meaningless. It was understood by both Tamils and Sinhalese as part of the state's criminalisation of Tamil agitation for political independence/autonomy. As such, neither the Tamil militant groups nor the 'Sinhala' state seriously sought to convince the 'other' community of the legitimacy of their respective causes. Indeed, it was a decade later that the state, amid a new counter-insurgency strategy, altered its rhetoric to differentiate 'LTTE terrorism' from 'Tamil terrorism', in part by insisting its military campaign was intended to 'liberate the Tamils from the LTTE.'[15] Just as the Sinhala perspective saw militant violence as conducted on behalf of and endorsed by the independence-seeking Tamils, Tamils saw violence by the state security forces as conducted on behalf of and endorsed by the dominant Sinhalese.

The identification of the LTTE with Tamil demands for political independence has been reinforced by the LTTE's early supremacy among the militant groups, as well as by the emergence of a *de facto* state in areas under LTTE control. The depth of popular support for political independence, rooted in entrenched perceptions of ethnic discrimination by the state, has meant that few Tamil voices opposed to the LTTE actually challenge the organisation's political goals. On the contrary as noted above, even Sri Lanka's four main Tamil political parties, once positioned by the state as an 'alternative' Tamil leadership, have recently united into an alliance backing the LTTE as 'sole representatives of the Tamil people'—and have subsequently enjoyed considerable electoral success in Tamil areas. Meanwhile, attempts to bridge the ethnic divide, including conciliatory efforts from within the 'civil society', have had little success. As Camilla Orjuela notes, Sri Lanka's civil society 'is to a large extent ethnically divided, and popular mobilization has through history been nationalist and violent rather than pro-peace'.[16]

## International centrality

Press coverage of the July 1983 pogrom and the sudden exodus of refugees to nearby India and Western countries raised the international profile of Sri Lanka's 'ethnic problem'—as did the sharp escalation of the conflict after July 1983. The rhetoric and logic of terrorism therefore became a key part of the international legitimacy of the state and its actions. This, combined with the domestic redundancy of the term, has shaped the discourse of terrorism in Sri Lanka from the outset and to the present. In short, both the state and the LTTE deployed and contested the label in any seriousness only in the context of shaping international opinion.

Sri Lanka's long-running conflict has sometimes been described, erroneously in our view, as 'the forgotten struggle'. The island's location astride the Indian Ocean sea routes and its proximity to India, the regional superpower, has always ensured a degree of international attention, not least New Delhi's (India's ill-fated intervention in 1987 to enforce the Indo-Sri Lanka pact resulted in thousands of casualties). And Sri Lanka's 'internal' conflict is affected by international developments in several ways. First, Sri Lanka's economy has failed to fulfil its potential as a consequence of the conflict and international financial assistance is vital to the state's continued functioning. Moreover, the economy is reliant on foreign markets, both for its export income and for remittances from migrant workers and expatriates. For its part, the LTTE has an extensive fundraising network among the Tamil diaspora, made up in large part by refugee and conflict-related flows into countries such as Canada, the UK, Switzerland, France, Australia and India.[17] Second, the central political issue of the conflict, which both protagonists agree is the demand for Tamil political independence, makes the international community important actors in the 'internal' conflict. It is in these contexts that international interpretations of the conflict become central to the protagonists' strategic objectives. The legitimacy of the LTTE's armed struggle—and hence the label of 'terrorism'—is at the centre of this interpretative contest.

Here there are some important parallels with the conflict in Bosnia. As David Campbell demonstrates, 'the settled norms of international society were...complicit and necessary for the conduct of the war itself'. Two predominant views of the war in Bosnia are evident: '[the Serb view] is the tale of a civil war in which antagonism between various groups emerged for a variety of reasons. The [Bosnian government view] is of international conflict, in which aggression from one state threatens another.' 'In their interpretation of the conflict, [the international community] adhered to a limited range of representations. Moreover, they are representations that have had more in common with the Serbian position than that of the Bosnian government.' This had a direct impact on international efforts to resolve the conflict and on the way it was reported by the international media. Not least, the logic of 'warring factions', 'ancient hatreds' and 'civil war' and a rejection of the 'genocide' claim precluded international enthusiasm for directly supporting the Bosnian government. Campbell demonstrates that the 'local' narrative which becomes accepted by international actors can be expected to drive their policies.[18]

As such, successfully ascribing or resisting the label of terrorism emerges as the most important ideational objective in the international arena. For the LTTE, it is the notion of a civil/ethnic war narrative that can best fit the arena of national liberation and political independence. For the state, it is the notion of terrorism that paves the way for both strong military action and non-engagement with the opposition's political demands. In the mid-1980s the LTTE rationalised its armed struggle in the framework of the self-determination of the Tamil people: 'Our struggle is for self determination, for the restoration of our sovereignty in our homeland. We are not fighting for a division or separation of a country but rather, we are fighting to uphold the sacred right to live in freedom and dignity. In this sense, we are freedom fighters not terrorists.'[19] Moreover, the LTTE, along with other Tamil groups, argued for resistance to state terrorism: 'under conditions of national oppression and the intensification of state terrorism and genocide against our people, the demand for a separate state became the only logical expression of the oppressed Tamil people. Our armed struggle is the manifestation of that logical expression.'[20] The state appealed to the internationally accepted rationale of maintaining stability. As National Security Minister Lalith Athulathmudali argued, 'no country in the world has succeeded by being soft on terrorism'.[21]

Both the LTTE and the Sri Lankan state have striven to promote their respective causes abroad. The state has used its diplomatic infrastructure overseas to lobby other states, international fora, the international media and leading human rights agencies in support of its fight against the LTTE. For its part, the LTTE has established representative offices in several key states and has also relied on efforts by Tamil diaspora community organisations to promote the Tamil nationalist cause among the same observers. This has been done through overt lobbying efforts such as public protests at critical times and through a range of diaspora-run media (websites such as www.eelam.com and www.sangam.org, newspapers such as *Tamil Guardian*, and television channels such as the global Tamil Television Network (TTN)). The complex interaction between the LTTE, Tamil nationalism and Tamil diaspora politics has blurred the distinction between the diaspora's sociocultural practice and its political support for the LTTE.[22] As a result, several Tamil organisations, such as the World Tamil Association (WTA), World Tamil Movement (WTM), and the Federation of Associations of Canadian Tamils (FACT), have been designated by the US State Department as 'front' organisations of the LTTE.[23] It is also worth noting that the ethnic divide that pervades Sri Lankan society is also reproduced to a large extent among the diaspora. Thus, while there are several Sinhala diaspora organisations that lobby on behalf of the state (www.spur.asn.au; www.sinhaya.com), multiethnic diaspora political groups promoting recon-ciliation are extremely rare.

### What's in a name?

A cursory survey of international responses suggests that neither narrative has been accepted in its entirety. The LTTE has been banned under anti-terrorism legislation by the USA (in 1997), UK (in 2001) and India (in 1991). Other countries, such as Australia and Canada (both in 2002), have prohibited its fundraising activities. Incidentally, the LTTE has not always been banned in Sri Lanka: a ban was imposed in 1978 under a specific law which was then replaced in 1979 by the PTA. An explicit ban was reimposed in January 1998, but lifted in September 2002 to enable negotiations. Yet, despite these proscriptions, the internationally backed Norwegian-brokered peace process is based on parity between the protagonists—including the acceptance in the ceasefire agreement of two separate controlled areas demarcated by a frontline—at least in so far as the negotiation process is concerned. For its part, the Sri Lankan state is compelled—especially through economic conditionality—to negotiate with the LTTE and hence recognise it in a political arena.[24] Moreover, international pressure is impelling the state towards a domestic taboo—a political solution to the conflict based on autonomy for the Tamil areas, albeit short of independence.

If the objective of the Sri Lankan and international bans on the LTTE sought to undermine the organisation's (military, political and administrative structural) growth, they have been demonstrable failures. Evicted from its stronghold of Jaffna in a Sri Lanka Army (SLA) offensive in late 1995, the LTTE retreated to the Vanni jungles and in 1996–98 was on the defensive against a series of further SLA offensives. The imposition of the US ban in October 1997 coincided with the largest military operation ever mounted by the SLA. Sri Lanka's own 1998 ban was thus imposed amid widespread belief that the LTTE was already on the point of collapse. However, in late 1999 the LTTE launched a series of counter-offensives that not only recaptured the territory it had lost since 1996 but also overran the SLA's largest base complex at the neck of the Jaffna peninsula. The defeats prompted the state to scramble for international assistance—which was quickly provided—to prevent Jaffna falling again to the Tigers. Moreover, in the fighting of 2000 and 2001, the LTTE unveiled a significant new conventional military force and seriously damaged the SLA's offensive capability. In mid-2001 the LTTE launched a major attack on Sri Lanka's sole international airport-cum-airbase in Colombo, destroying several military jets and airliners of the national carrier. The subsequent increases in insurance premiums on air and sea movement, and the decline in tourist arrivals, had a severe impact on the Sri Lankan economy, contributing to the first annual contraction since independence.

The military outcomes and, most importantly, the scale of these battles suggest the international and domestic prohibitions have failed to undermine the LTTE's ability to recruit and raise funds. Yet the timing of Sri Lanka's ban and the US proscription suggest they were less intended to weaken the LTTE—which at the time was considered on the verge of defeat anyway—than to undermine its political project, namely Tamil political independence. The US designation of the LTTE as a Foreign Terrorist Organization (FTO) is particularly important in this regard, given that the ban is intended to 'stigmatize and isolate designated terrorist organizations internationally, signal to other governments [US] concern about named organizations and deter donations or contributions to and economic transactions with named organizations'.[25] That the LTTE was not known to have a significant fundraising presence in the USA and that US security analysts had concluded that the LTTE 'does not pose a significant threat to the United States because [it has] not demonstrated high degrees of anti-US sentiment' makes its FTO designation even more intriguing.[26]

Part of the explanation for the banning of the LTTE by the USA and other states has to do with the challenge of the LTTE's political project of establishing an independent state rather than, say, with the direct threat the LTTE poses to their national interests. As US Secretary of State Colin Powell put it, 'we consider terrorism to be unacceptable, regardless of the [underlying] political or ideological purpose'.[27] Furthermore, no country has recognised the claim for Tamil self-determination.[28] As Adrian Guelke points out, there is a latent international resistance to the alteration of state boundaries, many of which are arbitrary products of post-World War II decolonisation.[29] Guelke also notes that the great powers would accept secession 'when it is limited to sub-units of states, with the further conditions that the right is exercised through the ballot box and [that minority rights are protected]. *Rejected, at least in principle, will be the carving out of new political entities by the use of force.*'[30] Furthermore, while political violence is 'self-legitimizing when applied to autocracies', conventional wisdom rules out the legitimacy of political violence in democracies: 'democracies are seen to provide dissenters with peaceful ways to achieve their ends. Political violence is less likely because there is no "need" for it.'[31] The US State department, meanwhile, describes Sri Lanka as 'democratic republic with an active multiparty system'—even as it admits that 'institutionalized ethnic discrimination against Tamils remains a problem'.[32]

The question of whether the LTTE is or is not considered a terrorist group by Western governments has not discernibly diminished its support base within the Tamil diaspora. On the contrary, the proscriptions may even have consolidated the resolve of the Tamil diaspora organisations to support the Tamil nationalist project and the LTTE.[33] Certainly the Tamil diaspora has lobbied hard in support of the LTTE, especially in the lead-up to the US and UK bans, even going as far as mounting a legal challenge in the USA.[34] The LTTE has also been manoeuvring diplomatically and politically to shake off, or at least cast doubt on, the terrorist tag.[35] Meanwhile, sections of the Sinhalese diaspora, supported by the Sri Lankan state, have also been involved in campaigning against the LTTE.[36]

## Contradictions

The LTTE is thus at the centre of several paradoxes in prevailing international norms. Despite increasingly hostile international attitudes to armed struggles (many of which are now framed by the discourse of terrorism), negotiation, rather than a military solution, is deemed the appropriate response to the LTTE's challenge to the Sri Lankan state. The LTTE has been banned in several countries, but negotiations with the Sri Lankan government brokered by Norway are proceeding on the basis that it represents Tamil political interests. The USA and the UK are actively promoting the negotiations between the LTTE and the Sri Lankan state, implicitly recognising the LTTE as the appropriate party to negotiate the terms of the Tamil region's autonomy. Their allies like Germany, Japan and Thailand have hosted the talks, while simultaneously supporting the 'war on terror' in other arenas. Following the LTTE's declaration in December 2002 that it was prepared to explore federalism as a possible solution to the conflict, LTTE delegations have toured a number of countries, including France, Spain, Switzerland and South Africa, to examine constitutional models and governance arrangements. Many important states (such as the UK, China, Germany, Italy and Japan) and international organisations (such as the World Bank, Asian Development Bank and several United Nations agencies) have, since the 2002 ceasefire, established diplomatic contacts with the previously ostracised LTTE. While this demonstrates an increasing willingness on the part of these actors to see beyond the terrorist label, even amid reports that it continues to develop its military ('terrorist') capability, limits on relations between the LTTE and international actors remain. The willingness of many actors to interact with the LTTE, even on 'universal' matters of human rights and humanitarian affairs, remains conditional on the Sri Lankan state's approval. International funding for rehabilitation work in LTTE-controlled areas remains controversial, despite guarantees of transparency via international auditing.[37]

In the meantime the labelling of the LTTE as a terrorist organisation affects efforts to resolve Sri Lanka's conflict in several ways. On the one hand, some argue that it was the inclusion of the LTTE in the US FTO list amid the international 'war on terror' that has compelled the LTTE to enter the peace process. While there is an element of truth in this, the effect of international pressure can be overstated. The argument that the LTTE has been forced into talks also ignores the considerable benefits that accrue to it from the peace process, not least its ability to consolidate its gains in the last round of fighting, its much easier access to supporters in SLA-controlled areas and, perhaps most importantly, its increased exposure to the international community.

On the other hand, the bans on the LTTE undermine the negotiation process in several ways. The availability of 'neutral' venues is limited, with those countries hosting talks contradicting expectations of the 'war on terror'. With regard to formulating a new constitution to resolve the conflict, the LTTE's access to constitutional knowledge is also restricted by its characterisation as a terrorist organisation: the USA has suggested that a federal model similar to its own might be appropriate for Sri Lanka, but LTTE officials seeking to study it cannot visit the USA or, for that matter, Canada given the LTTE's expressed interest in Quebec's model. The undertaking of humanitarian activities to deliver the 'peace dividend' to the people of the Northeast—something universally recognised as necessary to build support for the peace process—is problematic because the interactions between donor agencies and the LTTE's civil administration may be seen to constitute 'economic transactions' with a proscribed terrorist organisation.

These contradictions in international attitudes and practices raise important questions. If Western states are serious about defeating what they see as terrorism through the use of legal and military force, then the LTTE appears an important exception. If, however, the US-led 'war on terror' actually allows for more nuanced and gradual modes of conflict resolution, as appears to be underway in Sri Lanka, then it raises the question of whether anything has really changed. Guelke's argument that 'the weaker the credibility of international norms, the more likely that the outcome will be determined by the balance of forces within states and that the international community will be compelled to recognise (and thereby legitimise) whatever has been created on the ground—even if violence has played a large role in its determination' comes to the fore here.[38]

But it is within Sri Lanka that the rhetoric of terrorism has truly emerged as a serious impediment to peace. The deliberate conflation of 'terrorism' with the Tamil political project by successive Sri Lankan governments has produced a political culture in which the main (Sinhala) parties routinely vie to adopt more hard-line positions on the 'ethnic question'—a practice which began as long ago as 1956. As a result, a government's readiness to compromise at the negotiating table can easily result in its electoral defeat—

as the UNF administration that signed the ceasefire with the LTTE discovered in the elections of April 2004. The hard-line rhetoric from both sides of the political fence in Colombo, meanwhile, compels the LTTE to adopt an equally intransigent position at the table, not least to maintain its credibility and support base.

## Conclusion

As we have seen, the politics of naming the LTTE has been an important feature in Sri Lanka for several decades, with important discursive and material impacts. Domestically, these politics should be seen in the context of the essentialisation of ethnic politics and the conflation of the Tamil political project with terrorism. Moreover, the incorporation of the logic of 'fighting terrorism' into Sri Lanka's mainstream politics has reduced what ought to be serious debates on the constitutional structure of the country into an emotive and dangerous war of words. In short, using the politics of the terrorist label, the Sri Lanka state has managed to mask the broader questions at the heart of the conflict. Not only has this discourse made the conflict intractable, its continued prominence does not augur well for a permanent political settlement of the conflict.

Internationally, the LTTE has been designated by foreign states as a terrorist organisation, usually through its inclusion in lists of proscribed organisations in recent years. However, the attitudes of foreign states have more to do with their disapproval of the LTTE's political objective of establishing a separate Tamil state than with the perception that the LTTE represents a direct security threat to their national interests. In recent years, despite official censure and the 'war on terror', foreign states have shown that they are willing to work with the LTTE in shaping a political solution to the conflict. Taken together, these developments suggest that, while the label of 'terrorism' continues to be applied domestically and internationally to describe the LTTE, the politics of naming have not necessarily impeded the international community's pragmatic approach to conflict resolution in Sri Lanka.

## Notes

[1] AS Balasingham (on behalf of the Political Committee of the LTTE), *Liberation Tigers and the Tamil Eelam Freedom Struggle*, LTTE, 1983.

[2] Letter from LTTE leader Vellupillai Pirapaharan to Sri Lankan President Chandrika Kumaratunga, 28 March 1995, at http://www.tamilnation.org/conflictresolution/tamileelam/cbktalks/950328vptocbk.htm.

[3] W Claiborne, 'Sri Lankan leader says Marxists incited clashes to cover coup', *Washington Post*, 8 August 1983, p A15; and Claiborne, 'Sri Lanka presses military drive on rebels; Israeli aid reported', *Washington Post*, 9 August 1984, p A25.

[4] 'The success of the LTTE in resisting the Sri Lankan forces', *Jane's Sentinel*, 4 September 2000, at http://www.janes.com/security/international_security/news/sentinel/sent000904_6_n.shtml.

[5] 'LTTE announces tax relief measures', *TamilNet*, 14 December 2003, at http://www.tamilnet.com/art.html?catid = 13&artid = 10684.

[6] AJ Wilson & J Chandrakanthan, 'The de facto state of Tamil Eelam', in Wilson & Chandrakanthan, *Demanding Sacrifice: War and Negotiation in Sri Lanka*, London: Conciliation Resources, 1998, at http://www.c-r.org/accord/sri/accord4/.

[7]  'Tamil parties' alliance formed to support liberation struggle— TULF', *TamilNet*, 28 October 2001, at http://www.tamilnet.com/art.html?catid = 13&artid = 6422.

[8]  'President warns of terrorism', UPI, 6 June 1983.

[9]  See comments by British Prime Minister Margaret Thatcher and US President Ronald Reagan, in E Silver, 'Tamil terror tactics draw fire from Thatcher', *Guardian*, 13 April 1985; Visit of President JR Jayewardene of Sri Lanka, *Public Papers of the Presidents*, 20 Weekly Comp Pres Doc 891, 18 June 1984; and LL Knutson, 'Reagan backs Sri Lanka's anti-terrorist drive', Associated Press, 18 June 1984.

[10] R Herring, 'Making ethnic conflict', in MJ Esman & RJ Herring (eds), *Carrots, Sticks and Ethnic Conflict*, Ann Arbor, MI: University of Michigan Press, 2001, pp 140–174.

[11] *Ibid*, p 161, emphasis in the original.

[12] *Ibid*, pp161–162.

[13] *Ibid*, pp163, 160, 153.

[14] Interview with Graham Ward, *Daily Telegraph*, 18 July l983.

[15] EA Selvanathan, 'Has the Tamils' struggle ended?', *Green Left Weekly* (Australia), 17 July 1997, p 15, at http://www.greenleft.org.au/back/1996/238/238p15.htm.

[16] Camilla Orjuela, 'Building peace in Sri Lanka: a role for civil society?', *Journal of Peace Research*, March 2003, 40 (2), pp 195–212.

[17] D Byman *et al*, 'The LTTE and the Tamil diaspora', in *Trends in Outside Support for Insurgent Movements*, Santa Monica, CA: RAND Corporation, 2001, pp 41–60, at http://www.rand.org/publications/MR/MR1405/.

[18] D Campbell, *National Deconstruction: Violence, Identity, and Justice in Bosnia*, Minneapolis, MN: University of Minnesota Press, 1998, p 13, p 49, p 61.

[19] LTTE leader V Pirapaharan in an interview with Anita Pratap, *Sunday Magazine* (India), 11–17 March 1984, at http://www.eelamweb.com/leader/interview/in_1984/.

[20] Statement of LTTE and other Tamil groups made at Thimpu, Bhutan in 1985 during peace talks.

[21] Claiborne, 'Sri Lanka presses military drive on rebels'.

[22] D Sriskandarajah, 'Tamil diaspora nationalism', in CR Ember, M Ember & I Skoggard (eds), *Encyclopedia of Diasporas*, New Haven, CT: Yale/Kluwer, 2004, pp 493–501.

[23] http://www.state.gov/s/ct/rls/pgtrpt/2002/html/19991.htm.

[24] Tokyo Declaration on Reconstruction and Development of Sri Lanka, 10 June 2003, a joint statement by numerous foreign states and international organisations, at http://www.mofa.go.jp/region/asia-paci/srilanka/conf0306/declaration.html.

[25] US State Department, *Fact Sheet on Foreign Terrorist Organizations*, 30 January 2003, at http://www.state.gov/s/ct/rls/fs/2003/17067.htm.

[26] K Cagin & SA Daly, *The Dynamic Terrorist Threat: An Assessment of Group Motivations and Capabilities in a Changing World*, Santa Monica, CA: RAND Corporation, 2004, at http://www.rand.org/publications/MR/MR1782/MR1782.pdf.

[27] 10 September 2002, at http://www.state.gov/secretary/rm/2001/4852.htm.

[28] The USA and the UK limit themselves to acknowledging 'legitimate Tamil aspirations'. See comments by US Assistant Secretary of State John Armitage, 14 February 2003, at http://www.state.gov/s/d/rm/17752.htm and by UK Foreign Office Minister Peter Hain, *TamilNet*, 23 November 2000, at http://www.tamilnet.com/art.html?catid = 13&rid = 2000112301.

[29] A Guelke, *The Age of Terrorism and the International Political System*, London: IB Tauris, 1998, p 187.

[30] *Ibid*, p 187, emphasis added.

[31] DC Rapoport & L Weinberg, *The Democratic Experience and Political Violence*, London: Frank Cass, 2001, pp 2–3.

[32] US State Department, *Country Reports on Human Rights Practices 2001*, 4 March 2002, at http://www.state.gov/g/drl/rls/hrrpt/2001/sa/8241.htm.

[33] Sriskandarajah, 'Tamil diaspora nationalism'.

[34] *Humanitarian Law v Reno*, US 9th Circuit Court of Appeals, 3 March 2000.

[35] Letter from LTTE to US Court of Appeal Judges, 6 November 1997, at http://www.sangam.org/NEWSEXTRA/ltte.htm.

[36] See, for example, the Society for Peace, Unity and Human Rights in Sri Lanka, at http://www.spur.asn.au.

[37] Transparency International, Press Release, 11 April 2003, at http://www.transparency.org/pressreleases_archive/2003/2003.04.11srilanka.html.

[38] Guelke, *The Age of Terrorism and the International Political System*, p 188.

# Terrorists, bandits, spooks and thieves: Russian demonisation of the Chechens before and since 9/11

JOHN RUSSELL

Those engaged in studying the conflict in Chechnya are ruefully aware that public concern in the West over one of the bloodiest confrontations on the European continent since World War II remains low. How is it that the two Russo-Chechen wars (1994–96 and 1999 to date), which have cost perhaps as many as 200 000 lives,[1] mainly civilians, or more than one-fifth of the entire Chechen population, as well as those of 25 000 Russian forces,[2] are barely mentioned in any meetings of the G-8, NATO or the European Union, or even in national parliaments in Western Europe?[3]

Clearly, the geographic location of the conflict exacerbates what has been termed 'complexity fatigue'.[4] During the NATO campaign in Kosovo, memories were resurrected of Neville Chamberlain's infamous description of the German attack on Czechoslovakia as 'a quarrel in a faraway country between peoples of whom we know nothing'.[5] Demonstrably, people in Western Europe have found it difficult enough to get to grips with the consequences of the collapse of the socialist bloc in the Balkans and Central Europe, let alone comprehend the ethnic and territorial implications of the break-up of the USSR, including the constituent parts of the Russian Federation. Chechnya, which does indeed lie in the southeastern corner of Europe, remains for most West Europeans a faraway country, and the Chechens a people of whom they know little or nothing. Political leaders in Western Europe and the USA are well aware that this region only registers on their public's political radar screen at the time of such terrorist 'spectaculars' as 'Nord-Ost' in 2002 and Beslan in 2004 and, to the disappointment of those ngos and individuals that have engaged with the complexities of this conflict, appear to adopt a policy of 'appeasement' in allowing President Putin virtually a free hand in Russia's crude handling of Chechen self-determination.

Of course, the Chechen wars on occasions have hit the headlines in the Western press. However, as noted, this tended to be only when Chechen insurgents launched terrorist 'spectaculars'. In the first war these included the taking of hostages at Budennovsk (June 1995) and Kizlyar (January 1996) and, in the second, the Nord-Ost theatre siege (October 2002), the 'Black Widow' suicide bombings throughout 2003 and the Beslan school siege in September 2004. Significantly, the events of the first war were not generally referred to in the Western press as 'terrorist attacks', whereas those in the current war routinely were, especially after 9/11, since when the Western public has tended to perceive the Chechens, as it were, through Russian eyes. The 'rebels', 'armed resistance ' and 'freedom fighters' of the first war have been replaced in the public perception by the 'Islamic terrorists' of the second.

### Demonisation of the Chechens—the Russian and Soviet legacy

Paradoxically, thanks to the popularity in translation of the works written during the Great Caucasian War (1817–64) by Pushkin, Lermontov and Tolstoi, before the Russo-Chechen wars, and to some extent right up until 9/11, Western readers tended to have the same highly romanticised perception of the freedom loving, savage yet brave and honourable Chechens and their fellow mountain peoples as they did of the native American Indians as portrayed by James Fennimore Cooper's *Last of the Mohicans* (1826) or of the Scottish highlanders in Walter Scott's *Rob Roy* (1817). What all three groups represent, of course, is the romantic writer's nostalgia for a traditional tribal/clan-based way of life, tinged with regret that its suppression and extinction are inevitable given its incompatibility with the demands of modernising, 'civilised' societies.

The grim reality was that the military confrontation with modern civilisation, in these three cases, led to defeat followed by the *mukhadzhirstvo* (deportation) in 1864 for the Chechens, the Removal Acts for the Indians and the clearances for the Highlanders, all effectively destroying the old way of life.[6] A common experience, too, was that the injustice, brutality and unequal struggle that accompanied the suppression of the natives, however much this was justified by the perpetrators, left those on the receiving end with a sense of collective cultural superiority over the invading 'barbarians'. This is graphically described by Leo Tolstoi in *Hadji-Murat*, his tale set in Chechnya in the 1850s:

> Nobody spoke of hate towards the Russians. The feeling, which all Chechens large and small experienced, was stronger than hate. It was not hate, but a refusal to accept these Russian dogs as people and such repugnance, loathing and bewilderment at the clumsy cruelty of these creatures that the desire to destroy them, like the desire to destroy rats, poisonous spiders and wolves, was as natural a feeling as that of self-preservation.[7]

For their part, the Russians, although sharing a positive perception of the *djigit* (mounted mountain warrior), have always counterbalanced it with the negative 'bogeyman' image of the 'wicked Chechen' who 'whets his dagger keen' in Lermontov's famous 'Cossack Lullaby'.[8] Although the average Russian would be hard put to distinguish between a Cherkess or Kabardinian (let alone an Ingush) and a Chechen, it is the Chechens that have entered the Russian imagination as the epitome of this negative perception. This is not just because they are the most numerous of the North Caucasian ethnic groups, but also because even the neighbouring mountain peoples regard them as being the most aggressive and uncompromisingly hostile to Russian rule.

Before the first Russian incursion in the 19th century, the Chechens had already won a fearsome reputation for being the most skilled and daring raiders, sweeping down from the mountains to steal livestock, hostages and women and slaves. It was at the request of the Georgians in 1805 that Imperial Russia set out to finally suppress the Chechens. It is indicative that, in the first agreement of this campaign to be signed by Chechen elders in 1806 with Russian General Khudovich, setting out the terms upon which the Chechen people might become subjects of the Russian Empire, one clause states: 'Finally, if the Chechens do not refrain from carrying out raids, they must expect to be completely exterminated and destroyed'.[9] The message was clear: abandon your old ways or die.

The ambiguity of the Russians' perception of the Chechens is perhaps best summed up by the evolution of the word *abrek*. In Lermontov's time this meant a lone armed and mounted outlaw resisting Russian rule, traditionally portrayed, rifle in hand, on a hilltop silhouetted like a wolf against the moon,[10] but by the beginning of the 20th century it had acquired the less positive connotation of a *blagorodnyi razboinik* (noble robber).[11] By Soviet times, following fierce Chechen resistance first to the Bolshevik Revolution, then to the collectivisation of agriculture and, finally, to alleged support for the Nazi invaders, this word had become a totally negative 'enemy of the state'.[12]

Although Stalin used this epithet against millions of individuals during his reign of terror, he was selective in collectively punishing whole peoples, as he did the Chechens and nine other minorities before, during and after the Great Patriotic War (1941–45).[13] Along with the mass deportations to Turkey and the Middle East in 1864, the injustice of the enforced exile to Siberia and

Kazakhstan in 1944 of every last Chechen man, woman and child is etched deeply in the collective cultural narrative of the Chechen people

It has been argued that, apart from military considerations,[14] there was an ideological logic to Stalin's deportation of entire peoples. Steven T Katz writes:

> The Stalinist program of complete cultural conversion through migration... directly and indirectly caused up to 500 000 deaths. It is therefore a paradigmatic instance of ethnocide facilitated through mass murder. But it was neither intended, nor did it become in practice, an example of physical extermination of a minority nation. The intent was to destroy a variety of minority cultures and the ambitions built upon them, rather than to murder all the members of a specific people.[15]

Yet, in effect, Stalin's so-called 'socialist culture' was a thinly disguised version of the Russian culture that the Chechens had fought so hard for so long to resist. Paradoxically, therefore, it led to a strengthening in exile of the Chechen self-reliance and the *teip* (clan) structure that helped sustain this.[16] Unsurprisingly, the return to Chechnya failed in itself to resolve the Russo-Chechen relationship, the Russians still demanding assimilation to Soviet 'proletarian' norms and the Chechens seeking to restore their traditional customs (*adat*) and code of honour (*nokhchallah*).[17]

Unequipped or unwilling to follow the opportunities in the oil industry or collectivised agriculture available in the Soviet Chechen–Ingush Autonomous Republic, many Chechens turned to the nascent 'grey' and 'black' economies that were to thrive in the USSR under Brezhnev. This produced considerable profits for the Chechens and resentment from the Russians, who felt that they were being ripped off.

The link between the deportations and Chechen involvement in organised crime was encapsulated well in an interview given to a Western writer by a Moscow detective:

> They had a strong clan system, based on family ties...Every Chechen youth was taught to obey and respect his elders and distrust outsiders. They were also addicted to firearms as a way of settling disputes or merely demonstrating prowess...They seemed to me very similar to the Sicilian mafia...When the Chechens were finally permitted to return after the war, they discovered that their best land had been occupied by strangers. What else could many of them do but turn to crime?...It was a logical step to turn their clans into criminal groups.[18]

As the power and influence of the Chechen gangs grew, the transition in the stereotype of Chechens held by both the authorities and the public in Russia from that of *abrek* to that of *vor* (thief) or *bandit* (bandit) was not at all difficult. By the time the Soviet system collapsed in 1991, it was widely recognised that, of all the mafia groups: 'the most successful were the Chechens and their hallmark was extreme violence'.[19] Certainly, the Chechen mafia, established in the major Russian cities, was well placed to exploit the opportunities afforded by the post-Soviet transition to a market economy.

Historically, then, the relationship between the Russians and the Chechens has been characterised by the Russian willingness to use overwhelming might to suppress the Chechens' distinctive understanding of freedom,[20] and the Chechens sporadically fighting back while stubbornly refusing to submit to Russian rule. Given the asymmetry of the human and military resources in this confrontation, it is not surprising that the Russians have managed to subdue the Chechens for much of the past 200 years. Although it could be argued that, in contrast to the Nazis' attitudes to *Untermenschen*, neither the Russians nor the Soviets wished physically to exterminate the Chechens, but rather to resettle and re-educate them en masse, such has been the brutality employed against them as a people that Chechens find it difficult to distinguish 'assimilation' from 'genocide'.

### The years of the wolf: Russian demonisation under Yeltsin, 1991–99

From its declaration of independence in October 1991 until the outbreak of the first war in December 1994, Chechnya was *de facto* independent. Russia was more concerned with more immediate internal problems and was faced with a greater security threat on its borders, the civil war in Tajikistan, than that posed by the Chechens. By 1993 the Chechens were alone in refusing to sign the new Russian Constitution, even the Ingush having broken away in 1992 to join the Russian Federation. In 1994, when the Yeltsin administration finally focused attention on the rebellious southern republic, a series of botched armed insurrections and coups were launched, culminating in the humiliating capture and destruction in November 1994 of a column of Russian tanks masquerading as Chechen oppositionist forces. On 11 December 1994 Yeltsin launched a full-scale land and air attack on Chechnya to 'restore constitutional order', culminating in the disastrous assault on the Chechen capital, Grozny, on New Year's Eve.[21]

Once it was obvious that Yeltsin would not achieve the quick victory in Chechnya that he sought, public opinion in both Russia and the West turned sharply against the Russian federal forces. The disproportionate use of massive air power and artillery to flatten Grozny, ostensibly to 'save' its citizens, the incompetence of the Russian army and the heroic resistance of the Chechen defenders were all played out in front of the world's (and Russia's) media, with the result that support for the Chechen 'underdog' against the Russian 'top dog' was widespread.

Yeltsin's attempts to brand the Chechen resistance 'bandits' or 'terrorists', the regime 'criminal', and its leader Djokhar Dudayev as 'mad' sounded like hollow rhetoric to a considerable proportion of the Russian population, some 70% of whom remained opposed to the war throughout.[22] Because the Chechen fighters spoke Russian and were much more accommodating to both Russian and Western journalists and human rights activists than were the federal forces, the insurgents got more than their fair share of positive reporting and were generally held to have won the propaganda war.

A feature of this war of images between 1994 and 1999 was the identification of the Chechens, by themselves and by the Russians, with wolves. The Chechens adopted the wolf as their national symbol; it featured on the flag of independent Chechnya – Ichkeria and figured in the first line of their national anthem. A Chechen fighter was proud to be called a *borz* (wolf) and strove to uphold the spiritual affinity between the *abrek* and the courageous, lone wolf silhouetted against the moon.

The wolf, however, figures large in the Russian imagination, too, from the host of fairy tales to the machismo of the wolf hunt. Perceived to be a fearsome, cunning, fierce and untameable opponent, for the Russians the wolf came to symbolise the Chechen, a worthy enemy, but one that was wild and dangerous enough to warrant only destruction. Lupine epithets were given to the Chechen leaders: Aslan Maskhadov (President of Chechnya – Ichkeria from 1997)—'the wolf with a human face', Shamil Basayev—'the lone wolf' and Salman Raduyev—'the loony wolf'. [23]

The Chechen wolf theme had so caught the public imagination in the first war that it was quite easy for the media to resurrect it when fighting broke out again in 1999. This time, however, it was against the background of Russia's own 'Black September', after which the public mood swung decisively against the Chechens.

In the aftermath of the apartment house bombings in Moscow and other Russian cities in September 1999, *Izvestiya* headlined one of its reports of a Chechen connection 'Wolf tracks'.[24] *Argumenty i fakty* featured on its front page a pack of rabid wolves under the headline 'The Chechen wolves have been driven back to their lair, but for how long?'.[25] It was alleged that Russian guards at the notorious Chernokozovo detention camp in Chechnya would terrify male Chechen prisoners by calling 'Wolves, the hunters have come', before dragging them out and raping them.[26] The campaign by the Russian federal forces to rid Grozny of Chechen fighters on 1 February 2000 was called Operation Wolf Hunt[27].

The ordinary Russian soldiers picked up on the wolf theme but, as is usually the case in counterinsurgent operations, the troops soon came up with their own names for their opponents. Among these were *dukhi* (spooks), because of the way the Chechen fighters would appear as if from nowhere, especially at night, and melt away again; and *chichi* and *chekhi* (both shortened and distorted variants of *chechentsy*— the Russian for Chechens). 'Chichi' was also the name of the monkey known to all Russian children in Kornei Chukovsky's celebrated children's book, *Doktor Aibolit* (Doctor Ouch). The 'monkey' theme was quite popular among troops: even officers, such as General Mikhailov, would go on the record to foreign correspondents calling the Chechen fighters *obezyany* (monkeys). [28]

The Russian population at large, however, continued to call Chechens, as they did all other inhabitants of the Northern Caucasus *cherniye* (blacks), *chernozhopy* (black arses) or by the euphemistic acronym 'LKN', meaning *litso kavkazskoi natsional'nosti* (a person of Caucasian nationality). Sergei Sossinsky wrote in the English-language periodical *Moscow News*: 'Most city residents of peasant origin in Russia blame Jews or "Caucasians" (people who come from the Caucasus) for all their woes. Despite the fact that Caucasians (being Caucasians) are largely white-skinned, common Russians call them blacks or black asses. Police officials have even come up with a term "a person of Caucasian nationality".'[29]

Angry and ashamed at their forces' capitulation in the first war, and horrified at independent Chechnya – Ichkeria's slide into savage anarchy in the inter-war period, Russian public opinion was not minded to be magnanimous to its southern neighbours. This was reflected in the Russian media, significant sections of which had previously been sympathetic to the Chechen cause. When even Russian reporters who had supported the Chechens during the first war were caught up in the frenzy of hostage taking, an inevitable and significant shift occurred in Russia on the reporting of events in Chechnya.

Moreover, under Maskhadov, a leader who proved incapable either of stopping the excesses of the Chechen warlords, or of creating viable state institutions to tackle the wave of crime, sadistic cruelty and religious fundamentalism that subsequently engulfed it, Chechnya lost its image internationally as a brave 'David' fighting 'Goliath' and became perceived as yet another failed state like Afghanistan or Lebanon when these were ruled by warlords. The fact that Russia stood by and, effectively, allowed Chechnya to descend unaided into anarchy did little to redeem the Chechens in the eyes of a horrified Western world, which perceived the resurrection of some of the more gruesome native customs as barbaric, medieval and uncivilised.

In Russia, the shocking sequence of *Shari'a* beheadings and torture of Russian and foreign hostages by the Chechens, which were captured on videos and widely distributed by both sides for propaganda reasons,[30] raised anti-Chechen feeling to fever pitch and led to the Russian media introducing the term *oborotni* (werewolves) to describe the Chechen rebels.[31] Although not etymologically connected to the wolf in Russian, it did represent a transitional shift in the Russian perception of the Chechens from a wild animal to something as equally inhuman but much more sinister.

### The Chechen conflict as a springboard to power: 'iron' Putin takes control

Into this emotional maelstrom stepped Prime Minister Vladimir Putin, the virtually unknown Federal Security Service (FSB) security chief before he was promoted in the wake of the Chechen incursion into neighbouring Dagestan in August 1999. Although this ill-advised attack, initiated by the more militant Islamic faction of the Chechen opposition led by Basayev and Khattab, was condemned by Maskhadov, it served to heighten fears among Russians of a fundamentalist Islamic assault on Russia's soft underbelly in the Northern Caucasus and was a critical factor in winning over Russian public opinion for a renewal of military action against the Chechens. To this extent, Putin's rise to power—first as prime minister but by March 2000 as president—was linked closely to the hard-line policy adopted *vis-à-vis* the Chechens.

However, it was the apartment house bombings of September 1999 that killed over 300 Russians which finally provoked Russian public opinion into expressing its pent-up fury against the Chechens. Whatever one makes of the conspiracy theories that point the finger of blame for the explosions at the Russian authorities themselves, it is clear that the ethnic Russians believed that the Chechens were responsible.[32] A poll taken shortly after the bombings found that 64% of Russians wanted all Chechens expelled from the country and a similar percentage wanted Chechen towns and settlements to be bombed, effectively giving the Russian leadership a green light for an all-out assault on Chechnya. Moreover, Russia's media and politicians were accused of equating all Muslims with extremists and bandits.[33] Thus, Operation Whirlwind, launched in Moscow to round up suspects connected to the atrocities, affected people from all over the Caucasus.[34]

Upon coming to power, Putin immediately struck a chord with the Russian public by promising to 'waste the terrorists in the outhouse'.[35] The overwhelming majority of ethnic Russians, it would seem, agreed with their new leader and, two years before the West, perceived their renewed struggle with Chechnya as a frontline battle for survival against Islamic fundamental terror.[36] Putin at once set about linking this fear of Islamic terrorists to the deep-seated Russian prejudice against Chechen criminality, evoking the following warning from an American commentator on Russian politics:

> But the most serious consequences of Putin's continuing efforts to portray the Chechens as a uniquely criminal nation are likely to be felt elsewhere. Such charges may very well poison relations between ethnic Russians and non-Russian groups within the Russian Federation by opening the door to the possible demonization of others.[37]

Although the BBC reported, as early as 19 November 1999, that Putin had ordered all Russian news media to refer to the Chechen opposition as 'terrorists', this clearly took a little time to take effect. The shift was aided significantly by the rise in profile within the Chechen ranks of the radical Islamist field commander, Khattab, the Jordanian-born 'wahhabite' fighter who joined the first war in 1995, and by Shamil Basayev's conversion to the fundamentalist cause during the course of that war. This was reflected in the Russian press by horror stories about the 'wahhabites', along the lines of 'Diary of a Terrorist' and 'Concubine of the Wahhabites' printed under headlines in Arabic font.[38]

This was the background against which Vladimir Putin handily won the Russian presidency. At the very time in March 2000 when he was declaring the completion of the rout of the Chechen armed formations while likening their leaders to 'Nazi criminals', news was breaking of a major ambush in Chechnya led by Khattab, which had left 86 Russian paratroopers dead. Also in March 2000, as Interpol's new internet site placed the names of Basayev, Khattab and other Islamists in Chechnya alongside that of Osama bin Laden as wanted terrorists,[39] tank commander Colonel Yury Budanov was raping and killing the teenage Chechen girl El'sa Kungayeva, acts which served as the basis for the most high profile 'war crime' trial of the second war.[40]

The impact of these conflicting events on the Russian population was ambiguous; on the one hand, both Putin and the army were held to be doing a much better job than had Yeltsin and his forces in the first war. On the other hand, 63% of Russians were 'alarmed' by the situation in Chechnya (and another 7% 'ashamed'), against just 15% 'satisfied' and 2% 'delighted'. A mere 12% wanted the restoration of Chechnya to be paid for out of Russia's budget. Significantly, given the signals emanating from the Kremlin, the Russian population was not fooled into thinking that the war was over, 58% believing that the Chechen armed formations had not yet been routed.[41] These contradictory opinions—approval of Putin's strong leadership accompanied by a strong desire for a resolution of a conflict that sporadically gives rise to fear and insecurity over the situation in Chechnya—have characterised the Russian public's attitude to the war ever since.

It is clear that the Russian population had been traumatised by the events of September 1999, as were to be both the Israelis in September 2000 with the start of the al-Aqsah *intifada* and the Americans in September 2001 after 9/11. This was manifested in all three countries by intensified feelings of insecurity, an intolerance of any opposition to sometimes quite drastic counterinsurgency measures and an ambiguous attitude to both the norms of international law and the reaction of world public opinion. In all three cases, too, it was Islamic fundamentalist terrorism that was popularly perceived to be the biggest security threat.

Putin was the first leader to link Islamic insurgencies across the world when, on 6 July 2000, in an interview with *Paris Match* he noted that 'We are witnessing today the formation of a fundamentalist international, a sort of arc of instability extending from the Philippines to Kosovo'. In relation to Chechnya, he added, 'Europe should be grateful to us and offer its appreciation for our fight against terrorism even if we are, unfortunately, waging it on our own'. Although he repeated this warning at the G-8 summit in Okinawa later that month,[42] it was not until 9/11 that Western leaders really took note.

If Putin and the Russian population sought to eradicate the threat emanating from Chechnya, the Russian army generals were out for revenge against the Chechen people for the humiliation of the first war. In June 2000 General Vladimir Shamanov excused the killing of the wives of Chechen fighters, by asking 'How do you tell a wife from a sniper?'[43] A year later General Gennady Troshev called for the public hanging of captured Chechen fighters, stating 'This is how I'd do it: I'd gather them all on a square and string up the bandit and let him hang, let everyone see'.[44] With the army chiefs taking such a prejudiced view, it was not surprising that the lower ranks felt that they could act with impunity towards all Chechens. Unlike during the first war, with a few brave exceptions, neither Russian nor Western media were allowed free access to the conflict zone. The Russians had clearly learned the utility of 'information warfare'.

Having used the renewal of the conflict as a springboard to power, Putin's political future was tied intrinsically to the future conduct of the war. At any time between the enforced withdrawal from Grozny by Chechen forces in February 2000 right up until the summer of 2001, Putin could have satisfied Russian public opinion and sought a political settlement with his opponents.

By opting for the absolutist approach advocated by his generals, he was now going to have to find an alternative way out of the impasse into which his policies had driven Russia in Chechnya.

That policy was to be the 'Chechenisation' of the conflict, cutting Maskhadov and his 'moderate' rebels off from the political process and, in June 2000, replacing them with the Mufti of Chechnya—Akhmad Kadyrov—as his Chief of Administration. All those who continued to advocate Chechen, rather than Russian, choices for self-determination were demonised as 'criminals', bandits' and 'terrorists'. The humanitarian disaster in Chechnya was deliberately allowed to continue when it could, and should, have been ended. In a move to further strengthen his hand in Chechnya, in January 2001 Putin ordered the FSB to take over control of the counter-terrorist operation from the Ministry of Defence.

If 'Chechenisation' was to provide a political settlement in Chechnya, Putin wanted to ensure that it would be one controlled by *his* 'Chechens' and *his* 'Russians' from the outset. So, with the Russian public starved of information on the conflict and Western media and human rights organisations no longer free to operate safely in the region, all that was required for Putin's plan for Chechnya to be accepted internationally was for Western political leaders to acknowledge that the Russian president was on the front line of the struggle against Islamic terrorism. The dramatic events of 9/11 were to provide the most important piece in Putin's Chechen jigsaw.

### After 9/11: Putin on the side of 'right'?

By the summer of 2001 only 22% of Russians listed the largely forgotten war in Chechnya as a major concern, compared with 66% mentioning rising prices, 59% the level of poverty and 41% the rise in crime.[45] Although ngos in the West continued to hammer Russia for gross human rights' violations in their reports, the Western public appeared to be curiously disengaged from the suffering. In the absence of any meaningful criticism from Western governments, Putin could continue to operate as he pleased in Chechnya.

However, *Le Monde* reported on 6 April 2001 that, for the first time since the launch of the second war in October 1999, the percentage of Russians opposed (46.4%) to Moscow's Chechnya policy exceeded the percentage for (42.8%). In this respect the al Qa'ida attacks on New York and Washington on 11 September 2001 came at a juncture that was extremely fortunate for the Russian leader. Almost overnight, Russia became a key partner of the USA and its allies in the common struggle—the global war on terrorism—against a common foe—Islamic fundamentalism.

Members of the Putin administration were quick to draw the link between the Chechen rebels and Osama bin Laden, the presidential aide, Sergei Yastrzhembsky, claiming that 800 fighters from the Middle and Far East had been in Chechnya at the start of the second war.[46] Despite denials by the Chechen side, and doubt cast by journalists covering Chechnya as to the real number and influence of 'Arab' or 'Islamist' mercenaries, the importance of this linkage was accepted both by Western leaders and the Russian public.

Since 9/11 the terrorist attack in Bali and the Moscow theatre siege of October 2002, followed by a succession of domestic terrorist-related incidents in Russia and Chechnya, have not only kept the anti-Chechen sentiments high among Russians, but have done enough to persuade Western leaders that Chechnya is, indeed, on Russia's frontline in the war on terrorism. On receiving President Putin at Chequers in December 2001, Tony Blair drew parallels between the September 1999 bombings and the attacks on 9/11.[47] With such powerful allies as President Bush and Prime Minister Blair, Putin has been able to play the 'Islamic terrorist' card every time Chechnya appears on the agenda.

By April 2002, in his state of the union address, Putin felt secure enough to declare once more that the military phase of the war in Chechnya was over.[48] Predictably, within weeks the rebels hit back to prove that it was not, choosing symbolically 'Victory Day' (9 May 2002), when a bomb planted at a military parade in the Dagestani town of Kaspiisk killed 43 soldiers and family members and injured more than 100. Although Dagestani rather than Chechen militants were arrested subsequently, they could still be portrayed as part of an Islamic terrorist alliance and an enraged Russian public blamed the Chechens.[49]

Despite hostility from the Putin administration, but in line with preferences indicated in Russian public opinion polls, prominent Chechens, Russians and Americans were meeting, in the summer of 2002, to elaborate a peace plan for Chechnya. This culminated in Maskhadov's envoy, Akhmed Zakayev, attending a major conference in Liechtenstein in August 2002, alongside such Chechen representatives as Ruslan Khasbulatov and Aslanbek Aslakhanov, the Russians Ivan Rybkin and the late Yury Shchekochikin, as well as such US public figures as Zbigniew Brzezinski, Alexander Haig and Max Kampelman. The compromise peace plan that emerged would grant Chechnya autonomy within the Russian territorial space. Although the World Chechen Congress in Copenhagen was to endorse this Plan on 29 October 2002, the fall-out from the 'Nord-Ost' theatre siege effectively aborted this process.[50]

Perhaps to counter these positive developments, on 25 June 2002 Putin finally drew a distinction between the civilian population in Chechnya and the rebels, by claiming: 'As far as the negative image of Chechens is concerned, the Chechen people are not to blame for anything. I think this is the fault of the federal center that the Chechen people were left to the mercy of fate at some point...Our task is to destroy this image [of Chechens] as terrorists.'[51]

While this policy shift should have enhanced the prospects for an all-embracing political settlement, Putin's failure once more to distinguish between genuine 'terrorists' and those merely opposed to his policies robbed his initiative of any real political substance. Thus, no such tolerance was to be shown to any Chechen advocating a political solution other than that proposed by Putin. For example, Kadyrov, who had fought the Russians in the first war was, to all intents, given an amnesty, whereas such first war commanders as Turpal-Ali Atgeriev and Salman Raduyev, who also took no part in the second war, were tried, sentenced and died, in less than transparent circumstances, within a few months of each other in 2002 in Russian prisons.[52] FSB agents, meanwhile, had apparently assassinated the Arab field commander Khattab in April 2002.[53]

Putin's policy of demonising the Chechens certainly had borne fruit. The phenomenon of 'Caucasophobia' among ethnic Russians was spreading fast and, by October 2002, Lyudmilla Alekseyeva, Chair of the Moscow Helsinki Group, had identified it as 'definitely the most serious problem that Russia is faced with today. It is very widespread among the population in general, at all levels.' [54]It was exacerbated later that month by the 'Nord-Ost' theatre siege.

The circumstances around the 'Nord-Ost' siege in October 2002 have attracted as many conspiracy theories as had the Moscow bombings of 1999, with the finger of suspicion pointing at the Russian administration.[55] Whatever the truth, Putin came out of the affair well, representing a triumph for the policy of demonisation. Although the Russian special forces killed all but two of the 129 hostages and 41 hostage-takers, Putin was absolved of blame by his Western allies, with three groups led by Basayev being added to the US State Department's list of terrorist organisations.

The act of terror also further alienated the Russian public, which was quite ready to believe that the Chechens under Movsar Barayev were willing and able to blow up a theatre with more than 800 people in it. The prominence of the 'Black Widow' female suicide bombers reminded the public at home and abroad of the parallels between Palestinian and Chechen tactics in the international 'war on terrorism'.[56]

Putin moved immediately to put an end to the international peace plan process by seeking Zakayev's extradition from first Denmark and then the UK. At the same time he set in motion his own programme to hold a referendum in Chechnya in April 2003 on a new constitution, which would ban all political parties advocating Chechen independence.[57] Finally, in October 2003, Putin resolved to hold new presidential elections. Obviously the moves were so controlled and co-ordinated as to ensure that no one of Zakayev's persuasion would be allowed to participate in these 'democratic' processes, which as a result were not recognised as free and fair.[58]

By cutting out of the peace process all moderate opposition, Putin's policy effectively rendered impotent all those advocating diplomacy and inclusive negotiations as a means of reaching a political solution. Those intent on carrying on the fight switched their tactics to suicide bombing. In December 2002 trucks driven by suicide bombers destroyed the government head-quarters in Grozny, killing 80, and in May 2003 a further 59 in Znamenskoye. Throughout 2003 female suicide bombers struck in Moscow, in southern Russia and in Chechnya. Resulting in over 300 deaths, these attacks proved just as costly in human terms as the series of apartment blasts in September 1999.[59]

On 9 May 2004 (on Victory Day once more), the newly elected president Akhmad Kadyrov was assassinated in a bomb blast at a stadium in Grozny, an act for which Shamil Basayev has claimed responsibility.[60] As soon as

Putin had made clear that Kadyrov's successor would also be a Kremlin-approved candidate, even Aslan Maskhadov was moved to warn that any such 'Chechen president' would be the target of future assassination attempts.[61]

Since 11 September 2001 there has been a growing awareness of the danger of giving regimes countering insurgency *carte blanche*—a Report of the Policy Working Group on the United Nations and Terrorism in August 2002 warned that: 'Labelling opponents or adversaries as terrorists offers a time-tested technique to de-legitimize and demonize them'[62]. Nevertheless, in the post-9/11 world, Maskhadov's stance is not likely to endear him or his supporters to those advocating peaceful solutions to military conflicts. As in the wake of the recent tragedy in Beslan, in both the Russian and Western public's perception, it is Putin that emerges as the 'peacemaker' and his Chechen opponents as the 'terrorists'.

## Conclusion

By shamelessly playing the 'Islamic terrorist' card, Putin has effectively created in Chechnya a self-fulfilling prophecy. By offering those that still advocate any degree of Chechen separatism a choice merely between abject surrender and continuing a campaign of sabotage, any that follow the latter path are perceived in Russia and the West as advocates of the very Islamic terrorism against which Putin has warned.

Putin is under little pressure, either domestically or internationally, to acknowledge what is obvious to all who have engaged seriously with the Russo-Chechen conflict: that the war has much more to do with unresolved conflicts left over from previous eras than it has with international terrorism. By tolerating the existence of the 'black hole' of lawlessness on all sides in Chechnya and by continuing to portray even the most moderate of Chechen opponents as 'terrorists', Putin has created his own obstacles to peace in Chechnya.

Perhaps the debacle in Iraq or a broader realisation within Russia of the debilitating consequences that the war in Chechnya has on Russian civil society will put pressure on Putin to adopt a more humane and rational approach to settling the Russo-Chechen conflict. For the present, however, the Russian president appears to be firmly in step with the policies of such leaders as Bush and Sharon, who argue that the eradication of terrorism by force is the best way of tackling insurgency. Unless this changes then a further 'Palestinisation' of the conflict in Chechnya looks more likely than any 'Good Friday' type of agreement to end military hostilities.

The centuries-long failure of the Russians to accommodate the 'other' represented by the Chechens has turned a minor irritant into a costly fixation. Writing in the English-language publication *New Times* in December 2003, two Russian commentators noted that 'the impression has been created that our authorities have a sort of drug addiction to everything connected with Chechnya. And sometimes they react irrationally to it.'[63]

At times, Putin's irrationality *vis-à-vis* Chechnya is all too apparent, as demonstrated by his outburst in Brussels on 12 November 2002, when he responded to a French journalist asking probing questions about Chechnya by inviting him to Moscow for a circumcision![64]

The latest opinion polls show, however, that ordinary Russians are tired of the war in Chechnya, 63% in July 2004 favouring peace talks, with just 24% in favour of continuing military action.[65] Putin could demonstrate his diplomatic skills and bring an end to the Russo-Chechen conflict. Clearly, this is a compromise that he does not appear eager to embrace. He is aware that fear of Chechen terrorism in Russia remains high: before the tragic events in Beslan 88% of Russians polled expected a recurrence in the near future.[66] In continuing to play on these fears, by deliberately confusing Chechen self-determination with Islamic fundamentalist terror, Putin is avoiding having to engage with the complexities of Chechnya. Like Yeltsin before him, Putin has got a lot of mileage out of demonising the Chechens; he must now beware of reaping the whirlwind that he has sown.

## Notes

[1] If one adds together the casualties in all the conflicts in the former Yugoslavia, then this figure could be exceeded. See V Pupavac, 'Disputes over war casualties in former Yugoslavia', *Radical Statistics*, 69, 1998, at http://www.radstats.org.uk/no069/article3.htm. Like the conflicts in Bosnia and Kosovo, reliable statistics of civilian deaths in Chechnya are hard to come by and are prone to be inflated or understated for propaganda purposes by the warring sides. Akhmed Zakayev, the deputy prime minister of the separatist Chechen Republic of Ichkeria claims that 180 000 civilians have died in the two wars. *International Herald Tribune,* 18 June 2004. The highest aggregate for those killed in both wars of 250 000 was reported on a pro-separatist website, http://www.kavkazcenter.com/eng/article.php?id = 2899, 20 June 2004.

[2] Valentina Melnikova, of the Russian Soldiers' Mothers Committee, released the figure of 25 000 on 4 May 2004, during an interview on the radio station, Ekho Moskvy. See C Gurin, 'Group claims 25 000 Russian soldiers have died in Chechnya', The Jamestown Foundation, *Eurasia Daily Monitor*, 1 (3), 5 May 2004. By way of comparison, there were 14 751 combat deaths during the Soviet invasion of Afghanistan (1979–89). PF Kisak, 'Recently declassified Soviet War and US covert casualties', at http://www.geocities.com/echomoscow/warcasualties.html. The same source cites 8943 Russian combat deaths in the two Chechen wars up until the end of 2001.

[3] The pro-separatist Kavkaz Center accuses Western media and governments of paying more attention to animal rights issues than to the Chechen war. S Sattayev, 'Litsemeriye i nenavist'' (Hypocrisy and hate), at http://www.kavkaz.org.uk/russ/article.php?id = 23998.

[4] First identified in my forthcoming work, J Russell, 'A war by any other name…perceptions of the conflict in Chechnya: 11 September and the war against terrorism', in R Sakwa (ed), *Chechnya: From the Past to the Future*, London: Anthem Press, 2005.

[5] Paddy Ashdown, 'We must aim for a Kosovan protectorate', *Observer*, 28 March 1999. If one takes Iceland as the western, and the Urals as the eastern, extreme of Europe, then the midway line would run through Priština, placing the capital of Kosovo firmly in the centre of Europe!

[6] I have discussed the parallels between the Chechen and Scottish highlanders' experiences in J Russell, 'Mujahedeen, mafia, madmen: Russian perceptions of Chechens during the wars in Chechnya, 1994–96 and 1999–2001', *Communist Studies and Transition Politics*, 18 (1), 2002, pp 73–96.

[7] L Tolstoi, *Hadji-Murat*, Moscow: Khudozhestvennaya Literatura, 1965, p 110.

[8] 'Cossack Lullaby' by Mikhail Lermontov, translated in L Kelly, *Tragedy in the Caucasus*, London: Constable, 1977, p 207. The film about the current conflict, 'Chechen Lullaby' (Nino Kirtadze, France, 2000) commences with a reading from this poem.

[9] I Rybkin, *Consent in Chechnya, Consent in Russia*, London: Lytten Trading, 1998, p 157.

[10] See, for example, http://www.abrek.vov.ru/.

[11] The word *razboinik* (robber) can also be used in an affectionate, jocular sense, particularly when addressing children, to mean a 'scamp' or a 'scallywag'.

12  Yury Botyakov, 'Abrechestvo—real'nost' i predrassudki' (The Abrek way of life—reality and prejudices), *Nezavisimaya gazeta,* 29 August 2003.

13  Apart from the Chechens, the Ingush, Balkars, Karachai, Kalmyks, Germans, Greeks, Meskhetian Turks, Crimean Tatars and Koreans were deported en masse from their traditional areas of settlement, all for allegedly collaborating with the enemy. For the experience of the Chechens in exile, see M Pohl, '"It cannot be that our graves will be here": the survival of Chechen and Ingush deportees in Kazakhstan, 1944–1957', *Journal of Genocide Research,* 4 (3), 2002, pp 401–430.

14  The military case was undermined if only by the fact that some 300 Chechens and Ingush fought in the heroic defence of the Brest fortress in the summer of 1941, one of them—Magomed Uzuyev—being made posthumously a Hero of the Soviet Union for his exploits. See http://www.chechnyafree.ru/index.php?lng = eng&section = fwareng&row = 4.

15  ST Katz, 'Mass death under Communist rule and the limits of "Otherness"', in Robert S Wistrich (ed), *Demonizing the Other: Antisemitism, Racism and Xenophobia,* Amsterdam: Harwood Academic, 1999, p 280.

16  See Y Chesnov, 'Byt' chechentsem: lichnost' i etnicheskiye identifikatsii naroda' (To be a Chechen: individuality and ethnic identification of a nation), at http://www.sakharov-center.ru/chs/chrus04_4.htm.

17  On *adat,* see VA Dmitriyev (ed), *Adat; traditsii i sovremennost'* (*Adat,* traditions and the present day), Moscow and Tbilisi, MNIINK, 2003; on *nokhchallah,* see http://www.chechnyafree.ru/index.php?lng = rus&section = nohrus&row = 0.

18  S Handelman, *Comrade Criminal: the Theft of the Second Russian Revolution,* London: Michael Joseph, 1994, p 39.

19  M McCauley, *Bandits, Gangsters and the Mafia: Russia, the Baltic States and the CIS since 1992,* London: Pearson Education, 2001.

20  The traditional Chechen greeting is 'Be Free!' ('Marsha woghiyla' in the masculine form). See L Usmanov, 'The Chechen Nation: a portrait of ethnical features', at http://www.truth-and-justice.info/chechnat.html.

21  There exists a substantial literature in English on the run up to and conduct of the first Russo-Chechen war. Among the most valuable sources are C Gall & T de Waal, *Chechnya: A Small Victorious War,* London: Pan, 1997; JB Dunlop, *Russia Confronts Chechnya: Roots of a Separatist Conflict,* Cambridge: Cambridge University Press, 1998; and A Lieven, *Chechnya: Tombstone of Russian Power,* New Haven, CT: Yale University Press, 1999. For a Russian perspective, in English, that covers both wars, see DV Trenin & A Malashenko with A Lieven, *Russia's Restless Frontier: The Chechnya Factor in Post-Soviet Russia,* Washington, DC: Carnegie Endowment, 2004.

22  M Haney, 'Russia's first televised war: public opinion on the crisis', *Transition,* 1 (5), 1995, pp 6–8.

23  For Maskhadov, see the front cover of *Novoye vremya,* 38, 1996; for Basayev, *Moskovskiye novosti,* 18–25 June 1995, p 4; for Raduyev, *Moscow News,* 15–21 May 1997, p 1.

24  *Izvestiya,* 11 September 1999.

25  *Argumenty i fakty,* 38, 1999.

26  http://www.cdi.org/russia/johnson/4253.html.

27  http://www.rian.ru/rian/chechnya/en/02/06.html.

28  For *dukhi,* see V Mironov, 'Ya byl na etoi voine' (I was in that war), original from 1995, published online by http://www.artofwar.spb.ru:8101/mironov/index_tale_mironov.html. The English translation (by Alex Dokin), 'Assault on Grozny downtown' was published in 2001 online, at http://lib.ru/MEMUARY/CHECHNYA/chechen_war.txt. For *chichi,* see Igor Mariyukin, 'Tri nochi, chetyre dnya' (Three nights, four days), at http://www.artofwar.ru/mariukin/tale_mariukin_3.html. See also http://bestbooks.ru/Child/Chukovsky/0101.shtml. For *chekhi* (which means Czech in Russian) but appears to have derived from a combination *chechentsy* and *dukhi,* see V Rechkalov, 'Razboi na Ploshchadi Trekh Durakov' (Robbery on Three Fools' Square), at http://main.izvestia.ru/print/?id = 26227.

29  See his 'Our own and strangers', at http://english.mn.ru/english/issue.php?2002-5-15.

30  In the film *Chistilishche,* ORT Video, 1998, the Chechen commander has his *mujahideen* crucify the young Russian tank driver; on the weekend before the Russian invasion of Chechnya on 1 October 1999, Russian TV2 showed one of these gruesome videos of a stereotypical bearded Chechen cutting the throat of a fair-haired Russian soldier. See Jeffrey Taylor, 'Russia on the edge', at http://www.salon.com/travel/feature/1999/10/02/moscow.index.html.

31  See the video 'Oborotni', at http://www.compromat.ru/main/chechya/video1.htm.

32  Among sources pointing to a 'conspiracy' are Y Felshtinsky & A Litvinenko, *Blowing Up Russia,* New York: Liberty, 2002; D Satter, *Darkness at Dawn: The Rise of the Russian Criminal State,* New Haven, CT: Yale University Press, 2003; and the documentary film *Assassination of Russia,* Charles Gazelle Transparences Productions, France, 2002.

33  Sarah Karush, 'Mayor to crack down on unwanted guests', *Moscow Times,* 14 September 1999.

111

[34] For the poll, see *Novoye vremya*, 40, 1999, p 9; for 'Operation Whirlwind, see CNN report 'Turmoil in Russia', 28 September 1999, at http://www.cnn.com/WORLD/europe/9909/28/moscow.roundup/.

[35] *Nezavisimiya gazeta*, 25 September 1999.

[36] For a detailed account of Putin's handling of the 'Islamic factor' in Chechnya, see J Russell, 'Exploitation of the "Islamic factor" in the Russo-Chechen conflict before and after 11 September 2001', *European Security*, 11 (4), 2002, pp 96–109.

[37] See Paul Goble, 'Russia: analysis from Washington—criminalizing politics', at http://www.rferl.org/features/1999/10/F.RU.991020133930.asp.

[38] For an account of Chechen attitudes to 'wahhabism', see A Nivat, *Chienne de Guerre: A Woman Reporter Behind the Lines of the War in Chechnya*, New York: Public Affairs, 2001, pp 1–30. For a brief introduction to 'wahhabism', see http://www.pbs.org/wgbh/pages/frontline/shows/saudi/analyses/wahhabism.html; and for 'wahhabite' horror stories see *Argumenty i fakty*, 38, 2000, p 6, and 44, 2000, p 23.

[39] ITAR-TASS, 6 March 2000; and A Kachmazov, 'V Internete poyavlilis' seti Interpola: chechenskikh boevikov nakonets priznali terroristami' (Interpol site appears on the internet: at last the Chechen fighters have been recognised as terrorists), *Izvestiya*, 7 March 2000.

[40] http://www.compromat.ru/main/chechya/budanov.htm.

[41] http://www.wciom.ru/?pt = 43&article = 490.

[42] http://www.sptimesrussia.com/archive/times/589/opinion/army.htm.

[43] From an interview published in *Novaya gazeta*, 19–25 June 2000. Shamanov was later elected governor of the Ulyanovsk Region. See B Kagarlitsky, 'Insane "heroes" of our time', *Moscow Times*, 25 June 2002.

[44] http://www.cnn.com/2001/WORLD/europe/06/04/russia.execution/.

[45] http://www.wciom.ru/?pt = 48&article = 341.

[46] *The Jamestown Monitor*, 7 (197) 11 October 2001.

[47] *Guardian*, 22 December 2001.

[48] http://news.bbc.co.uk/1/hi/world/europe/1936998.stm.

[49] 'Vzryv v Kaspiiske, 9 maya 2002 goda' (Explosion in Kaspiisk, 9 May 2002), a *Novaya gazeta* special investigation, at http://www.novayagazeta.ru/rassled2/vzrivi/karta-kaspiysk.shtml.

[50] http://www.peaceinchechnya.org/peace/peace_liechtenstein.htm.

[51] http://www.rferl.org/newsline/2002/06/1-RUS/rus-250602.asp.

[52] http://www.rferl.org/newsline/2002/12/161202.asp.

[53] http://www.rferl.org/newsline/2002/04/260402.asp.

[54] Z Sikevich, 'The Caucasus and "Caucasus phobia"', translated by Robin Jones for Rosbalt News Agency, 18 December 2002, at http://www.rosbaltnews.com/2003/02/07/60777.html. For the Alekseyeva quote, see http://www.csce.gov/pdf/101502CSCEbriefing.pdf.

[55] John Dunlop has analysed Kremlin involvement in the 'Nord-Ost' drama, in 'The October 2002 Moscow hostage-taking incident', *RFE/RL Organized Crime and Terrorism Watch*, 18 December 2003, 8 and 15 January 2004.

[56] See articles by B Lo, 'No compromises', J Thompson, 'Telling lies' and J Russell, 'On the side of might', *The World Today*, 56 (12), December 2002, pp 13–18.

[57] Article 8, point 4, forbids the creation and functioning of social organisations that aim to violate the territorial integrity of the Russian Federation. The Russian president is also given the right to remove the elected president of Chechnya (Article 72d). See http://www.chechnya.gov.ru/republic/const/.

[58] Officially, the turnout in this referendum was 89.48%, with 95.97% approving the Constitution. For a sceptical account of the vote, see International Helsinki Federation for Human Rights, 'The Constitutional referendum in Chechnya was neither free nor fair', at http://www.osce-ngo.net/030328.pdf. On the presidential elections, see Andrei Riskin, 'Kak "izbirali" Kadyrov' (How Kadyrov was 'elected'), *Nezavisimaya gazeta*, 6 October 2003. The Zakayev extradition hearings at Bow Street Magistrates' Court in London, in which I appeared along with Tom de Waal as an expert witness for the defence, supported by the evidence given in court by Sergei Kovalev, Andrei Babitsky, Yulii Rybakov, Ivan Rybkin and Aleksandr Cherkassov, lasted from December 2002 until November 2003.

[59] http://news.bbc.co.uk/1/low/world/europe/3020231.stm.

[60] J Russell, 'Primed to explode', *The World Today*, 60 (6), 2004, pp 20–21.

[61] See interview given to Chechen press website on 1 August 2004, at http://www.chechenpress.info/news/2004/08/01/07.shtml.

[62] Paragraph 14, see http://www.un.org/terrorism/a57273.htm.

[63] N Hovsepyan & L Tsukanova, 'Chechnya and Russia: war and peace', at http://www.newtimes.ru/eng/detail.asp?art_id = 535.

[64] See R Wielaard, 'Chechnya query incenses Putin', *Washington Post*, 13 November 2002.

[65] http://www.levada.ru/chechnya.html.

[66] http://www.levada.ru/takoemnenie.html.

# Savage wars? Codes of violence in Algeria, 1830s – 1990s

JAMES MCDOUGALL

On a trip into the Algerian Sahara my friends and I gave a lift in our car to a blind man who had been stranded with his stick, a small bag and a huge terracotta serving-dish at a petrol station in an isolated village. He had been waiting all day in a gusting light sandstorm for a bus to his home town, but every one that had passed was crowded to its seams. Si el-Haj, as we all automatically referred to the older gentleman, rode beside me in the back seat and, perceiving that I was the only European in the party, quizzed me intently for a while in the usual amalgam of Arabic and French about the war in Iraq, my knowledge of Islam, what I thought constituted democracy, etc. He chatted to my friends about life in the area and the forthcoming saints' festivals, led their prayer by the side of the road, and when we dropped him off at his home, insisted that we come in for tea and the local dried dates that taste like thick, dark chocolate. We sat on the floor in a clean, spartan reception room whose only furniture was a long, low table, a huge, chiselled French-style dresser and a recent, wide-screen television. Si el-Haj told a story about a local theft and complained about corruption in local bureaucracy; we stayed a respectable length of time and, after being warmly embraced, thanked and duly offered a fare for the lift, which we duly refused, we left. It was all perfectly pleasant and conventional. We learned shortly afterwards that Si el-Haj, who had been a locally prominent Islamist militant, had spent much of the past decade in prison. When he was arrested, we were told, a cache of arms had been found at his house along with a list of local dignitaries marked for assassination. It was in prison that he had lost his sight.

The purpose of the anecdote is not soothingly to suggest that Algeria's Islamist insurgents, whose campaigns of violence in the mid-1990s led simultaneously to the isolation of the country and to the internationalisation of a particularly horrific image of its internal politics, are basically decent, hospitable and ordinary people 'underneath', any more than it is sensationally to 'prove' that even the most apparently pleasant and benign individual encountered in this part of the world can turn out to be a 'terrorist' 'underneath'. Both readings of the story miss the point.

## 'If an Algerian says: "I'll kill you"—he really will kill you':[1] violence as caricature

Algeria has experienced so distressing a degree of violence in the course of its recent history that images and accounts of the country routinely reiterate two perceptions. First, a supposed ubiquity of violence, endured and inflicted, in Algerian society and its history—so that the infliction and suffering of violence becomes an explanatory factor in Algerian history and social organisation, rather than a problem to be explained. Second, the exceptional intensity of this apparently pathological fact. Nor is it only observers inclined to neo-Orientalist clichés or post-imperial nostalgia who acquiesce in this imagery. Other people from places in Africa and the Middle East which have their own terrible histories, from Iraq, Palestine, Sudan, can be heard (anecdotally) to say much the same thing. The image of endemic, ubiquitous and unusually extreme violence as a constitutive element of Algeria, whether in media clichés or in the spontaneous ethnography of casually informed observers as close by as Morocco and Tunisia or as far away the USA, or in the more ostensibly sophisticated garb of academic analysis, is a first and most readily apparent aspect of the problem of naming violence in this context, from the colonial conquest to the present. It should also be immediately apparent that this representation of a society so 'plagued', as Algeria's incumbent president, Abdelaziz Bouteflika, himself put it in a re-election speech of early 2004, that all the other people of the world must keep a safe distance, itself does much violence to a country and a people who can only be caricatured, and who cannot begin to be understood, in these terms. The point of departure for an examination of violence in Algeria must be to acknowledge, but recuse, not reiterate, the caricature of 'savagery' with which Algerian history has been burdened, and which has generally debilitated understanding of this experience, rather than enlightening it.

Some understanding of the meanings of violence in Algeria, then, needs first of all to escape from this very old stereotype, in all its more or less elaborate forms. Conflictual social relations are as constitutive of this society as of any other; extreme forms of overt violence are not, by some particularly perverse streak of 'national character', nor by inculcation through a long colonial oppression, themselves characteristic of Algerians. Any explanation—and I do not presume to offer one here—of those particular forms which physical violence has taken, in the war of independence and again in the 1990s, would have to begin with the social and political conditions in which such practices arose. And it would have to account for the choices made in resorting to a violence that is no more instinctive to Algerians than to anyone else.

To do this, however, would not mean *rationalising* violence, either (at the crudest extreme) as the expression of a peculiar culture, history and social organisation, or (at the most sophisticated) as 'a virtue' in a peculiarly Algerian political imaginary, constructed across several centuries in which violence served as the most effective means of accumulating symbolic capital.[2] Such rationalisations in fact offer only another form of that naturalisation which we began by recusing. On the contrary, any more adequate account will have to find ways to address the very irrational, unimaginable unnaturalness of a violence which is, precisely, 'foreign' to most ordinary Algerians, to their self-conceptions, world-view and morality.[3] At the same time it should be recognised that certain narratives which have 'naturalised' a vision of the past as constituted by permanent and reciprocal violences—in official history, public commemoration and political discourse—have had their own effective force in shaping decisions and behaviour in the present.[4] If it is true, however, that the echoes of past violence, remembered and narrated, do indeed constitute an important part of the symbolic universe of Algerian culture, history and politics, it is crucial to understand the particular formulation, deployment and reproduction of such symbols in terms of their specific historicity.

This article examines three distinct moments of the social production and cultural encoding of the various forms of violence, physical or euphemised, which have entered into the constitution of social relations in Algeria, as well as playing a part in their crisis and breakdown. These three narratives move from the colonial obsession with an imagined 'native' savagery, which both produced and exonerated the spectacular exercise of colonialism's own violence, through the institution of a legal system of inflexible repression which came to dominate the nationalist imaginary of the colonial period and of its own history, to the complex afterlife of the war of independence and the emergence of new codes of legitimate warfare in the 1990s. The links between each moment are neither direct nor determining. Rather, each obeys a specific logic of its own, reflecting a particular constellation of circumstances. Si el-Haj, our Saharan fellow traveller and sometime alleged terrorist, is not a cipher for either the banality or the exoticism of violence in Algeria, but rather a man in a particular place and time with his own history, and his own view of history.

### Piracy, banditry, fanaticism: the alterity of violence

Imperial depictions of an empire's subject populations and territories are adept at externalising the violence of the empire's own exercise of power, projecting it onto its victims as inherent to *them*. Rather than a specifically situated practice, with its own social and cultural logic, arising at a particular moment, 'native' violence is, in imperial eyes, necessarily irrational, instinctive, 'savage'. Imperial power projection, on the other hand, is only ever conceived of as the necessary policy response to a specific situation: as deliberated, calculated (and now, of course, 'precision targeted'). While modern Europe led the world in the practice of organised violence— economic, symbolic and physical, and on an increasingly apocalyptic scale— from the early 16th century onwards its accounts of the world simultaneously became increasingly effective at portraying, not the effects of the vertiginous expansion of its own capacity to produce and direct coercive force, but the mortal danger faced by its legitimate interests and civilising works among the anarchic, despotic or barbaric zones of disorder in Africa, Asia and the Americas.

One of the first theatres of this developing conception of civilised selfhood and barbarian otherness was the western Mediterranean, where long-standing patterns of trade and warfare underwent significant changes of meaning in correlation with both the developing structures of early modern European states and these same states' expansion of colonial plantation slave economies across the Atlantic.[5] The original European stereotype of Algeria, as a fleshpot haven of renegade villains, a nest of pirates whose infamous depredations not only harried legitimate commerce but also enslaved white (and, by the early modern period, free-born) Christian subjects and citizens of Europe, is one of the earliest and most tenacious modern images of the alterity of violence.[6] The blanket bombardment of Algiers in 1816 by the British navy, which fired some 34 000 shells into the city in nine hours, and the French invasion and conquest in 1830 found their justification in the Algerines' limited, and economically almost insignificant, return to a moribund corsairing which had in any case been forced upon them at the end of the 18th century when the European fleets effectively closed off to them any less overtly rapacious commerce.[7] This fact, of course, like the death and destruction inflicted by Lord Exmouth's cannon and the 'pacifying' armies of de Bourmont, Lamoricière and Bugeaud,[8] was erased from the imperial narrative.

The point here is not simply to highlight the selective and self-serving automystification of imperial fantasies of power; it is, rather, to suggest that a fundamental psychological and ideological mechanism of colonial rule—one of the several ways in which Europeans not only produced imperialism, but contrived to live with it in perfectly good conscience, indeed in the conviction of its 'greater good'—has been the externalisation of imperialism's own violence onto its victim. This does not mean, of course, that the colonised internalised this projection, that they did in fact *become* 'the sneering face of [Europe's] own evil shadow' which early colonial observers thought they recognised on the Mediterranean's southern shore.[9] On the contrary, colonised populations were and remained, in this respect, the entirely innocent objects of a developing European world-view, one to which African and Asian peoples remained external precisely as their bodies and territories were incorporated into the domain of European power projection. The efficacy of this operation lay not in the minds and practices of Algerians, but in those of Europeans.

Colonial violence was encoded, in Algeria as elsewhere, as defensive, preventive—even, already, as pre-emptive—a necessary response to the putative, and very really feared, instinctive, unpredictable and unlimited violence that the 'native' supposedly bore always within his breast, and of which his occasional self-assertion in rebellion was simply proof. All the early colonial typologies of Algerian violence—pirate at sea, bandit on land, religiously inspired fanatic, unremittingly suspicious xenophobe—are variations on this same obsessive theme, and the apologetics of the conquest's war criminals are perfectly clear and, one imagines, of perfectly good conscience, on the subject:

> Little does it matter if France in her political conduct goes beyond the limits of common morality at times. The essential thing is that she shall establish a lasting colony and that as a consequence she will bring European civilisation to these barbaric countries. When a project which is of advantage to all humanity is to be carried out, the shortest path is the best. Now, it is certain that the shortest path is terror; without violating the laws of morality, or international jurisprudence, we can fight our African enemies with powder and fire, joined by famine, internal division, war.[10]

Nor was this basic ideological operation limited in scope or efficacy to the period of conquest and the wars of pacification from 1830 to 1870. The alterity of violence underpinned a crucial, constitutive reflex common among the European population. While never simply collectively shared by all—one cannot speak of a monolithic and undifferentiated 'settler psyche'—it was a powerful presence in widespread socialisation processes and in the consensus of the colony's internal politics. It remains present, even if only in the form of a cipher, in Camus' *L'Etranger*, and reached its suicidal acme in the ultra-colonialist terrorism of the Organisation de l'Armée Secrète (OAS).[11] The conviction of quotidian colonial racism—'the Arabs are cut-throats'—which so effectively held Algerians as invisible to settler society and, when visible, as intolerably threatening,[12] was itself an acute form of symbolic and psychological violence, simultaneously inflicted and endured (as an hysterically internalised fear of the 'native') by Algeria's Europeans. It also served as the unspoken, since self-evident, ground of justification for the spectacular exercise of physical violence against Algerians by both regular armed forces and the settlers' own militia. This is most obviously visible on a large scale in the reprisal massacres at Sétif and Guelma in May 1945[13] and later in the OAS death-squad murders of 1961–62. In these cases colonial violence was a massively and demonstratively disproportionate reaction to Algerian resistance. Not so much the suppression of the actual acts of violent resistance which Algerians had carried out, these spectacles of force were ferociously self-assertive pre-emptions of any conceivable resistance, a terrified exorcism of the latent 'savagery' of the 'native'. As a divisional army commander after Sétif reported, the repression exacted was intended to bring 'peace for ten years'.[14] The poet and playwright Kateb Yacine, who witnessed the events of Sétif at first hand at the age of 16, and later located the emergence of his own nationalist commitment in that experience, set the European settlers' response in a striking fictional dialogue, published in 1956, as the war of independence gathered pace:

F: This time they've understood.

N: You think so? I'm telling you, they'll have another go. We didn't do it properly.

Mme N: My God, if France doesn't deal with them … we can't defend ourselves alone!

F: France has had it. They should give us arms, and let us get on with it. There's no need for law here. They only understand force. They need a Hitler.

Mme F, caressing [a schoolboy] R: And to think they go to school with you, dear [. . .]

R: Oh, things will change. We were scared before. There are lots of them in my class—there are only five of us who are French, not counting the Italians and the Jews.

Mme F: Take care, dear, they're savages![15]

The massacres of May 1945 and the indiscriminate serial assassinations of the OAS were seen by their perpetrators as *defensive* actions, prompted as they were by the same fear (the same simultaneously internalised and externalised, endured and inflicted, violence) that Fanon, in one of his most astute passages, puts in the mouth of a metropolitan French child: '*Regarde le nègre!. . .Maman, un nègre!. . .maman, le nègre va me manger*'![16]

### 'Order' and armed struggle: the law of violence

Underlying these occasional conflagrations there was a more euphemised, everyday and insidious means of assuring imperial rule and of keeping Algerian 'anarchy' in check, through the juridical 'incarnation of the violence of the coloniser'[17] in special native-status legislation, the *indigénat*. Enacted in 1881 as a transitional, emergency measure, it remained in force in various forms until 1944. Overtly a wartime law, a set of emergency regulations for the suppression of revolt, but maintained thereafter in what was notionally a time of peace, the *indigénat* both symbolised and, in the exactions it entailed, made manifest that aspect of the colonial state which constituted an apparatus of permanent, routinised low-intensity warfare.[18] This, alongside the generalised extrajudicial regime of daily indignity suffered by a non-citizen, mostly disenfranchised and expropriated subject population, was a crucial pillar of the colonial order and constituted a major aspect of ordinary Algerians' experiences of colonialism. In the nationalist historical vulgate, this aspect is indeed the *only* face of colonial history, and it is this century-long story of inflexible, unreformable,[19] total oppression which leads, inexorably and as if by an equally iron law of historical evolution, to the

118

taking up of arms and the ultimate, supposedly military, defeat of the occupier by a corresponding, and obligatory, revolutionary violence.

This 'law of violence' in the unfolding of a collective Algerian destiny, a homogenising meta-narrative in which total, reciprocal conflict is understood as the determining law of history, has done much to obscure the intense complexities and contradictions of both colonial relations of power and the emergence of nationalism and armed struggle. The entirety of the colonial period, in the 'official' national history and its rhetorical commemoration, is seen in flat monochrome. As Jacques Berque, the eminent (and entirely sympathetic) historian and sociologist of Islam who grew up in colonial Algeria, observed: 'the violence of the liberation struggle nourished a bitter, sometimes frenzied, literature denouncing the wounds inflicted by colonialism. In short, the literature retained from the colonial dialectic only the outer layer, and of that only what was destructive.'[20] The many deeper 'layers' of the long and viciously intimate colonial dialectic are as invisible to the nationalist orthodoxy as was the injustice of its domination to colonialist self-justification.

Principal among the crucial factors written out of this account is the long and impassioned search of Algerians for a workable reform of the colonial system, for a *peaceful* solution to the intolerable condition of their subject status within the free and egalitarian republic. Or for one which would liberate both communities in the colony ('Algerians of long date'— presumably including the ancient local Jewish population—and 'Algerians of recent date', as one leading nationalist and Islamic scholar expressed the difference between the indigenous and settler societies as late as 1951[21]) from the mutually destructive relationship of violence which would ultimately consume them both. The francophone intellectuals who sought accommodation with and emancipation within *la mère patrie* from around 1908 up to the end of the 1930s are dismissed as at best misguided, at worst treacherous, 'assimilationists',[22] or grudgingly rehabilitated (and miscast) as precursors of the ultimate revolt in a preparatory phase of 'political resistance'. This very notion is manifestly tributary to the later, and more worthy, 'mature' phase of armed struggle whose centrality determines, in this teleological re-reading, the meaning of all previous history since the conquest. In this interpretive dynamic, which seems to have emerged in the mid-1940s can be traced the deeply ingrained suspicion of its own intellectuals prevalent in Algerian political culture. The arabophone scholars and teachers of Islam, whose political programme was similarly reformist, gradualist and opposed to the use of violence, and who saw themselves as the 'awakeners', guides and spokesmen of the nation (whose 'self-awareness' they considered to be of their own making) are similarly drafted after the fact into the unifying teleology of 'the national movement' as the spiritual fathers of a revolution whose paternity was decidedly not theirs.[23] Read backwards from the exhilarating vantage point of victory, through an intensely divisive and traumatic war which could, nonetheless, be quickly enough re-imagined as the triumphant climax of one long, unending struggle over 132 years, the whole history of colonial Algeria appears to conform exclusively, unremittingly, to the law of violence.[24] A violence to which no alternative was *ever* possible, against which no possible political victory (including that which in fact eventually occurred[25]) could be won, but which could only be overcome by a corresponding recourse to violence.

Reducing the complex totality of this history to the simplicity of total conflict, the 'law of violence' underpins an important post-independence political myth of the war of national liberation, as the divinely guided act of the People (in the singular) arising *en bloc* against the monolithic force of oppression. In the words of Algeria's leading nationalist poet, in an epic text officially commissioned to celebrate the writing of Algeria's national(ised) history, the voluntarist insurrection launched by a small fraction of radical nationalists on the night of 31 October – 1 November 1954 becomes an act of the entire people under God, telescoped into Islamic religious history:

> Your Lord announced the Night of Destiny/ And cast a veil over a thousand months/ The people said: Your command, Lord!/ And the Lord replied: Your enterprise is mine!/ ...November...you changed the course of life/ And you were, November, the rising dawn/ You recalled to us, in Algeria, the battle of Badr/ And we arose, as the Companions of Badr.[26]

The official history of the revolution is that of a glorious epic in which only extremes of purity or corruption are possible, in which 'men were snatched from their mediocrity to become the "sublime heroes" or the "absolute traitors" of the unfolding tragedy'.[27] For Algerian historian Mahfoud Kaddache, 1 November was 'the beginning of a new and glorious page of the history of Algeria'.[28] The constitution of 1976 asserted in its opening paragraphs that the war of national liberation 'will remain in history as one of the great epics marking the resurrection of the peoples of the Third World' and that 'Algeria today holds a place of the first order in the international arena thanks to the worldwide influence of the Revolution of 1 November 1954'. It further asserts 'the continuity and reaffirmation of the noble ideals which have animated, from its beginnings, the great Revolution of 1 November 1954'.[29] As the original point of reference for the independent state, its supplier of legitimacy and principal symbolic resource, the revolutionary epic was instituted at the very centre of Algeria's political imaginary, the founding aporia of the nation's forgetful memory.[30]

This social memory of the seven years' war of decolonisation as the founding experience of modern political community, of the single myth of origin for contemporary Algeria and Algerians has had an important series of consequences. The first is the erasure from official history and social memory of the actual divisions and conflicts of the revolution, of the means by which an activist fringe of the radical nationalist movement, having launched the insurrection on its own initiative in order to transcend the factional crisis of its party,[31] thereafter inspired, persuaded and coerced the loyalty of the masses, and eliminated or absorbed their rivals along the way.[32] As everyone is perfectly aware but as it is perfectly impossible to admit, the Front de Libération Nationale (FLN)'s revolution, whose slogan remains 'by the people and for the people', in fact was made 'by the FLN for the

120

Nation…with the support of the People whenever possible and against the opposition of the People whenever necessary'.[33] The role of the active minority of revolutionary militants who in fact sparked the war is, of course, recognised. Indeed, the 'men of November' are particularly celebrated,[34] but they, and the counter-state institution of the FLN which succeeded them and eventually assumed power, are imagined as the expression of 'the People' (in the singular), not as their own, wilful, emancipatory–coercive selves, sometimes followed, sometimes opposed, and who certainly did not naturally subsume the whole of 'Algeria'.[35]

A second effect is the apparent converse of this—the actual expropriation of Algeria's people (in the plural) from the revolution and from the emancipation and self-determination it was supposed to bring. While the armed struggle is said to have mobilised *le peuple tout entier*, simultaneously a military elite issued from the revolutionary army, while proclaiming that the 'sole hero' was indeed the people, lost no time in asserting its right to rule over the people, a right which it considered had been earned in the prosecution of the war. While the war was said to have been the act of the unanimous nation, it in fact constituted a unanimist state out of the conflicts which split Algerians (Europeans from Muslims, and each community against itself), under the aegis of a postcolonial authoritarianism, alienating the state from 'its' people and eventually, in the eyes of many of the people themselves, considering them only with *hogra,* 'contempt'.[36] The doctrine of the historical necessity and inevitability, the supremely uncompromising virtue, of armed struggle (as against the necessarily compromising practice of politics) in the overthrow of colonial domination, and the legitimacy gained by engagement in that struggle—especially late in the war, after the early heroes of the guerrilla were mostly dead, and men flocked from the French army and from civilian life suddenly to swell the ranks of the ALN on the brink of victory[37]—required that all 'the People' be implicated in it, but only in the person of those who themselves incarnated the people's destiny, not through *any* destiny that the people themselves might, eventually, choose.

### Terrorists, patriots, victims and martyrs: the inheritance of violence

This complex underside of the foundational political culture of revolutionary legitimacy begins to explain the strange ambivalence of the social memory of the war of independence as, outside the political field, it is actually experienced in Algerian life. There is a tension, tangible in private and in certain public expressions (the press, cinema, literature), between the war remembered as enactment, the epically memorialised active prosecution of the guerrilla in the maquis, and the reality of the war as the endurance of massive counter-insurrectionary violence at the hands of the French army. Of these two aspects, the latter is, if anything (and unsurprisingly, given the numbers of people involved), more prevalent, more acutely felt and more generally remembered. The FLN maquisard (*mujahid*) remains a ubiquitous summarising symbol of national virtue and honour, expression of Algeria's greatest trials and triumph, and repository of society's values and

121

commitments. The kind of poster one can see on the walls of a youth association office—with the text of the national anthem, *Qassaman* (written by the same poet mentioned earlier), unfurled above an artist's impression of a company of uniformed *mujahidin* running into battle amid the explosions of French bombs—and the imagery of schoolbooks and popular histories, as well street names and their commemorative portraits and plaques, exude this message. At the same time, however, there is, at a deeper level of popular imagination, the predominant image of a war fought against, rather than by, Algerians, of the people of Algeria, as a whole, as having endured the war fought against their emancipation rather than having actively fought a war for it. Fifty years after the outbreak of the insurrection many small towns and villages, or distinct quarters of towns, are still easily identified as having been established by the colonial army as 'regroupment centres', forced-relocation camps where the rural population, driven away from their homes and off their lands (which were razed, napalmed and cordoned off as free-fire zones) were resettled in squat, cramped shelters under the observation of a local garrison. The memory of the cordons and *ratissages* ('raking-over', the systematic, intrusive searches of urban districts, or combing of whole rural zones), the uncounted disappearances, internments, summary executions, torture and rape, involved, of course, far more people as objects of a violence visited upon them than were ever under arms (or engaged in any other active capacity) as agents of revolutionary war.

These two sides of the conflict are in a sense complementary, and the figure of the *mujahid*, marching victoriously under the national flag across the frontier at independence, is the obverse image of the 'one and half million martyrs' which the war is routinely said to have cost Algeria.[38] The dead, both the civilian victims of colonialism and the actively fighting martyrs fallen 'on the field of honour' in the maquis, are perhaps the strongest of all postwar national symbols. Beyond the structural symbolic complementarity of these aspects of Algeria's social memory, however, there remains a certain malaise, an unspoken recognition of the horrific tragedy of the war, below the 'glorious' rhetoric of its celebratory myth. In Merzak Allouache's 1976 masterpiece, *Omar Gatlato*, internationally recognised as one of the first Algerian films to break the mould of postwar heroic epic and portray a deeper, more intimate and multifaceted reality of Algeria, the revolution is an acknowledged but distant backdrop. It is referred to explicitly, almost as pre-history, in Omar's opening speech but then more subtly in the guise of an occasional tattoo-drumming soundtrack cut with views over the Algiers rooftops, a neat reference to Gillo Pontecorvo's *The Battle of Algiers*, shot in the city a decade earlier. In *Omar Gatlato* there is a remarkable sequence where the hero is assailed, one imagines for the *n*th time, by his braggart uncle evidently fabricated tales of heroism during the revolution, and does his best to pay no attention. Throughout the scene the main character's elderly relative, a man who has himself quite obviously witnessed and lived through colonialism and the war, sits unmoved in the corner of the shot, his eyes fixed on the television—and says nothing.

122

The figure of the 'fake *mujahid*' *(faux mujahid)*, a scammer who, in independent Algeria, has forged testimony of his wartime service so as to receive the substantial benefits available to a recognised, card-carrying ex-maquisard, is the grotesque complement of the torch-bearing freedom fighter whose lofty statue adorns the base of the colossal martyrs' monument on the Algiers skyline. The question of the numbers of *faux mujahidin* (and of whether, in fact, there are any) is hotly disputed and occasionally the scandal gives rise to exasperated ire in the press. The country's favourite and most infamous caricaturist, Ali Dilem, portrays a card-wielding loafer in conversation with his signature female figure (who stands in all his work as a cipher for Algeria): 'That's it, I've got my card.'—'You fought in the war?'—'No, I filled in the form!'[39] Another Saharan anecdote may also contribute something in this regard. On our return trip from the desert, a distinguished gentleman with spectacular white whiskers hitched a short ride with us. He was, he said, a former maquisard himself (he exhibited his card, to our great curiosity), and was now engaged in a local self-defence group, one of the militia units armed by the state during the 1990s to fight Islamist guerrillas and, reportedly, not infrequently constituted by FLN veterans. Most of these *patriotes*, the generic term applied to all such militia, have since been stood down and (at least officially) disarmed, but his group had continued to exist as an auxiliary arm of the customs service, tracking contraband traffickers across the desert. When the man had left us, one of my friends remarked speculatively that the story, in this case, might actually have been true. In his own experience genuine former *mujahidin* generally do not introduce themselves as such, rarely have the famous card, and are intensely reluctant to talk about it.

The societal inheritance, then, of this history which is said to be 'inhabited by violence' is, at the personal, familial, local level, and at that of national political culture, the rhetoric and monuments of commemoration and the narratives of official history, a most ambiguous one. In this context, the notion of violence, in any one of a series of historical guises (Ottoman corsairs, anti-colonial *mahdi*s, nationalist revolutionaries) as having simply provided a generic model of political behaviour for replication in all subsequent moments of Algerian history, is clearly too simple. There are, undoubtedly, aspects of the insurgency and repression of the 1990s which explicitly echo, in the language and self-view of the actors involved, the codes of earlier violence. Islamist militants are *mujahidin* fighting a holy war for the recovery of Algeria's 'authentic values' and the popular sovereignty of the *mustad'afin* (the oppressed, the new 'wretched of the earth') against the corruption and tyranny of those who have 'betrayed' the promise of the revolution, against the traitors of the 'party of France' *(hizb fransa)* who have compromised Algeria's true destiny. The army and its auxiliaries are *patriotes* fighting the alien and un-Algerian terror of 'sons of *harkis*',[40] who have betrayed the nation through their allegiance to the 'Islamist international' and seek to destroy the republican state created by the revolution, condemning Algeria through 'programmatic regression' to a barbaric medieval theocracy. Some, at least, among the Islamist insurgents in the early 1990s explained their strategy of terror—the murders of low-level state functionaries, police officers, artists and intellectuals—with reference to the war of liberation. In a contemporary documentary film, a woman recalls the explanation given her by a family acquaintance and member of an armed group, after his colleagues have murdered one of her relatives, a woman police officer: 'It's just like in the war of independence'.[41] And, correspondingly, the senior army officers behind the suspension of elections in January 1992, and the subsequent repression of the Islamist opposition, explain their move as a 'patriotic act' and a 'Novembrist' engagement for the salvation of the state and nation.[42]

But this has not been simply the instinctive reiteration of culturally entrenched patterns of political behaviour. Rather, such expressions reflect a continuous, deliberate reinvention, and struggle for the appropriation, of the strongly valorised and widely diffused inheritance of the war of independence and the nationalist register of legitimacy in a situation of political implosion where the symbolic order has been fragmented, and where symbolic goods are up for repossession. The necessity and legitimacy of armed struggle, inherited by the army as 'shield of the revolution'[43] or by Islamist maquisards as new *mujahidin*, and of Islam as the core component of national belonging (despite the opposition to this doctrine in the councils of the wartime FLN[44]), find new significance in the entirely altered circumstances of the new political and social struggles emerging in the 1980s and 1990s. To these already established registers are added new, previously unthought elements, introduced from elsewhere. Doctrinal imports from the Middle East include a reinvented notion of the 'Islamic state' influenced by the Taliban emirate in Afghanistan, the practice of *takfir* (declaring 'nominally' Muslim rulers and regimes to be apostates) as theorised by Egyptian Islamist radicals, and the sacralisation of redemptive *jihad* even against Muslim civilians who are reluctant follow the Islamist 'call'. (Omar Carlier, in this regard, points to the contrast with the peasant insurgents of early 20th century colonial Algeria, who, even amid the frantic bloodletting of millenarian revolt, allowed Europeans to live who consented to utter the *shahada*, the formulaic expression of testimony to Islam.[45]) The emergence of this reinvented lexicon, pressed into the service of a radical, transnationalist, utopian and chiliastic Islamism, is part of the new conflict's geopolitical context, just as Bandung, self-determination, socialism and Third Worldism were in a previous time.

The comparison most often drawn between the forms of violence enacted during the war of independence and those of the 1990s—the mutilation of bodies, the extreme, exhibitionist atrocity against one's physical adversary which leaves 'the body of the victim without even the value of a sacrifice, [being] ostensibly dehumanised'[46]—also requires more subtle reading than that furnished by the label of 'Algerian savagery'.[47] A beginning might be made in the decryption of 'the accumulation of tensions occasioned by the unravelling of each and every mechanism of social solidarity'which Algerian society has endured in its multifaceted (urban, rural, demographic, economic, educational, linguistic, political) crises since the early 1980s.[48] The most recent reproduction and recoding of the recourse to political violence in

Algeria is the product of its own, specific context of crisis, and of the ways in which this crisis has been managed, or mismanaged, exploited and exacerbated, by particular actors.[49] Such conditions of crisis, with which Algeria has been particularly terribly afflicted, have nonetheless been shared, in varying degrees, with other parts of Asia and Africa. They are not intrinsic to Algeria, its social organisation, cultural values or political ideas, and no more are the forms of terribly extreme overt conflict which, in this case, have arisen out of it. Each moment of the breakdown or recomposition of social order presents its own possibilities within its own context of constraints, but no ingrained societal or political structure of violence, as an innate characteristic or determining law of history, inherently precludes the creation of alternatives. However difficult such choices are and however unlikely such alternatives may appear given the circumstances of the past decade,[50] they undoubtedly remain possible. However many savage wars Algeria may have suffered, Algerians have not thereby been collectively brutalised into thinking with savage minds.

## Notes

[1] Tunisian saying (reported in personal communication, 1999).

[2] L Martinez, *La Guerre civile en Algérie*, Paris: Karthala, 1998, p 9.

[3] Thus the early actions of armed Islamists in the 1990s were initially attributed in public opinion to 'foreigners'.

[4] H Remaoun, 'La Question de l'histoire dans le débat sur la violence en Algérie', *Insaniyat*, 10, 2000, pp 31–43; A Moussaoui, 'Du danger et du terrain en Algérie', *Ethnologie française*, 31, 2001, pp 51–59; and J McDougall, 'Martyrdom and destiny: the inscription and imagination of Algerian history', in U Makdisi & P Silverstein (eds), *Memory and Violence in the Middle East and North Africa*, Bloomington, IN: Indiana University Press, forthcoming 2005, ch 8.

[5] G Weiss, 'Mediterranean captivity and the language of slavery in early modern France', paper presented to the Society for French Historical Studies, Paris, June 2004; and Weiss, 'Barbary captivity and the French idea of freedom', *French Historical Studies*, forthcoming 2005.

[6] For a recent restatement of the theme, see RC Davis, *Christian Slaves, Muslim Masters. White Slavery in the Mediterranean, the Barbary Coast and Italy, 1500–1800*, Basingstoke: Palgrave, 2003. For an incisive analysis of the relationship between imperial vulnerability and imperial power, see L Colley, *Captives. Britain, Empire and the World, 1600–1850*, London: Jonathan Cape, 2002.

[7] D Panzac, *Les Corsaires barbaresques. La fin d'une épopée, 1800–1820*, Paris: CNRS, 1999; and L Valensi, *On the Eve of Colonialism. North Africa before the French Conquest, 1790–1830*, New York: Africana, 1977, ch 5.

[8] Respectively, the commander of the Anglo-Dutch naval expedition of 1816 and the early generals of the French army of Africa.

[9] Valensi, *On the Eve of Colonialism*, p xiii.

[10] Quoted in M Bennoune, *The Making of Contemporary Algeria. Colonial Upheavals and Post-Independence Development*, Cambridge: Cambridge University Press, 1988, p 40.

[11] The 'ultra' terror group formed in 1961 by militant European settlers to resist the abandonment of 'Algérie française'.

[12] While individually an Algerian could be *mon pôte Ali* ('my mate Ali'), visible, collective self-assertion was intolerable, as is evidenced, for example, by the fact that, before independence, organised (and authorised) demonstrations by Algerians in the city of Oran which dared to leave the so-called *village nègre* and descend the main boulevard toward the Place d'Armes in the European *centre-ville* were met with police repression. On both of the only two occasions that such marches occurred before 1962, there were deaths among the demonstrators.

[13] On 8 May 1945, and for several days following, an abortive insurrection in these districts of eastern Algeria was followed by massive retaliation by military, naval and air forces, and (especially in Guelma) by local militia armed and supervised by the local sub-Prefect (who had been a wartime hero of the anti-Nazi resistance). Around 200 Europeans were killed in the initial rioting; the most reliable estimates of Algerian casualties seem to range between 15 000 and 20 000 (the official nationalist figure

being 45 000). See J-P Peyroulou, 'La milice, le commissaire et le témoin: le récit de la répression de mai 1945 à Guelma', *Bulletin de l'Institut d'histoire du temps présent*, 83, 2004, pp 9–22; and J-L Planche, 'La répression civile du soulèvement nord-constantinois, mai-juin 1945' in D Rivet *et al*, *La Guerre d'Algérie au miroir des décolonisations françaises*, Paris: Société Française d'Histoire d'Outre-Mer, 2000, pp 111–128.

[14] Quoted in A Horne, *A Savage War of Peace: Algeria, 1954–1962*, Basingstoke: Macmillan, 1996, p 28.

[15] K Yacine, *Nedjma*, Paris: Seuil, 1996, p 220.

[16] F Fanon, *Peau noire, masques blancs*, Paris: Seuil, 1971, pp 91–92.

[17] C Collot, *Les Institutions de l'Algérie durant la période coloniale (1830–1962)*, Paris: CNRS/Algiers: OPU, 1987, pp 190–200 (quote at p 200).

[18] A simultaneously unyielding and highly flexible system (since almost anything—from travelling to gathering firewood to pasturing one's flocks—could be constituted, in particular circumstances, as an infraction), the *indigénat* was based on the (constitutionally illegal) premise that certain acts not normally punishable under French criminal law were in fact crimes if committed by persons of 'native personal status' (ie after 1870 and until 1944, most Algerian Muslims).

[19] The (only partially enacted) new dispensations of 1944–47, which finally removed the *indigénat*, established parity of elected representation for the European and Muslim communities, bracketing the Muslim vote in a second college, where 1 300 000 electors, voting on behalf of a population of eight million, voted for the same number (60) of Algerian representatives as the 532 000 voters of the first (overwhelmingly European) college. J-C Vatin, *L'Algérie politique. Histoire et société*, Paris: FNSP, 1983, pp 260–261. Subsequent elections, most notoriously those held under Marcel-Edmond Naegelen (Governor-general from 1948 to 1951—a socialist and anti-fascist resister during World War II), were notable for the blatant fraud deployed by the administration.

[20] Berque, *Dépossession du monde*, quoted in Valensi, *On the Eve of Colonialism*, p xiii.

[21] Interview with shaykh Larbi Tebessi, *Alger républicain*, 10 November 1951.

[22] The classic formulation of their position was made in a newspaper article of 1936 by the liberal leader, Ferhat Abbas, whose stand was considered 'treachery to the national cause' by the radical nationalists.

[23] J McDougall, 'S'écrire un destin: l'association des 'ulama dans la révolution algérienne', *Bulletin de l'Institut d'histoire du temps présent*, 83, 2004, pp 38–52. For more detail on the *'ulama* (Islamic scholars), see McDougall, *History and the Culture of Nationalism in Algeria*, Cambridge: Cambridge University Press, forthcoming.

[24] In the words of Houari Boumédienne (Algeria's iconic president from 1965 to 1978): 'This generation has not only fought colonialism, but has known the signal honour of achieving victory. There resides the difference between ourselves and our ancestors.' Speech made in 1976, quoted in H Remaoun, 'Pratiques historiographiques et mythes de fondation', in Ch-R Ageron (ed), *La Guerre d'Algérie et les Algériens, 1954–1962*, Paris: Armand Colin, 1997, p 317. Evoking the leader of 'primary resistance' in the 1830s to1840s, an Algerian historian asserts what became conventional truth: 'The revolution in Algeria began with 'Abd al-Qadir, and never ceased since his time'. Muhammad al-Tammar, *Ta'rīkh al-adab al-jazâ'irí*, Algiers: SNED, nd (1969) , p 278.

[25] Independent Algerian official memory cultivated a myth of victory by arms, but the revolution was, in fact, ultimately successful not on the battlefield (which remained dominated at the end of the war by the French), but through its international political efforts and the creation of a situation of critical instability to which the only solution, for the French, had to be political and not military (as de Gaulle eventually understood, although his rebellious generals did not).

[26] M Zakarya, *Ilyadhat al-jaza'ir*, Algiers: Ministry of Original Education and Religious Affairs, 1972, p 45 (p 23 in accompanying French translation). The 'Night of Destiny', *laylat al-qadr*, celebrated on 26–27 Ramadan, is the night on which the first of the Qur'anic revelations is held to have been vouchsafed to the Prophet (Q97). The battle of Badr, fought in 2 AH (623–24 CE), was a crucial battle of the Prophet's campaigns in the Arabian peninsula.

[27] B Stora, 'La Guerre d'Algérie quarante ans après: connaissances et reconnaissance', *Modern and Contemporary France*, 2 (2), 1994, pp 131–139 (quote at 131).

[28] M Kaddache & D Sari, *L'Algérie dans l'histoire. (t5) La Résistance politique (1900–1954; Bouleversements socioéconomiques*, Algiers: OPU, 1989, p 127.

[29] *Journal officiel de la République algérienne*, 15(94), 1976, p 1042.

[30] B Anderson, *Imagined Communities*, London: Verso, 1991, ch 11.

[31] The Parti du Peuple Algérien (Algerian People's Party—PPA), founded in 1937 and clandestine since 1939, and its (legal) electoral cover, the Mouvement pour le Triomphe des Libertés Démocratiques (MTLD), established in 1946.

[32] The most violent confrontations, both in the maquis and, especially, in the emigrant community in France, occurred between the FLN and the rival Mouvement National Algérien which was formed by dissident ex-militants of the PPA/MTLD.

[33] H Roberts, *The Battlefield: Algeria, 1988–2002. Studies in a Broken Polity*, London: Verso, 2003, p 211, n 1.

[34] The original leader of the Front Islamique du Salut (FIS), Abassi Madani, derived his own legitimacy from having been one of this select band. The prevention of the FIS's victory by the interruption of the electoral process in January 1992 was correspondingly declared a 'Novembrist' act by its architects in the military.

[35] M Harbi, *Le FLN, mirage et réalité, des origines à la prise du pouvoir (1945–62)*, Paris: Jeune Afrique, 1980; and Harbi, *L'Algérie et son destin: croyants ou citoyens*, Paris: Arcantère, 1992.

[36] '*Hogra barakat*', an end to the disdain of the powerful for the powerless, is a leitmotiv slogan of recent protests against the political status quo in Algeria.

[37] The ALN, the FLN's revolutionary armed forces, were constituted as such at the Soummam conference in 1956. The late flood of adherents to the struggle at the moment of the ceasefire in March 1962 gave rise to the term *marsiens* (a laconic pun on the homonymous *martiens*, Martians).

[38] The official '*milyun shahid*', an enduring repetition whose value is not historical but symbolic, is generally recognised as an ideologically inflated figure. While calculations are hotly disputed, the likely true figure of Algerian war dead appears to be around 300 000. See Ch-R Ageron, 'Pour une histoire critique de l'Algérie', in Ageron (ed), *L'Algérie des Français*, pp 7–13; and X Yacono, 'Les pertes Algériennes de 1954 à 1962', *Revue de l'Occident musulman et de la Méditerranée*, 34, 1982, pp 119–134.

[39] Cartoon appearing in *Liberté*, 17 November 2002. The original reads: 'Ça y est, j'ai eu ma carte'. 'T'as fait la guerre?' 'Non, j'ai fait la *demande*'.

[40] The *harki*s were auxiliary counter-insurgency and 'self-defence' troops recruited among the Algerian population. The term has come to signify any Algerian held to have collaborated, in any capacity, with the French army during the war.

[41] J-P Lledo (dir), *Chroniques algériennes*, 52 mins, Algiers–Paris: Audience productions/Planète, 1994.

[42] K Nezzar (Minister of Defence in 1992), *Algérie: Échec à une régression programmée*, Paris: Publisud, 2001, and his various interventions in the press, especially *Le Soir d'Algérie*, 11 October 2003, 3 February 2004; and interview with Nezzar by A Shatz, 'Algeria's ashes', *New York Review of Books*, 18 July 2003.

[43] According to the 1976 constitution, art 82.

[44] Particularly in the various Algerian student unions (UGEMA, UNEA, UEAP), where membership contingent on adherence to Islam was a point of contention, and most importantly in the drafting of the Tripoli programme, the unfulfilled constitutional document of 1962, most of whose artisans were in favour of a secular republic and opposed to the designation of Islam as religion of state.

[45] O Carlier, 'D'une guerre à l'autre, le redéploiement de la violence entre soi', *Confluences Méditerrannée*, 25 (1998), pp 123–137.

[46] *Ibid*, p 136.

[47] R Delphard, *Vingt ans pendant la guerre d'Algérie. Générations sacrifiées* (a memorial account of the war as seen by young French conscripts), Paris: Michel Lafon, 2001, ch 11.

[48] Carlier, D'une guerre à l'autre', p 136.

[49] H Roberts, 'Doctrinaire economics and political opportunism in the strategy of Algerian Islamism', in J Ruedy (ed), *Islamism and Secularism in North Africa*, Basingstoke: Macmillan, 1994, ch 8.

[50] Possibilities included the short-lived presidency of Mohamed Boudiaf in 1992; the Sant'Egidio (Rome) reconciliation platform in 1995; and the civil concord of 1999. Each of these episodes is, of course, controversial (on the latter, see especially International Crisis Group, Africa Report 31, *The Civil Concord: A Peace Initiative Wasted*, Brussels, 9 July 2001). The possible outcomes of the second presidential mandate gained by Abdelaziz Bouteflika in April 2004, on a platform of 'national concord', peace and stability, remain to be seen.

# Israeli snipers in the Al-Aqsa intifada: killing, humanity and lived experience

NETA BAR & EYAL BEN-ARI

What is it like to kill another human being? This paper presents an analysis of Israeli snipers who served in the Israeli military during the current Al-Aqsa intifada. We use this case in order to explore the complex of factors—cognitive, emotional, social, moral and organisational—that centre on the lived experience of these soldiers. Our starting point is a challenge provided by the data we gathered. Zizek has argued that '"enemy recognition" is always a performative procedure which brings to light/constructs the enemy's "true face"...[I]n order to recognize the enemy, one has to "schematise" the logical figure of the Enemy, providing it with the concrete features which will make it into an appropriate target of hate and struggle.' Indeed, the consensus among scholars who have written about killing is that, for such acts to take place, perpetrators have to somehow dehumanise—either demonise or objectify—their enemies.[1]

In our interviews with Israeli snipers who have served in the current conflict, however, we found that they actually held several contradictory views concurrently. Palestinian enemies were curiously portrayed both as an 'other' and as 'like us'. In our discussions with these soldiers it was not only 'terrorist', 'Arab' or 'armed person' that were the common terms used to refer to the Palestinians they had killed. Rather the designation 'human being' (*ben-adam*, literally 'son of Adam') was one no less frequently used. In addition, while terms such as 'neutralize', 'take down' or 'hit' that blur the act of killing were sometimes employed, the simple, naked phrase 'I have killed a human being' was one that appeared in many cases, even if the act was not easy for the killer. Accordingly, the question that stands at the base of our analysis is all the more poignant: what is it like to take the life of another being whose basic humanity is recognised by the killer?

The background to our project centres on the recognition that, however personally and politically problematic the issue, in order to understand the dynamics of any violent conflict one needs to study the perpetrators of violence as well as its victims. Yet when one looks at studies of killing by soldiers one encounters a certain gap. Scholarly writings about combat often concentrate on such issues as courage and discipline, leadership and motivation, the camaraderie of battle, or stress and the terror of impending death. Similarly, scholars have shown how exposure to the death of friends and the guilt of the survivors may precipitate emotional damage.[2] But the act of killing, the ultimate act of war, is often absent from scholarly discussion. Even in Israel, a society marked by decades of armed conflict, scholars have analysed issues such as the personal meanings of service, control of emotions in combat, or soldiering and manhood, but not the taking of life. As Bourke sardonically comments, sometimes one gets the impression that soldiers are there to die and not to inflict death and destruction on others. Given that the military is the organisation most strongly identified with the legitimate use of violence and that soldiers are trained in wielding weapons and wreaking destruction, this lack of scholarly attention is surprising.[3]

In his important book *On Killing* Grossman argues that the experience of killing another person is a private, intimate occurrence of tremendous intensity. For this reason humans have an intense, biologically based resistance to killing other humans. Our common humanity and this biological mechanism make killing a difficult task that inevitably leads to feelings of guilt and pain. Similarly, other scholars have argued that internal prohibitions on killing have pathogenic potential to bring about a range of psychological and behavioural problems. Another, more anthropologically oriented strand of research contends that violence forms a problematic phenomenon because it threatens the very basis of social order and questions the basic humanity of members of any social group. And yet, despite this intense internal resistance and social depreciation, under the appropriate circumstances soldiers regularly take the lives of other human beings.[4]

Why snipers? In contrast to the previous intifada which was characterised by mass beatings and arrests, a major feature of this conflict has been the policy of targeted killings through the use of helicopters, planes and elite units.[5] Snipers—who selectively shoot from a distance—play a major role in this 'precision warfare' and have been used extensively over the past few years. However, there are also theoretical reasons for analysing snipers. Most cases of killing in modern wars are impersonal. Only extremely small minorities of soldiers actually shoot their guns at enemy individuals and kill them. In the majority of cases the act of killing is blurred by distance. Snipers function at a distance from which the average infantry soldier can see the enemy but cannot kill him without special weaponry. Snipers, however, are unlike aircraft pilots, tank gunners or artillery troops in that they are able to see the effects of their shooting. They are also unlike regular infantry soldiers for whom killing involves physical exertion, danger to life and limb and uncertain reality of combat. For snipers, killing and wounding are thus not hidden behind some 'fog of combat' or technical distance. Rather, they present a case in which distance from the enemy is closely combined with a heightened awareness of the effects of their actions. Theirs is a paradoxical kind of killing: shooting takes place from a distance of hundreds of meters but is, at the same time, closer that many other kinds of killing. Moreover, most snipers do not act out of the passions of combat but shoot when composed and determined. It is this combination of personal mark, intense emotional concentration and heightened awareness that interests us. It is the certainty of killing involved in the work of snipers that forms the focus of our analysis.

Between 2000 and 2003 we interviewed 31 soldiers. Twenty-three of these soldiers served as snipers (in various infantry units), five were sniper instructors (three of these were female), and the final three were more senior (and older) officers serving as commanders of the snipers' school. The majority of the interviews were held within the framework of the military (in various camps and bases) and a few in people's homes. In all the interviews we made it clear that we were studyir.g the ongoing violent conflict with the Palestinians and that we wanted to understand what a sniper's life is like.

Methodologically, one could well question the ways in which our social standing influenced soldiers' responses to our questions. Both of us are civilians, middle-class and clearly belong to the academic world. However, Bar served as an Israeli Defence Forces (IDF) officer for four years and Ben-Ari served in the military reserves for over two decades.[6] In truth, some interviewees did try to give us the 'party line' and were at times suspicious of our intentions during the first parts of interviews. Given the sheer variety of difficulties and qualms they talked about—fears, violence perpetrated against Palestinians, and social pressures within small units—we think that they were honest with us, as the excerpts in the article show. Another methodological problem centres on the extent to which we focus on what may be termed 'the' sniper experience. As will be evident from the excerpts we cite in the text, our data are based on all the interviews we carried out with the snipers (and to a more limited extent with their officers and instructors). The variation in voice and tone that we heard from the troops is very much one that is based on personal inclination and reflection. Thus we did not find any significant differences in outlook between snipers from different units, holding different political views or with shorter or longer experience in the military. This does not mean that there is some kind of homogeneous sniper experience but it does imply that the standard sociological variables do not 'explain' divergent positions. We use the masculine form of denotation for snipers since there are no female snipers in the IDF.

## Positioning ourselves

The Al-Aqsa intifada has been going on for more than four years and the end of the bloody conflict between Israelis and Palestinians seems to recede farther into the future everyday. The heavy price of this conflict, in terms of human lives, continues to grow. Some of the Palestinian victims are the outcome of the actions of the snipers we have studied. For both of us who had been studying the military for some years, listening to, and then trying to make sense of, the actual acts of death and killing was a rather harrowing experience. We are fully aware that our article could be read by different groups as either condoning the killing of Palestinians or as an anti-Israeli tract. Rather than leading our analysis in an explicitly political direction, we purposely take a distanced view (perhaps the only one possible for us as Israeli anthropologists) to understand the intense, often horrendous, act of killing another human being. Thus we strive to listen very carefully, to analyse the wider context, and to explain the lived experience of the Israeli snipers.

In order to foreshadow our argument about the contradictions and complexities of their experience we begin with the voices of the soldiers talking about the problematics of killing. We then go on to talk about the 'enjoyment' of killing and the mechanisms of dehumanisation that accompany such actions. It is against this background (which takes off from much of contemporary social scientific scholarship) that we turn to the last sections of the article, in which we demonstrate how soldiers liken Palestinian enemies to themselves and see them as human beings. In the conclusion we offer an analysis of some of the wider issues raised by our argument.

## The problematics of killing

The operational guidelines provided to snipers by the IDF have changed over the course of the current conflict. At the beginning of the conflict soldiers were instructed to shoot only armed Palestinians who were actively engaged in armed aggression against soldiers or Israeli citizens. Later the rules were changed to include any armed Palestinians or those coming near various IDF outposts and positions. Within these rules snipers have had to obtain explicit permission from commanders at the company or battalion levels to shoot their weapons. It is on the basis of reports from the snipers themselves, intelligence data provided to the commanders and the latter's assessment of a specific situation that orders to kill or wound someone have been given. The criteria for ordering snipers to shoot have been immediate threat to IDF soldiers and Israeli citizens or the belief that targeted Palestinians belong to one of the armed Palestinian groups. Any drift from these orders is considered a violation from the rules of engagement and has usually been dealt with informally inside military units and much more rarely through formal disciplinary measures.

Turning to snipers, because such violent acts are so visceral and palpable, their actions deeply concern them. Take the words of a paratroop sniper:

> It does not become simple, but you, you understand, the [sniper] squad, it killed a person only once and then I was in shock for two days. I can tell you that apart from that we did not have a chance to kill...I thought that in the field I would be more excited, I would shoot who I have to shoot...Afterwards you have all the time to think. Suddenly you realise that you have killed someone.

Another soldier who was very satisfied with his successful hits (wounding rather than killing armed Palestinians) was nevertheless surprised at the reaction of a fellow sniper who had killed a man by mistake:

> For a full day, X felt really bad because after all he did not want to kill the man who threw rocks, he was not about to kill anyone. So he...was really depressed. He had a talk with the company commander, with the guys, and in the end we calmed him down...But me, I don't know how I would feel. I thought about it and told myself that I don't think that I would feel terrible...but you never know because here X suddenly feels bad like that.

Another combatant went to prison because he fired his rifle without permission and killed someone by mistake. He initially told us that he too did not have a bad conscience about what happened. Then, after a short break in his words, he added 'not very much' and immediately went on to talk about his experiences in prison. Later in the interview he went back to the killing and the influence this had on him.

> I began to read. Not that I became crazy or anything, I just began to read all sorts of things about spiritual awakening; all sorts of things like that...Not really important...I really changed after that thing, very much...I became a better person: more helping, more considerate, much less angry...

Yet another soldier who also told us that he does not regret his action nevertheless went on to say that afterwards he had thought about 'many things'.

> I may sound stuck-up, maybe, mainly his family, his friends, all sorts of things. I thought a lot about how he is beginning his process of decay. That thing sat really hard in my head...But he had it coming, he was a Hamasnik, belongs to the Hamas organisation and walking around with a weapon. He wasn't a guy who just came there to play games.

Among the psychological syndromes most identified with warriors in general, and Vietnam veterans in particular, is that of post-traumatic stress disorder; research has found that it was higher among those who had killed than among those who had not killed other people.[7] In our case, the chances of finding real trauma were low, since we did not interview any snipers who had been defined as psychologically damaged.

At the same time, however, the 'little' traumas—if they can be so labelled—came up time and again. One sniper (an immigrant from the former Soviet Union) who had hunted animals since he was 10 said decidedly that 'every person that a sniper kills, he sees him sometime'. 'When, under what circumstances?' one of us asked, and he answered, 'In dreams, when you don't sleep well'. Female sniper instructors could easily remember soldiers who had proudly said that they had 'taken someone down'. Although it was more difficult to remember those who had problems grappling with the results of killing, one instructor recalled:

> They do really important work, really hard, and it's a fact that many snipers after the first time when they kill someone then they come to tell us and that it was not easy for them when they see the man dead, because they see it in a magnified way...After that you have those that have nightmares about it, they dream about it at night. There are all sorts and then when they continue, it sort of goes away somewhere.

Another sniper in an elite unit talked about a 'tweak' that was caused when he heard the wife and friends of the person he killed mourn him. His slight vacillation says much more than the words themselves:

> At the basic level we understand that here is a man with a weapon and that he is about to go and carry out the attack, to kill innocent civilians and then we are not sorry about it. Even when you feel this tweak afterwards when his buddies and his wife, they beg...sort of sho...shouted, they shouted and cried. So it causes a tw...a tweak, because here is someone whose friends love him, and I am sure that he is a good person because he does this out of ideology, but we from our side have prevented the killing of innocents so that we are not sorry about it.

Thus even in cases where soldiers see a clear justification for killing or wounding, there are persistent thoughts and emotions that bring them back to the moment of violence. What is significant is the recurrent recognition of the humanity of enemies. One man, a shy soldier with a smile, killed six people. During the interview, he used few words and did not make an effort to explain his inconsistencies. In the following passages one can sense, at one and the same time, the great difficulties of being a sniper and his readiness—even his desire—to continue killing:

> I hit him in the head. At the beginning, the first time you shoot and hit a person in the head, its not so nice [smiles] all the...All the brain.

> Q: The whole brain was smashed?

> Yes exactly. Or it flew out the other side. A bullet hits, for example, when a bullet hits the head, where it hits is only a small hole and on the other side half the head is missing. The first time it is hard. Hard, so hard...I don't know, hard to look at it, hard to see a man fall like that, and his brain explodes.

> Every person that you kill it is not such a happy thing because he is also a human being. But you have to do it because it's either that he, as a terrorist, kills our women and children and explodes in the middle of the country, or we take him down and he can't do that. It's simple: less of our citizens are going to get killed. That is why we do this work...It's very hard to kill people, but you have to do it, someone has to do it.

134

Q: What do you like about your work?

Let's say that I like it and I don't like it. I like teaching people. To give something new, to find something new, new techniques...[of] shooting, aiming, that are comfortable for you. To become a professional.

Q: And what don't you like?

Don't like bringing people down. At this stage, I have not had the chance for more. If it works out [to shoot more people] then it works out.

Q: But you prefer not to?

Me? No, why? I do prefer to do it.

Q: You do prefer it?

Less terrorists in the territories.

Q: Despite the fact that you said that you don't like doing it.

[Nods in approval].

This kind of ambivalence comes out directly or indirectly in other interviews. One soldier paints a horrible picture: after the shooting, night falls, and then the mothers and the children of those killed arrive. In the dark, only the sounds of the crying are heard by the sniper. This situation is emotionally moving enough to sow doubts in his mind about the act of killing. But soon he remembers the terror attacks that are being waged on the urban centres of Israel and his doubts recede.

> After we finished shooting, we went back to our positions, and you begin to think...We stayed there and then they came to carry off the bodies at night. And the mothers there cried next to the bodies and started to cry...OK, when you think about it...like these mothers who are crying now for the two terrorists, when you hear their crying, everything is dark, and you hear the mothers crying and the mosque in the background, and it's, you don't really understand what is happening. You begin to think suddenly, why? And after all he was with a weapon. After that you say, they shoot at people, you think about the security situation in the country and that the mothers cry for their children here in Israel in the same way. There are terror attacks on buses and we here killed two and there 16 are killed in one day. So in general you say 'If another one will come out now you take him down'.

The hesitancy, doubts and often moving emotional reactions to killing another human being form the basis of how snipers talk about their military work. But there are other dimensions that must be taken into account.

## The enjoyment of killing

It is disturbing to acknowledge that killing may be a source of pleasure. A strong social stigma prevents soldiers from admitting that they enjoy such actions and scholars from being open and receptive to such revelations. The argument that killing is characterised by joy, satisfaction and spiritual elevation does not preclude the distress, difficulty and guilt associated with it. Conflicting human emotions can exist side by side. The problem is that scholars have almost always proceeded from the assumption that the enjoyment of killing is abnormal and that trauma is the reasonable reaction. A more open approach would seek to integrate the dimensions of pleasure into the analysis. In this respect, we emphasise that the enjoyment of killing is not identical with the joy of battle or the desire for action that many soldiers feel upon embarking on war. Nor is it identical with what Americans call being 'trigger happy', the feeling of satisfaction and liberation that the shooter may feel from pulling the trigger and the flow of bullets from the barrel.[8] We are talking about the enjoyment or satisfaction derived from killing another human being.

What is the source of such enjoyment? One proposition is that, because combat is fraught with mental and physical stresses, shooting is the only available means for soldiers to feel that they are still alive within a scene of horror. Shooting at enemies may combine release, relief and the masking of fear and thus make it easier for soldiers, especially if they are shooting as part of teams. Yet this contention evades the issue of killing, since it focuses on the situation within which it take place rather than on the act itself. According to Grossman, people who enjoy killing belong to the 2% of sociopaths found in any population: those clinically defined as having an anti-social personality and who do not feel normal resistance to killing or the guilt that accompanies it. This view, linking the enjoyment of killing to pathology, is reinforced by Lieblich, who contends that two of her interviewees who talked about enjoying killing were angry men who already had a tendency to violent outbursts before their military service. If the former explanation dismisses the evidence for enjoyment of killing through arguing about the situation which engenders it, the latter explanation distances the experience from the realm of 'normal' people.[9] Both explanations do not clarify the enjoyment that ordinary people may find in slaying and the possibility that death and killing are fascinating for the human race. After all, during some eras and among certain groups, humans (most often the ones in power) did possess a common habit of enjoying the sight of blood-letting in gladiator tournaments, bull fights, wrestling and boxing, or the slaughter of animals.[10]

One explanation for the fascination with killing is its appealing aesthetics. Hollywood cinema (like film makers in India, Hong Kong and Japan), for example, uses the beauty of death—in scenes of slaughter, images of running blood, or large-scale shootings—to attract crowds to theatres. Violence is very photogenic and it seems that death has a seductive allure. In the wake of such imagery, soldiers often grow up on childhood heroes like Rambo or Luke Skywalker and then develop romantic images of war and of themselves as warriors. As Bourke suggests, part of the enjoyment of killing may derive from an imagined similarity between reality and magical screen images.[11] Yet, as she notes, not all soldiers imagine themselves to be film heroes, not everyone finds beauty in death, and many do not feel that they are in a movie in the midst of a firefight.

There is another image that soldiers use: they imagine themselves to be god. Control over life and death, according to this view, is given to higher powers—god or the state—and not to ordinary humans. In the battlefield, however, soldiers sometimes suddenly have the terrible right to influence the fate of other humans. The higher authorities award soldiers the right to break the highest moral code without being accountable for their actions. It is not surprising, then, that soldiers derive much gratification from this awful power.[12] One soldier elaborated:

> There is a saying that the head of the snipers' course taught us, that the sniper is like god in that he decides who will live and who will die on the battlefield. It's really a bold statement but in reality it's quite right.

And another man said:

> Many times, the weapon's role is like god's role. You look through the sights and you can see the man and know that these are going to be his last moments and he doesn't even know that you are there.

To be sure, given the strict command and control of snipers, their perception of themselves as 'god' may seem to be an illusion, since shooting is dependent on strict authorisation and they are very rarely able to fire freely. Nevertheless at the phenomenological level of their experience, the feeling of being 'god' is very strong.

A related theme comes up in Krin's research on Israeli soldiers who served in the first intifada.[13] She found that most of her interviewees enjoyed inflicting violence during their service. The soldiers did not necessarily kill, but they beat Palestinians, shot rubber-coated steel bullets, threw hand grenades and used live-fire against the local population. While the enjoyment that comes out in their stories is often told in a relatively mild manner, Krin's interviewees did express intense pleasure derived from the combination of danger and power in violent situations.

A further related attribute that provides pleasure is the fact that the sniper works as an individual and that success is attributed to his personal talent. Accordingly, the enjoyment of shooting is related to receiving positive feedback, actualising professional capabilities or craving for 'action'. An infantry sniper:

> If I have my 'personal mark', that I know that only I was the one that shot and that I hit [him] without a doubt. Then I think that the feeling is good...If everyone is waiting for the result of your work and in the end it succeeds, then everything is great.

How can we explain the existence of emotions that have a strong potential to contradict each other? Snipers, it seems, are aware of the humanity of their enemies, of the import of their actions and the sorrow they are causing. And yet they inflict pain and sometimes kill without hesitation. The killing that they carry out seems neither banal nor traumatic and at times enjoyable. It is not easy, but is not unbearable and is sometimes pleasant. The problematic aspect of killing is seen by the snipers as natural and reasonable but as something that passes. Whereas during a specific act of shooting snipers do not get confused and rarely have doubts, it is in their thoughts and dreams that the people they have killed and injured appear.

## Distancing, emotions and the enemy

What kind of process underlies the ability of the snipers to kill? As Grossman suggests, distancing between soldiers and enemies is crucial in order to be able to kill adversaries.[14] In the scholarly literature there appear to be two ways to construct such distancing: dehumanisation, implying the negation of enemies' humanity, and demonisation, entailing the attribution of evil characteristics to their image. Despite certain confusion between the two, each distancing mechanism is accompanied by different emotions and implies different ways of behaving.

*Dehumanisation*

The enemy's human-ness is negated by various technological means or by the sheer physical distance between the killer and the killed. Thus, for example, range is important: pilots and artillerists belong to the maximal distance (where victims cannot be seen without mechanical aides), tank crews are at a reach where the average soldier can see his enemy but cannot kill him without special weaponry, infantry soldiers using rifles are at the medium range and finally soldiers who kill with a spear or knife are closest. In our case, de-personalisation of the enemy is facilitated for the sniper by the use of telescopes or field glasses that make the shooting appear as though on television screens or computer games. One sniper observed:

> When you look out a window, everything appears less human. Also when you ride a car and look outside it looks less human...That's what makes a difference between riding in a car or on a motorcycle...It is much, much harder to shoot a man, and the fact that I look at him through a [rifle] sight it is like looking at something on television more or less. Of course, you know to differentiate between them because this is real, but to look through the sight makes things less human.

Hence, in a poignant manner, the consequence of telescopes (whose aim is to make shooting more effective in a technical sense) is the de-humanisation of antagonists. Without this depersonalisation, killing, it seems, would become unbearable. As Holmes puts it:

> a soldier who constantly reflected upon the knee-smashing, widow – making characteristics of his weapon, or who always thought of the enemy as a man exactly like himself, doing much the same task and subjected to exactly the same stresses and strains, would find it difficult to operate effectively in battle.[15]

In the Israeli army, as in many other armed forces, soldiers use an array of metaphors taken from the world of machines to describe killing: for instance, to 'neutralize' or 'clean up'. These terms hint at a perception of the enemy as an object that has to be handled in a rational and unemotional manner.[16] Indeed, the Al-Aqsa intifada has spawned its own sanitising language, especially around the metaphor of 'surgical' action. Terms used by the IDF include 'focused prevention', 'focused assassination' or 'pinpoint assassinations'. While part of the conventional military parlance emphasising precision, the use of such expressions appears to blur the fact that on the 'other' side are humans, and turns killing into simple technical actions. One sniper seemed to be surprisingly aware of this process:

> From my view, I have a target, an object that is now carrying out certain actions that threatens the force that I am working with. And the object is the enemy. And I neutralised [him]...Sometimes when I say 'neutralised' it's like Freud, it's a sort of repression. Listen, I know what I am doing and believe in what I am doing...But try to disengage from the fact that this is a human being and it becomes an object that is shooting and threatening the situation. I neutralised him and he no longer does what he does and won't do it in the future.

A closely related mechanism is the process of turning the enemy into a collection of body parts. This point is evident in the next passage:

> I aimed at the thigh, from the hips down. We usually shoot from the knees down but the guy was sitting in such a manner that if I would have aimed at his knees it would have endangered him because the bullet would have penetrated his stomach or heart. The thigh was the most salient part. As I let off the bullet I immediately recharged the rifle...Then, it's something you don't forget, I identified the hit. The man just grabbed his leg, bent backwards from the force of the bullet.

Snipers often divide the bodies of enemies into parts. There are body areas that one aims at according to the kind of damage to be inflicted: in order to kill from a distance the sniper will aim at the centre of the body's mass, the chest and stomach. To kill with one bullet from a short distance he will aim at the head, and to neutralise the leader of a demonstration he will aim at the knees and lower. The division of the body into areas and parts is not unique to snipers. Indeed, many surgeons turn the bodies of patients into an anatomical map.[17] In such cases, as in sniping, the body is 'reduced' under the examining eye to body parts without thinking of the human behind the parts. And, in both cases, those of surgeons and snipers, de-humanisation appears to allow the avoidance of possible feelings of guilt or emotional turmoil.

What prevents soldiers from becoming uninhibited killers when the taboo against taking the lives of others has been lifted? In his research on the IDF, Ben-Ari found that de-humanisation is usually not accompanied by demonisation of the other side. The objectification is there, but enemies are not perceived as evil and so emotions of hate and disgust are not usually created. This argument fits with Shalit's findings about the relatively low rates of reported hate for the enemy among Israeli combat soldiers as opposed to support forces. This kind of attitude allows, Ben-Ari suggests, a rational handling of the enemy with relatively little space for emotional outbursts.[18]

*Demonisation*

By contrast, the ascription of evil or demonic attributes to enemies, or their portrayal as forces with unnatural powers, contributes to the emergence of fear and hate and to the use of uncontrolled violence in such acts as atrocities.[19] In other words, portraying the enemy as malicious and repulsive creates feelings that make killing easier. In this regard the Israeli situation stands in contrast to that of the US forces, which were characterised for long historical periods by an almost obligatory demonisation of enemies and their portrayal as the foes of civilisation. Fussel, Cameron, Dower, Eisenhart and Shatan all contend that enemies were demonised by the US military during World War II, Korea and the Vietnam War. Kennett suggests that, while the German soldier inspired no strong detestation, the strong animosity to Japanese soldiers was based on a combination of racism and religious legitimation. Twenty years later, as Shay remarks, the Vietnamese 'were thought of as monkeys, insects, vermin, childlike, unfeeling automata, puny...inscrutable, uniquely treacherous, deranged, physiologically inferior, primitive, barbaric and devoted to fanatical suicide charges'. Against this background, it is perhaps not surprising that American soldiers had the (unofficial) 'mere gook rule' which declared that killing a Vietnamese civilian did not really count.[20]

There were relatively few instances of comparing enemies to animals in our data, but they do appear. Notice the slippages in the following sniper's words:

> We simply had a talk...and it was said that it is now spring and when it warms up a bit they will come out of their eggs because in the rain it's not very nice to be walking around outside. They, not we. So they came of their houses and that is what you see.

The use of the word 'eggs' instead of 'houses' and the process of emergence when it becomes 'warm' raise associations of dangerous reptiles. Another form of demonisation is found in the words of a soldier talking about an 'inciter' he shot during a demonstration in Hebron:

> I really caught the guy from the beginning; the minute I saw him I said to myself this is a troublemaker because he seemed like that, dressed in black, with jewellery (gormette), he looked like a Hamas operative, really a Hamas operative.
>
> Q: Did he wear a mask?
>
> No he looked regular, hair and gel and so, and you see that he is bad like...Saturday noontime...again that guy is in the same place at the centre of things. This time I didn't wait too long and said that I identify that guy from yesterday. I gave him the name 'the man in black'. He seemed to be the centre of the incident. I asked, 'Can I shoot? I would like permission to shoot.'

It appears that precisely because the person's humanity was evident through the telescope there was a need to 'blacken' his face. Yet, because of the relatively rarity of demonisation in the IDF, these characterisations of enemies still allow rational and highly regulated reactions and do not lead to uncontrolled infliction of violence.

## The snipers and wider understandings

Here one could ask as to the extent to which such understandings reverberate with the perceptions that occur at broader societal and group levels. Snipers' attitudes and understandings may be compared with three other levels. First, the snipers we interviewed showed remarkably similar attitudes to other combat troops of the IDF. Indeed, in a project Ben-Ari has been carrying out on Israeli ground forces in the current conflict, he found a similar diversity of means of labelling and naming armed Palestinians. Where snipers do diverge, however, is in the actual experience of killing, as we have been showing here. Second, in regard to Israeli society in general, public opinion polls and newspaper reports have consistently shown that, on the whole, the Jewish–Israeli public has been much more extreme in its views of Palestinians and armed Palestinians. Thus, as Harel and Isacharoff contend, before Operation Defensive Shield, when Israel reconquered the urban centres of the West Bank, the majority of Jewish Israelis saw the Palestinians as having a 'murderous desire and will to take control of the territories within [Israel proper]'.[21] Finally, there is probably a difference between the ways in which the snipers perceive themselves and the ways in which they appear in media accounts. While an examination of this issue is beyond the limits of this paper, it would seem that the difference centres on the minority of rather sympathetic reports that see their work as part of Israel's policy of restraint and the majority of accounts that see their work as part of the Israeli state's ruthless policies against Palestinians.[22]

## Enemies and likenesses

Up to this point our discussion has developed a perspective that centres on the need for soldiers to see their enemy as the 'opposite' of themselves. But is this perspective always correct? As we argued in the introduction to this article, in many cases enemies do not necessarily become distanced objects or epitomes of evil but may actually be mirror images of soldiers. The likeness between soldiers and enemies is expressed on three levels.

The first is a process that may be termed 'reverse dehumanisation'. Dehumanisation aimed at the self is related to intra-psychic processes by which people protect themselves from emotionally loaded and threatening situations. Rieber and Kelly suggest that in stress-prone situations (such as medicine or law enforcement) dehumanisation involves two kindred but distinct processes. In the self-directed dehumanisation, individuals protect themselves, while dehumanisation of the other involves the process whereby individuals depersonalise others. These processes are intensified in situations of combat. In his ethnography of an infantry unit during the first intifada, Ben-Ari found that machine metaphors were often used in regard both to members of Israeli units and their enemies. During the same period members of another unit studied by Krin dehumanised both themselves and their enemies through the use of metaphors centred on animals.[23]

Second, the categorisation of enemy soldiers forms the basis for a scale of prestige or stature. Accordingly, in previous times, participation in battles in war was more prestigious than participating in engagements during 'peace-time'. And both activities used to be considered more impressive than border patrols where 'nothing happens'. In the present conflict the status of the sniper increases directly in relation to the threat posed by the enemy he shoots. Take the distinction one man drew between ordinary soldiers who shoot imprecise rubber-coated steel bullets and himself, up against an adversary with the binoculars.

> In the midst of a protest demonstration I observed a man...who was constantly observing our force. We had a force that was going into the village in a concealed way, three or four soldiers that took great risks. They went deep inside and shot rubber bullets from a short distance that unfortunately were not precise and then went back out. Now this man with the binoculars was constantly observing us...I didn't like it and reported it...At the beginning I did not get permission [to shoot] and continued to report and I tell them all of the time, 'Listen the man is obstructing the work of our team'.

Then, he receives permission to shoot:

> In short, I am at 380 meters and sitting on him and waiting... I don't want to shoot because all of the time there are people next to him. Till suddenly, he decides to get out and sit, like with his legs open wide; sits and looks...The man threatened the lives of the soldiers, threw a Molotov cocktail. How dare he do things like that to the IDF?

Indeed, grappling with an equal enemy (and projecting one's capabilities on him), rather than the humiliating struggle with civilians, increases the importance of the sniper. Accordingly, one interviewee told us:

> Sniper against sniper? Look, a sniper is the most frightening. OK, I'll tell you straight, if I know that opposite me is a sniper I will hide under a boulder, I will jump from one place to the next as quickly as possible, I will be as professional as possible.

In this respect, we see that the snipers' recognition of enemies as human beings and thus as fellow warriors owed respect may lead them to identify with them. Indeed, in those few cases where snipers recognised that they had killed someone who was not defined as a threat to Israeli civilians and troops, they experienced the killing or wounding as less professional and prestigious.

The third way in which the similarity between soldier and enemy is expressed centres on training, because the same practices of dehumanisation found in training camps are often used later in regard to enemies. In the US military during certain historical periods, 'hate training' was rampant. Accordingly, during Vietnam, rage at superiors fostered during training was transformed and channelled into fury at the enemy. The 'logic' of such practices was an attempt to demean and debase troops in a manner that could later be directed towards antagonists in Southeast Asia. Verrips, more generally, suggests looking at how, in order to earn self-respect and to enter the military group, the newly mobilised civilian has to adopt new standards. After he has survived basic training, he enters the 'in-group' and then uses the same practices used against him towards others. It is thus reasonable to assume that trainees learn on their very bodies how those who do not belong should be treated and then remember—consciously or unconsciously—that they too were once non-members.[24]

The Israeli army, in general, refrains from extreme forms of humiliation as part of training. Moreover, the five-week course for snipers is characterised by strict professionalism and there are no hazing and degradations because the course begins a full year after soldiers have entered service and a good few months after basic training (where soldiers are 'broken' and then 'built anew'). Indeed, by far the major part of the course is devoted to drills on shooting ranges where the snipers concentrate heavily on learning the proper body techniques and control that will enable them to shoot accurately. Sniper training is thus very different from the instruction given to regular infantry soldiers. Snipers not only learn to control their bodies but to be very reflective about this control. Moreover, within the snipers' course, the emphasis is very much on realistic, concrete instruction. The instructors quoted in Gilbert, for example, argue that it is critical to train snipers realistically since, if this is not done, during 'real' time they may be surprised by the sight of men, by their humanity. In fact, realistic training—for example, where spring figures are included—tends to increase the rate and percentage of fire of weaponry.[25] In the IDF camp where snipers train such targets are used as well as standard ones made of cardboard figures (that have the shape of soldiers with helmets aiming their guns). Thus, it is not surprising that, while later in the field snipers do not face helmeted individuals, they have been habituated to human forms and thus can shoot humans with cool precision and careful consideration. Thus, although there may be a contrast between the helmeted soldiers presented in training, and the types of situations and targets that the snipers face in the territories, the governing idea for the snipers is that they are shooting at threatening human beings.

This point is also important because of the sniper's ability to kill from a distance under cover: there is a high probability that he can kill the enemy, but a very low probability that the enemy can kill him. This is a very different situation than that faced by the infantry soldier going into battle—or by soldiers armed with rubber bullets deployed against street protestors. Along these lines, because snipers wage war with relatively impunity, their acts raise questions about the morality of what they are doing. At its most basic, it may be argued, they appear to be engaged in a fight that is not 'fair'. As we have shown, the reasoning of the snipers centres on the wider understanding that they only kill selected individuals who are particularly defined as threatening to IDF soldiers or Israeli civilians. In this sense their ability to kill with impunity is not an issue, just as their social control by commanders is not something that they deliberate upon. All the snipers we interviewed drew upon the justification of a conflict between two peoples as a basis for perpetrating violence.

## The enemy as 'human being'

As we explained in the introduction to this article, 'human being' is the most common term found in our interviews when snipers refer to their enemies:

> From afar, I identified a man that was climbing the fence with a ladder and when I got there I simply shot him...And then I was worried a bit about the fact that I had killed a man at that moment and then the inquests began.

In view of the repeated use of the word 'human being', one can hypothesise that the snipers do not completely deny or repress the humanity of the people they shoot. This argument is sustained by such passages as the one from the sniper who saw the body of the man he had killed lying in the street. These sights (and sounds) do not escape the vigilant snipers, and it seems that they are not wholly concealed through the use of the rich array of metaphors and images that dehumanise their victims. In addition, the snipers do not convey emotions of anger or hate, but rather deep persuasion in the justice of the act. The 'situation' of conflict against concrete threats justifies soldiers' actions and thus questions of conscience are unnecessary. As one of our interviewees stated:

> What's this whole matter with conscience? The situation is terrible and you hear all of the time about civilians being killed [by terror attacks] so really you don't have the strength to think about this poor guy...

The assumption that soldiers have to be distanced from their enemies, seen by scholars as being indispensable for killing, is not wholly vindicated in our case. Not only are identical terms used to describe soldiers and enemies, but much of the terminology does not dehumanise or demonise the two sides. In fact, some snipers are aware of this situation and one put it thus:

> If you don't see the enemy as a human being, you really become a war machine. You lose your humanity if you don't think about him as human.

The following two passages echo such sentiments:

> G: There's no hate, I don't feel that I hate people...Look, someone that is arrested because he is going to commit suicide, then you...you see a human being that is going to commit suicide. Then when you later see him in handcuffs, you say 'Wow, a regular human being'. He doesn't look bad or something...You hear of other units that hit them. I don't. We never did such things and...You don't feel any hatred towards them, even while you know that they are suicide bombers.

> H. I don't know what to tell you, every human being is a human being. I see many Arabs here and I don't hate any one of them. Each one has his own truth. I also don't want to kill anyone of them. But the minute I see anyone go out to a terror attack, someone with a weapon comes to our area, I will shoot him without any guilt because that is the situation here in the country.

It may thus be possible to recognise the humanity of an enemy and concurrently be deeply persuaded about the justice of your cause so that you can kill time and again. Perhaps it is possible to recognise the similarity between you and the enemy and still explain the taking of life based on a clear logic of justifiable conflict.

## Conclusion

The question that guided our analysis centred on the lived experience of killing other people. Our argument was twofold: snipers do not always need to dehumanise their targets and they experience killing in conflicting ways, both as pleasurable and as disturbing. This argument challenges dominant explanations of how human beings deal with slaying other human beings. Thus we have underscored the simultaneous use of distancing mechanisms: dehumanising enemies and a constant recognition of their basic humanity. In this sense we accept previous scholarship which has emphasised the ways in which enemies are turned into 'others' so that violence may be perpetrated against them, but continue on to argue that the reality within which soldiers—and in our case snipers—operate is much more complex.

Indeed, by focusing on the level of lived experience, we can comprehend the ways in which feelings of guilt, recurring dreams, sudden flashes of pictures and persistent doubts exist side by side with feelings of satisfaction, achievement, enjoyment and joy. Indeed, these conflicting emotions are part of the way in which snipers continued to perform their military role. We have not heard of cases where snipers have refused to continue serving in their capacity, nor have we found cases of completely unjustified berserk behaviour. Snipers continue to do their work in a cool and calm manner out of a full belief in the justice of their cause. Indeed, the belief that they are preventing the next terror attack or suicide bomber is a key motivator for them.

As we showed when describing their victims/targets, snipers often associate Palestinian individuals with the label 'terrorists'. Yet this assignation does not imply the mandatory dehumanisation of Palestinians. Indeed, our argument is not a simplistic one based on the dehumanisation of others through the use of various appellations: one can be a terrorist and human. For snipers the Palestinians they shoot are threatening human beings, threatening to them, to their fellow soldiers and (potentially) to Israeli civilians. Thus the assignation of 'terrorist' should not be understood as necessarily contradictory to their being humans. Terrorists, for the snipers, as for the majority of Israeli combat troops, do not belong to some category of evil non-human beings but are human beings who are perceived to be dangerous.

It is within this dynamic that the perception of enemies as humans should be understood. To be sure, the snipers talk about enemies as 'them' versus 'us' soldiers. They also dehumanise enemies by objectifying them and (at times) demonising them. But they also understand them to be human beings. What is interesting is that this understanding does not hinder their ability to kill and wound those people whom they perceive to be their enemies. Thus the killing is at times banal and not traumatic; it is not too easy, nor too hard to bear. Within the context of contemporary Israel, marked as it is by a widespread consensus about the threat armed Palestinians pose, the killing is understood as normal, justified, clear and unquestionable. In fact, one could argue that, because the IDF is very widely understood as necessary and trusted by Israeli Jews, the snipers are less traumatised.

To be sure, the process of 'naming' or labelling is akin to the process that Zizek (quoted in our introduction) terms part of the 'schematisation' of enemies so as to make them into appropriate target of hate and struggle. But as our work shows this is not a linear process but one based on tension and contradiction. Our work thus questions the unidirectional argument found in much scholarly literature about the necessity for a totally negative construction of enemies in order to carry out violence against them. Based on our case study (and its limitations), we offer a cautionary message. Sometimes one does not have to turn enemies or foes into lawless beings, unordered entities or evil life forms in order to intervene violently. Rather, enemies may labelled as humans and as 'like us' but violence is still perpetrated against them. In other words, we argue that strict dichotomies of us/them, inside/outside, or human/non-human are much more complex than most of the scholarly literature brings out.

Take the label 'human being' as it was used by our informants. This label forms part of a classificatory system that is intimately connected to the justification for killing. The snipers' reasoning is closely linked to a Zionist text in the sense of connecting their personal understanding to the grand narrative of the IDF protecting the very survival of the Israeli nation-state. In this manner their actions during the Al-Aqsa uprising are subordinated to the *a priori* Zionist text.[26] In this respect the discursive act of aggregation by which the snipers 'name' all offensive actors—whether participating in rallies, directing protests or as armed aggressors—as 'terrorists' should be seen as part of that wider Zionist myth. Let us be very clear: our argument is not that by characterising Palestinians as 'humans' the snipers somehow depoliticise their acts. In fact, quite the opposite: we argue that this very classification is based in a wider model of political conflict and opposing forces using violent means against each other. It is not so much a process of dehumanising which is of significance here but rather the rules of legitimate violence, the culturally specific ideology of violence at work in this case. Israel has been the site of confrontations for so long—and the Palestinians have been a key opponent in these conflicts—that there is a now a rather widespread legitimacy for such killings and woundings as carried out by our interviewees. Our point is thus that snipers classify, make a choice and act, and that their actions are fateful.

Finally, we do not argue that killing by snipers is somehow emblematic of all violence. We do contend, however, that, as scholars, we must be wary of an automatic attachment of negative value to violence. With all the moral difficulty involved in making this point, it is important to understand how people may perpetrate violence through indifference or sometimes enjoyment. Violence does not only belong to the realm of the pathological but is woven into the very fabric of normal everyday life. Thus we do not see violence as something that is inherently pathological or traumatic.[27] One needs to proceed with a careful phenomenological account of violence from the perspective of its agents. Thus there are soldiers who may not feel anything during an act of killing but may feel intensely guilty afterwards; and it is possible to kill easily out of deep personal conviction, to enjoy it and to feel guilty at the very same time. All these facts shed light on one of the most hidden arenas of modern war, but which is in fact a common one among soldiers.

## Notes

We wish to thank Michael Bhatia, Uzi Ben-Shalom, James Burk, Edna Lomsky-Feder, Don Handelman, Don Seeman and Bettina Prato for very helpful comments on a draft of this article. We would also like to thank participants in a panel of the biannual conference of the Inter-University Seminar on Armed Forces and Society and seminars at the US Naval Postgraduate School and the Department of Anthropology of Gothenburg University for their comments.

[1] D Grossman, *On Killing: The Psychological Cost of Learning to Kill in War and Society*, Boston: Little, Brown, 1995; R Holmes, *Acts of War: The Behavior of Man in Battle*, New York: Free Press, 1985; and S Zizek, 'Are we at war? Do we have an enemy?', *London Review of Books*, 24 (10), 2002, at http://www.lrb.co.uk/v24/n10/zize01_.html.

[2] Grossman, *On Killing*; Grossman 'Human factors in war: the psychology and physiology of close combat', in M Evans & A Ryan (eds), *The Human Face of Warfare: Killing, Fear and Chaos in Battle*, London: Allen and Unwin, 1995, pp 5–24; I Hacking, 'Memory science, memory politics', in P Antze & M Lambek (eds), *Tense Past—Cultural Essays in Trauma and Memory*, New York: Routledge, 1996, pp 67–88; WE Kelly (ed), *Post-Traumatic Stress Disorder and the War Veteran Patient*, New York: Brunner/Mazel, 1985; RS Laufer, MS Gallops & E Frey-Wouters, 'War stress and trauma: the Vietnam veteran experience', *Journal of Health and Social Behavior*, 25 (1), 1984, pp 65–85; J McManus, *The Deadly Brotherhood—The American Combat Soldier in World War II*, Novato, CA: Presidio Press, 1998; HZ Winnik, R Moses & O Mortimer (eds), *Psychological Bases of War*, New York/Jerusalem: Quadrangle/Jerusalem Academic Press, 1973; and A Young, 'Bodily memory and traumatic memory', in Antze & Lambek, *Tense Past*, pp 89–102.

[3] B Boene, 'How unique should the military be? A review of representative literature and outline of synthetic formulation', *European Journal of Sociology*, 31 (1), 1990, pp 3–59; P Bourdieu, 'Rethinking the state: genesis and structure of the bureaucratic field', in George Steinmetz (ed), *State/Culture: State-Formation After the Cultural Turn*, Ithaca, NY: Cornell University Press, 1999, pp 53–75; and J Bourke, *An Intimate History of Killing*, London: Granta Books, 1999.

[4] Abbink, 'Preface', in Grossman, *On Killing*; and E Tanay, 'The Vietnam veteran: victim of war', in Kelly, *Post-Traumatic Stress Disorder and the War Veteran Patient*, pp 29–42.

[5] J Peteet, 'Male gender and Rituals of Resistance in the Palestinian Intifada', *American Ethnologist*, 21(1), 1994, pp 31–49; J Ron, 'Varying methods of state violence', *International Organization*, 51 (2), 1997, pp 275–300; Ron, 'Savage restraint: Israel, Palestine and the dialectics of repression', *Social Problems*, 47 (4), 2000, pp 445–472.

[6] E Ben-Ari, 'Masks and soldiering: the Israeli army and the Palestinian uprising', *Cultural Anthropology*, 4 (4), 1989, pp 372–389; and Ben-Ari, *Mastering Soldiers: Conflict, Emotions and the Enemy in an Israeli Military Unit*, Oxford: Berghahn, 1998.

[7] A Fontana, 'War zone traumas and post traumatic stress disorder symptomatology', *Journal of Nervous and Mental Disease*, 180 (12), 1992, pp 748–755; N Krin, 'Violence in the life narratives of soldiers who served lengthy periods in the intifada', unpublished masters thesis, Department of Psychology, Hebrew University of Jerusalem, 1998 (in Hebrew); and RM MacNair, 'Perpetration-induced traumatic stress in combat veterans', *Peace and Conflict*, 8 (1), 2002, pp 63–72.

[8] Bourke, *An Intimate History of Killing*; Grossman, *On Killing*; and B Shalit, *The Psychology of Conflict and Combat*, New York: Praeger, 1988.

[9] Grossman, *On Killing*; A Lieblich, *The Spring of Their Lives*, Jerusalem: Shocken, 1987 (in Hebrew); and McManus, *The Deadly Brotherhood*.

[10] Grossman, 'Human factors in war'; K-YV Ho, 'Butchering fish and executing criminals: public executions and the meanings of violence in late imperial and modern China', in G Aijmer & J Abbink (eds), *Meanings of Violence: A Cross Cultural Perspective*, Oxford: Berg, 2000, pp 141–160; and R J

Lifton, *Home from the War—Vietnam Veterans Neither Victims nor Executioners*, New York: Touchstone, 1973.

[11] Bourke, *An Intimate History of Killing*.

[12] *Ibid*; Holmes, *Acts of War*; and Lifton, *Home from the War*.

[13] Krin, 'Violence in the life narratives of soldiers'.

[14] Grossman, *On Killing*.

[15] Holmes, *Acts of War*, p 361.

[16] Ben-Ari, *Mastering Soldiers*.

[17] S Hirschauer, 'The manufacture of bodies in surgery', *Social Studies of Science*, 21, 1991, pp 279–319.

[18] Ben-Ari, *Mastering Soldiers*; and Shalit, *The Psychology of Conflict and Combat*.

[19] Tanay, 'The Vietnam veteran'.

[20] C Cameron, *American Samurai: Myth, Imagination, and the Conduct of Battle in the First Marine Division, 1941–1951*, Cambridge: Cambridge University Press, 1994; J Dower John, *War Without Mercy: Race and Power in the Pacific War*, New York: Pantheon, 1986; P Fussel, *Wartime: Understanding and Behavior in the Second World War*, New York: Oxford University Press, 1989; W Eisenhart, 'You can't hack it little girl: a discussion of the covert psychological agenda of modern combat training', *Journal of Social Issues*, 31 (4), 1975, pp 13–23; L Kennett, *GI—The American Soldier in World War II*, New York: Scribner, 1987; CF Shatan, 'Bogus manhood, bogus honor: surrender and transfiguration in the United States marine corps', *Psychoanalytic Review*, 64, 1977, pp 586–610; and J Shay, *Achilles in Vietnam: Combat Trauma and the Undoing of Character*, New York: Touchstone, 1995.

[21] For public opinion polls, see http://truman.huji.ac.il/; and A Harel & A Isacharoff, *The Seventh War*, Tel Aviv: Yediot Ahronoth Books, 2004 (in Hebrew).

[22] A somewhat sympathetic account is found in S Anderson, 'An impossible occupation', *New York Times Magazine*, 12 May 2002, while a very critical one is found in International Federation of Human Rights Leagues, 'Operation Defensive Shield', in Reporters Without Borders (eds), *Israel/Palestine: The Black Book*, London: Pluto Press, 2002, pp 70–95.

[23] Ben-Ari, *Mastering Soldiers*; RW Rieber & RJ Kelly, 'Substance and shadow—images of the enemy', in RW Rieber (ed), *The Psychology of War and Peace: The Image of the Enemy*, New York: Plenum Press, 1991, pp 3–39; and Krin, 'Violence in the life narratives of soldiers'.

[24] Bourke, *An Intimate History of Killing*; Shay, *Achilles in Vietnam*, pp 103, 202; and J Verrips, 'When grammatical otherings implode', paper prepared at the workshop 'Grammars of Identity/Alterity: A Structural Approach', 7th Biennial EASA Conference, Copenhagen, 14–17 August 2002.

[25] A Gilbert, *Stalk and Kill: The Thrill and Danger of The Sniper Experience*, New York: St Martin's Paperbacks, 1997; and Grossman, *On Killing*.

[26] R Paine, 'Anthropology beyond the routine: cultural alternatives for the handling of the unexpected', *International Journal of Moral and Social Studies*, 7 (3), 1992, pp 183–203.

[27] E Lomsky-Feder, *As If There Was No War: The Perception of War in the Life Stories of Israeli Men*, Jerusalem: Magnes, 1998 (in Hebrew).

148

# Words as interventions: naming in the Palestine – Israel conflict

JULIE PETEET

Although oft repeated, the dialogue from *Alice in Wonderland* over words and their meaning continues to resonate:

> 'When I use a word,' Humpty Dumpty said, in a rather scornful tone, 'it means just what I choose it to mean—neither more nor less.'
>
> 'The question is,' said Alice, 'whether you can make words mean so many different things.'
>
> 'The question is', said Humpty Dumpty, 'which is to be master—that's all'.

This paper examines the practice of naming events, actions, places and people by the participants in the Palestine – Israel conflict. It explores the way colonialism and the national project utilises transformations in naming to construct place and identities and craft international imaginaries about these places. While Palestinian naming practices are outlined, the paper focuses more on naming by the Israelis because of its status as an objective, conscious part of the project of crafting a national identity and claiming the territory of Palestine for a Jewish homeland and state.

Words to refer to people, places, events, actions and things are critical building blocks in the linguistic repertoire. Names, and their meanings, form part of the cultural systems that structure and nuance the way we see, understand and imagine the world. As such, they are always more than simple reflections of reality, referencing a moral grammar that underwrites and reproduces power.

Terminology is subject to the historical process. Names are thus not only components of a repertoire of mechanisms of rule and a prominent part of historical transitions but are, methodologically speaking, themselves a means of tracking power in this process. Contests over names in the Palestine – Israel conflict, in which the two parties are vastly disparate in terms of weaponry, support from the USA, the prevalence and circulation of narrative and voice in the West, and institutional infrastructure, are certainly an example of this and thus changes in naming should be traced along the lines of power. It is axiomatic that history is written as conceptualised and narrated by the winners. More recently, the same argument could be applied to official Western media sources, where dissenting or alternative views, or even complex argumentation, have been marginalised and muted. Similarly, the words that circulate most profusely and effectively are usually those of the dominant forces as well. Their categories and terms of discourse render domination natural, and part of the taken-for-granted, if you will, as if there were no other possible alternatives. Words are extraordinarily important for the way they embody ideological significance and circulate moral attributes. In other words, in a conflict setting the words chosen from a vast lexicon to describe events, actions, peoples, places and social phenomena reverberate with, uphold or contest power. They constitute moral worlds and the humanity of participants and thus, ultimately, the distribution of rights. A prime example is found in the debate in the USA over the legitimacy of torture; the very possibility of a debate over the potential use of torture was only realised in the context of a 'war on terror' where no one seems able, or even necessarily willing, to define or locate the enemy but is sure they are everywhere. If the 'terrorist' membership in the human community is in doubt, that opens a space to torture 'terrorists' legitimately.

The words deployed to describe adversaries are articulated to particular objectives and world-views. Israeli domination and hegemony in the arena of discourse and terminology is not meant to sway the natives to their ideological and political position; they aim not to convert the natives, so to speak, but simply to pacify them. There is no acquiescence by the Palestinians in the lexical repertoire of Israeli domination. Their words are intended for a largely American audience, which provides the support necessary to maintain the state. Indeed, the lively dialogue and debate in the press in Israel could hardly be printed in the USA without arousing quick and widespread opposition. For example, revisionist scholarship initiated discussions of the Palestinian displacement in 1948 that implicated the Israeli military. In this campaign Palestinian narratives, voices, and their lexicon have been consistently marginalised or silenced in an attempt to structure how the conflict is written, understood and ultimately enters popular, academic and official discourse, imagination and the historical record. Neo-conservatives and prominent American Jewish organisations have engaged in what Beinin calls a 'sustained campaign to delegitimize critical thinking about the Middle East'.[1]

150

## Lost Palestinian narratives

The historical process of de-legitimising Palestinian perspective and voice has unfolded over the decades in several contexts: the invented traditions of modern colonialism, accompanied by a sustained Palestinian resistance, and the field of power between the USA, Israel and Palestine. With its vastly unequal power relations, colonialism typically generates a set of terms and discourses to describe conquered lands as uninhabited, virgin territory, *terra nullius*, uncharted and undiscovered territory, the frontier, wasteland, wilderness, untamed and unoccupied, regardless of the presence, often extensive and hardly unnoticed, of the indigenous population. Inhabitants of these colonised or subjugated areas have been referred to as savages, heathens, barbarians or primitives; more recently they are 'terrorists'. Gasteyer and Flora outline a pattern in the colonial process in which rhetoric about the natives as backward and dangerous surfaces once the initial romantic view of the landscape gives way to the reality of native opposition and often violent responses to settler attempts to appropriate their lands and resources.[2] Early on, Israeli colonisation of Palestine followed this path. Yet, like all such colonial settings, this one produced a unique set of discursive features and patterns. Not only were the natives branded as primitive and later as terrorists and their land described as empty, but the settlers renamed themselves and the places they settled.

More recent colonial and imperial adventures describe subjugated areas as under-utilising their resources, in need of democracy, or as threats to world peace. Whatever the case, names, terms and discourses are pivotal to these projects, part of transforming landscape, identities and forms of power. The Zionist project to colonise Palestine and settle it with Jewish immigrants continues to generate its own particular set of discourses and terms to which Palestinians are highly attuned. They have a visceral experience of what it means when a settlement in occupied territories is referred to as a 'neighbourhood' in the international media. Or when resistance to occupation is widely, and uncritically, accepted as terrorism.

Words circulate and acquire meaning and intensity in a field of power. In the 'hierarchy of credibility', the dominant group's narratives are accepted as 'objective and legitimate'; while those of the lower-ranked, often defeated, group are derided as crudely fashioned propaganda and thus met with contempt.[3] In the end they often fade away, or alternatively, they form the core of an alternative discourse or world-view.[4] To illustrate, Israel refers to 1948 as the year of its 'independence', while Palestinians refer to same set of events during that fateful year as *al-nekba*, the catastrophe or disaster. For both, it was a watershed year; Israel declared statehood and emptied the area of anywhere from roughly 710 000 – 780 000 Palestinian inhabitants and has consistently refused to allow their or their descendants' return.[5] The Israeli narrative of a small, besieged and plucky group of Jews facing a massive, co-ordinated Arab assault took hold in the West and, until recently, was firmly entrenched in the standard historical record, particularly after the 1967 war.

The Palestinian narrative, which claims that a well armed, well trained and well supported military with institutions of state faced disorganised, ideologically disparate, under-armed and leaderless Palestinians and an inefficient and weak set of Arab forces with outdated weaponry, was silenced outside the Middle East until quite recently when the turn in Israeli scholarship towards a revisionist history of the period more-or-less confirmed the Palestinian narrative.

Naming that historical moment 'Independence', 'facilitated the narrativization of history, the transformation of what happened into that which is said to have happened'. Furthermore, the act of naming occludes process and shifts the focus to the single event and its trajectory. The Jewish state arose from the destruction of Palestine, as a political entity and as a particular geosocial space. Sustained attempts have been made to deny Palestinian memories and narratives of what transpired in 1948. That 15 May is annually celebrated as 'Independence Day' in Israel is a sign of the Israelis power to define the historical events of the time 'cleansed of traces of power'.[6] Many of the attempts to deny a Palestinian voice and memory are concerned with obstructing the emergence of an image of the Palestinian as a victim. Just as two natives can not occupy the same territory and claim origins and sovereignty neither can there be two victims making a claim for their narrative and memories to prevail.

Recently, naming and rhetoric were easily reconfigured to incorporate the USA's restructured global role in a post-11 September world order of absolute dualities, where Israelis (allies of the West) are civilised and Palestinians (forces of evil and darkness) form part of the vast global terror network and where US and Israeli goals and visions increasingly converge and appear almost seamless. Israeli Prime Minister Ariel Sharon quickly capitalised on 11 September to declare that 'Together we can defeat these forces of evil'.[7] Criticism of the Bush administration's handling of US foreign policy and actions in the Middle East and Afghanistan have been muzzled and dissenters, or even those who posed questions, were labelled unpatriotic. This mirrored and mimicked the pattern of response to criticism of Israel's policies, which bring forth quick accusations of anti-Semitism.

## Naming and action in Palestine

What is the relationship between naming and action? Do rhetoric and particular forms of naming and renaming inform particular kinds of actions? Representations, discourses and imagery of Palestinians are neither inert and innocuous nor do they produce an effect on their own. Discourse engenders, naturalises and legitimises certain actions because it occurs in the institutional context of power, in this case, settler–colonial rule.[8] Although not always neatly orchestrated, a synchronisation between forms of knowledge and practice is identifiable where the organisation of power is such that those producing knowledge of a subject are in a position to *enact* as well as sustain and reproduce it. Discourses can be indicative of and embody elements of predictability. Carefully calibrated wars of words often precede actual military conflict, portending action. One need only think of Hutu radio broadcasts in the months preceding the massacre of the Tutsi and moderate Hutus and more recently of the terms used to refer to the people of Darfur in the Sudan. The issue here is how Zionist discourses, representations, imagery and forms of knowledge are articulated and accompanied by sociopolitical practices and institutions to structure communal relationships and practices towards the Palestinians.

In the politics of place representations are replete with meaning.[9] Words and names form the substance of representations and as such they form a field of intense meaning and activity. Representations, often circulated as authoritative, are hardly inert; they can and do inform actions, endowing them with legitimacy and justification. Shifts in Israeli, Lebanese and Palestinian representations of Palestinians in Lebanon and their camps provide an index to the refugee experience in Lebanon, tracking its vicissitudes and its power.[10]

Naming a place functions as a public claim. Repeating a name, standardising it, and displacing former names normalises it. The names that endow place with meaning and resonance, particularly in settler–colonial settings are often ideological invocations, part and parcel of an imaginative, often violent geography, that are then standardised by the state and often the academy. In other words, naming is an assertion of power. In the context of the Israeli–Palestinian conflict, naming can be a diagnostic of power; conflicts over naming reflect and are integral to contests over control and ownership. Each party tries to superimpose its name over territory, places, actions and interpretations of events. Whose nomenclature prevails derives from the ability to have one's narration and lexicon accepted as the standard one. Naming is also part of constructing collective memories and traditions. All national projects spawn and must necessarily form narratives of a past in order to craft a sense of a collective present and future.

The colonisation and dispossession of Palestinians involves what Said has called 'at least two memories, two sorts of historical invention, two sorts of geographical imagination'.[11] Each of these involves a highly contrasting set of words, names and discourses. Yet these are not symmetrical sets. Indeed, the Palestinian voice has been silenced or muffled and always juxtaposed to an Israeli interpretation and voice. Indeed, a Palestinian voice and narration cannot stand alone in the media or the academy and is rarely unaccompanied or not followed by an Israeli counterpoint. Yet the reverse is rarely the case.

## Crafting places, peoples and identities

Landscapes are culture before they are nature; constructs of the imagination projected onto wood and water and rock...But it should also be acknowledged that once a certain idea of landscape, a myth, a vision, establishes itself in an actual place, it has a peculiar way of muddling categories, of making metaphors more real that their referents; of becoming, in fact, part of the scenery.[12]

*Places*

In a state based on a settler – colonial movement and ideology, Israeli naming strategies have an overlapping two-fold purpose. First, these strategies attempt to nativise Israelis by consciously and methodically elaborating historically deep ties to place. Second, they accomplish this by, in part, erasing a Palestinian presence and history, and thus any claim to the land of Palestine and legitimate rights to reside there. Palestinian naming strategies occur in the context of mass displacement, dispossession and a sustained resistance movement. The names they use are less suggestive of a project of remaking place, than of a retention of legitimate rights to reside there.

The imposition of particular names on place is an ideological invocation that is integral to the more encompassing project of claiming territory and creating sentiments of belonging. Thus, from the beginning, the practice of naming has pointed to a contest over names and rights to place in Palestine. Settler – colonial movements engage in conscious renaming, aware of its pivotal role in creating a sense of place, ownership and identities. Naming is a practice that contributes to the construction of place, distinguishing it from other places and endowing it with particular, culturally meaningful attributes. In this way naming can be an act of intervention, a way of organising and giving meaning to place and thus staking a claim and imposing ways of conceptualising and navigating in it. Finally, once in circulation, they gain a currency which can then be difficult to dislodge.

The Zionist project of forging a link between the contemporary Jewish community and the land of Palestine was a project of extraordinary remaking: of language, of place and relation to it, and of selves and identities. Naming, a form of symbolic intervention, points to a cultural politics of landscape and competing nationalisms. In this instance naming a place facilitated claiming it and endowing it with a particular history articulated to state-building and nationalist images of historical depth and religious imagery. Names can evoke or commemorate certain historical, religious or political events or eras. Thus the currency of place names can be an indication of power arrangements and is heavily implicated in the politics of landscape. Between a Jewish presence in the biblical era and modern Zionism, Palestine was conceptualised as a wasteland. The Zionist project understood naming as serious business and established the Names Committee in the 1930s. With statehood, the new Israel Place-Names Committee replaced the Names Committee and was charged with changing place names to either biblical or national/Zionist ones. Israeli journalist and former deputy mayor of Jerusalem, Meron Benvenisti, writes that 'every Arabic name, even if no ancient Hebrew name had preceded it' was erased from the map, an act he equated with a 'declaration of war' on Palestinian heritage, attributed to the Zionist 'desire to make direct contact with their own ancient heritage'. Noting the centrality of naming to nationalist territorial claims, Benvenisti comments on his father's leading role in devising a 'new Hebrew map of the land, a renewed title deed'. Renaming was intended to further the 'recreation of a Biblical ancient homeland' and the severing of 'any bonds with the Diaspora'.[13] Linguistic kinship between Hebrew and Arabic meant this was often easily accomplished. For example, al-Bassa became Betzet, Saffuriyyah became Tzippori, and Baysan became Beit Shean. Renaming places with Hebrew or biblical names establishes a 'narrative of "origin" and therefore "originary rights"...the history of the place is then constructed as a moral history, with a specific and proper distribution of rights and entitlements'.[14] In other words, transforming the landscape via names, making it an artefact of the imagination, but also displacing the natives and settling it, making it a real artefact, was supposed to bring it in line with the biblical era on the one hand and modern colonial ideology on the other.

In exile in Lebanon, through culturally grounded practices of ordinary living, Palestinians imposed their social organisation, cognitive–spatial maps and names on camp spaces, thus crafting a geosocial space of Palestine in exile. Naming units of space produced place, as did the social activities and relationships enacted in them, attesting to the remarkable human capacity to create new cultural and social forms of daily life and meaning from monumental loss. Organising and naming camp space by pre-1948 Palestinian villages crafted both a memory-scape and a practical, spatial enactment of the lost homeland. Palestinian refugee camps were intended as transit centres in preparation for local integration. Yet instead they became oppositional spaces appropriated and endowed with alternative meanings.

The inscription of a Galilean landscape in the camps launched the crafting of place out of space and made apparent the simultaneous continuity and transformation of social life. Villages were relocated, newly landscaped and socially reconfigured, while their original geographic spaces were renamed and occupied by foreigners.[15] The practices of simply dwelling and naming may impose the most basic features of place-making. Bourj al-Barajneh camp was constituted by a spatial array of a number of northern villages in six named areas: Kweikat, Tarshiha, al-Kabri, Sheikh Daoud, al-Ghabisiyya and al-Chaab. 'Ayn al-Hilweh had named quarters for the villages of Saffuriyya, 'Amqa, Loubia and al-Bassa/al-Zeeb, among others. To move around inside many camps, one passed from one named village to another. In daily usage, the term *'ahl'* (people) referred to people of a particular village, for example 'ahl al-'Amqa', temporally compressing place and locating people, individually and collectively, in terms of particular places. Named village areas in the camps were actually family or clan units of particular villages that settled together.

The larger the village, the more distinct its area. Smaller villages occupied spaces intermediate to larger, more visible and marked villages. Thus Palestinian settlement and naming of places of exile by villages, however partial, asserted an intimate claim to now distant, re-landscaped and occupied space, forging a connection between time and space which was inherited by successive generations through dwelling in these camp areas and being part of a social world organised, in part, on a village model. In a sense, village areas have been the physical and symbolic memory, transmitting the space of Palestine to the present, giving the displaced a deep, visceral and everyday connection to past time, place and social relationships. With the rise of the resistance movement new names appeared to overlay or coexist with village names. Resistance clinics and offices became new geographical markers. Later, the civil war in Lebanon, the Israeli invasion of 1982 and the camp wars (1985–88) pitting Palestinians against the Lebanese Shi'ite militia 'Amal devastated the refugee camps. Sieges and massacres spawned new names for old, familiar places. Alleys formerly known by the name of families living on them were re-named 'sniper's alley'. The main thoroughfare running alongside Chatila camp in Beirut was re-named 'Street of the Massacre' after the 1982 massacre of Palestinians and Lebanese civilians by the Israel-supported, -armed and -led Christian right-wing Lebanese militias.

### Naming individuals and the national project

In the Hebraisation project, renaming encompassed individuals as well. In 'returning' to Israel, the Zionists were also remaking themselves. Zionism was a rejection of the Jewish diaspora and the image of the effeminate Jewish male, unable to defend himself, family and community against the murderous violence of the non-Jew. With settlement in Palestine, the 'New Jew' would emerge, militant, tanned, close to the soil and able to defend self and community.[16] The new Jew, the *sabra* was conceived as the antithesis of the "Old World" European Jew'.[17] Taking a Hebrew name was integral to the process of becoming a new person, akin to a rite of passage, where one emerges from a liminal state with a new identity and position in society. For example, immigrants such as David Gruen of Poland became David Ben-Gurion; Golda Meyerson (née Mabovitch) became Golda Meir; Ariel Scheinerman became Ariel Sharon; Moshe Smolansky became Moshe Ya'alon. More recently young settlers in the occupied territories continue the practice of adopting Hebrew names.[18] In many cultural settings names embody a sort of magical property and power. They create sacred linkages between past and future, between the contemporary and distant times and spaces. Zionist renaming attempts to connect history and the sacred by telescoping to craft the appearance of an intimate and deep connection between past time and place and the present. Legitimacy derives from the sacred nature of this linkage.

Although Palestinians did not engage in nationalism as a modern project of construction to the same degree as the Zionists did, mass dispossession, exile and the formation of a national liberation movement did initiate the beginnings of an objectified approach to national identity. Palestinians had less need to craft a relationship to place and land carefully and purposefully; they did, however, have to refashion themselves as militants in order to respond to their predicament. Self-naming played a role in Palestinian fashioning of new selves and identities. Upon joining the resistance movement, many young men, especially those in official positions or in the guerrilla units, adopted a *nom de guerre*. On a practical level these were intended to disguise one's true identity and thus were part and parcel of the

156

secrecy involved in guerrilla warfare. On another level new names signified participation in the resistance movement as a catalyst in the remaking of selves. Men followed the common Arab practice of teknonym (naming by relationship to someone else) whereby males are referred to by the name of their first born son, so that Abu Ali, for example, is the father of Ali. Most of these young men had not sired sons but the practice of naming oneself as such suggests an assertion of masculinity. Yasser Arafat was for long known as Abu Ammar, although he never fathered a son. He was also referred to as *al-khatiyar* (the 'old man'), again suggesting patriarchal power and the wisdom of age and tradition. Some men adopted *noms de guerre* of famous heroes of national liberation movements such as 'Che' or 'Castro' or 'Guevara' or 'Gaza Guevara'. Others adopted names that reflected profound sentiments in response to dispossession or occupation, such as Abu Ghadab (father of wrath). In short, naming was critical in a masculine remaking of the self as militant and revolutionary. Women militants simply adopted female pseudonyms with little nationalistic, revolutionary or emotive character. During the resistance era of autonomy in Lebanon (1968–82), baby girls were given names of villages and towns in Palestine; for example, Baysan and Jenin, towns in Palestine, became popular girls' names, as did Rami, a village in the Galilee, for boys.

Palestinian self-remaking through names parallels in some significant ways the Jewish practice of adopting Hebrew names. In both cases renaming follows on the heels of large-scale disaster, where masculinity and the ability to respond were in question. Where Jewish renaming was a reaction to the image of the effete, passive Jew unable effectively to resist the onslaught of genocidal anti-Semitism, the Palestinians have longed questioned themselves as to why they were unable to mount an effective response to Zionist colonisation. Their self-image emphasised the naive peasant who did not truly comprehend the magnitude of the Zionist intent to build a Jewish state in Palestine and they saw themselves as duped by a largely urban-based Palestinian leadership more concerned with its own survival.

### Natives as non-natives

The Zionist goal of establishing a Jewish state in Palestine also presented a tremendous linguistic challenge: the revival of the Hebrew language. As Palestinian writer Anton Shammas so astutely noted, this process involved not only the displacement of the Palestinians from their homeland but that of their vernacular as well.[19] They lost not only homes and lands but also their voice. They were absorbed by a larger Arab world to which the Israelis had physically and linguistically confined them. In part this illuminates the Israeli shirking from the term 'Palestinian' and the subsumption of Palestinians under 'Arabs'. The term 'Palestinian people' only appeared in Israeli official documents in the 1990s.[20] Before that the official Israeli stance was encapsulated by Golda Meir's now infamous remark: 'There is no such thing as a Palestinian'. With the suppression of Palestinian narratives, and Palestinians, from any but a menacing presence in their national narrative,

Zionists intended the Palestinians to disappear as a political question subsumed under the broader Arab category. The intifada and the peace process that followed in the 1990s changed this.

With the first intifada (1987–91), the once 'inaudible' and 'mute' Palestinians gained a voice. The 'Arab–Israeli conflict' was now joined by, but never superseded by, the 'Israeli–Palestinian conflict'. Shammas claims that 'The real dispute has always been over speech, over the language of discourse, and not over the identity of the speakers. That's why the Israelis seem to be saying that only territorialized states can speak and negotiate; the Palestinians are stateless, so they cannot speak, let alone negotiate'.[21] It also implies that non-state forms of resistance are illegitimate.

The Zionist movement engaged in an elaborate discursive construction of the Palestinian population through categories of time, space, belonging and rights, as well as notions of relation to and power over place.[22] The central issue in the construction of a Zionist self was relation to place, the practice of producing it, and nativising the European Jew. The term of reference for Jewish settlement in Palestine/Israel is 'return', a term that draws upon religious texts for legitimacy in the modern period. The suffix 're-' implies to 'do again', to 'repeat' and indicates a previous state of being to which one is returning. To return is to reclaim and to re-establish; for Zionists who desired to 'return' to Israel, the land was to be 'reclaimed' and a Jewish community 're-established' in order to make Israel itself reappear. Through their efforts the desert would bloom, the swamps would be drained and the barren plains would be made to produce once again. Returning to a place implies that they once owned it and were now taking repossession. Thousands of years of a complex history and ethnic and religious pluralistic social life were simply telescoped and disappeared. To return and reclaim and re-establish a Jewish presence meant nativising the Jew.

However, a Palestinian majority was an obstacle to this project of a Jewish state in Palestine. A land heavily populated by another people undermined the notion of Jewish claims to ownership, of a 'return' to a place imagined as empty, even though it was teeming with inhabitants. If the Jews were the natives, what were the Palestinians? Israelis, particularly the more ardent and religiously motivated, often refer to Palestinians both in Israel and in the occupied territories as 'foreigners'. In summer 2004, as acres of olive groves were being uprooted to make way for construction of a 24-foot high concrete wall extending well into Palestinian territory, and enclosing the rest of Palestine into numerous walled enclaves dotted with checkpoints that control mobility, protesters asked soldiers guarding the bulldozers why they were destroying cultivated Palestinian fields. The heavily armed soldiers pointed their rifles at the protestors and yelled, 'They are foreigners here. This all belongs to us'. In a poignant display of performative emotion, an elderly Palestinian woman from the village stood in front of one of the few remaining olive trees in a devastated field of uprooted trees littering the landscape and, holding an olive branch, angrily chanted, 'They can come from Poland, they can come from Russia, they can come from America, and they can come from Ethiopia, but this will always be ours! This is Palestinian land.'

*Naming territory*

While the Israelis would not concede the use of the term Palestinian or Palestine until the past decade, the Palestinians for their part, spent decades referring to Israel as the Zionist entity or occupied Palestine. In WAFA (the Palestinian news agency), radio broadcasts and news about Israel were given a byline that referred to them as originating from 'Occupied Palestine' or the 'Zionist Entity'. With the beginnings of the 'peace process' and the PLO's recognition of Israel in the late 1980s, use of these names diminished.

With the advent of the 1967 war and Israel's occupation of the remainder of historic Palestine, the West Bank and Gaza Strip, Israel began to refer to the West Bank by its biblical names of Judea and Samaria. Which terms Israelis use—Judea and Samaria, administered territories, or occupied territories—is indicative of the former's ideological and political stances on Israel's biblical right to this area, the idea of trading land for peace and recognising a Palestinian presence and the Palestinians' right to form a sovereign state. In the 1990s the US media went from calling the West Bank and Gaza 'Israeli occupied territories' to 'disputed territory' or 'Israel's occupied territory'. In Arabic they are referred to variously as Palestine, the West Bank, Gaza Strip or the Occupied Territories.

Settlements in the West Bank, Gaza Strip and East Jerusalem, illegal in international law, are now often referred to in the media euphemistically as 'neighbourhoods' for example, Gilo, a settlement in the suburbs of Jerusalem, is a common example, referred to routinely as a 'Jewish neighbourhood" in the US media. Likewise, the swath of Jewish settlements around Jerusalem is called 'Jewish neighbourhoods'. In May 2002 the Israeli newspaper *Ha'aretz* reported that the Israeli media had been prohibited from using the terms 'settlements' or 'settlers'. CNN had already adopted a policy of referring to Gilo not as a settlement but rather as 'a Jewish neighborhood on the outskirts of Jerusalem, built on land occupied by Israel'. CNN had been under fairly intense pressure from a number of pressure groups to adopt this policy.[23] As Fairness and Accuracy in Reporting (FAIR) noted in its media advisory of 2002, CNN, the *New York Times* and National Public Radio's reporting on suicide bombings neglected to mention that they occurred in areas of Jerusalem such as French Hill and Gilo, which have been occupied since 1967.[24] While this certainly would not excuse such actions, this kind of reporting glosses over the international legal context of occupation in which the Palestine–Israel conflict takes place, where settlements are illegal, the occupying power is forbidden from settling its own population in these areas, and the Palestinians are denied basic human and civil rights.

*Jerusalem*

The city of Jerusalem (*al-Quds* in Arabic and *Yerushalaim* in Hebrew) is a contentious site in the Palestinian–Israeli conflict. Claimed by both Palestinians and Israelis as the capital of their states, the words used in their contrasting narratives and lexicons are thoroughly and unequivocally saturated with political, religious and ideological meanings. What Israelis refer to as the unified city of Jerusalem, Palestinians refer to as occupied Jerusalem, or East and West Jerusalem, to signify the absence of unity and East Jerusalem's international status as occupied territory. Although part of Jerusalem is officially occupied territory, the media commonly refer to it as part of Israel. The Hebrew word derives from the Aramaic and means 'city of peace'. In English, *Yerushalaim* becomes Jerusalem. Arabic speakers call the city *Bayt al-Maqdis* (House of Sanctity) or more popularly *al-Quds al-Sharif* which in daily contemporary usage is shortened to *al-Quds.*[25]

For the past 1300 years the skyline of Jerusalem has been dominated by the golden Dome of the Rock which sits atop the Haram al-Sherif (Noble Sanctuary), the massive rectangular stone structure on Mt Moriah. The peak of Mt Moriah is where it is believed that God ordered Abraham to sacrifice his son. Muslims believe that the prophet Mohammed landed at the site after his night flight from Mecca to Jerusalem. The site of the first Jewish temple, built by Solomon around 3000 years ago, is thought to be beneath or very close to the Dome. Over this site a second temple was constructed by Herod and destroyed in 70 AD. All that remains of the temple is the Western Wall, or Wailing Wall, now a site of Jewish prayer. In the disciplines of art history and history, the term *Haram al-Sherif,* which refers to the whole complex, has been standard use.

In the past couple of decades a group known as the Temple Mount and Land of Israel Faithful Movement has called for 'liberating the Temple Mount from Arab (Islamic occupation)'. They refer to the Dome of the Rock and al-Aqsa Mosque, which sit atop the *Haram al-Sherif*, as 'pagan shrines'. Their ultimate goal is to build a third temple. Such an endeavour requires the destruction of the Islamic sites. Since the 1967 occupation of the area and the rise of the national-religious right in Israel, the term has been gradually displaced by referring to the area as the Temple Mount. The US media, Israeli tourism and Israelis in general routinely refer to the *Haram al-Sherif* as the Temple Mount. By the 1990s Temple Mount had acquired widespread currency, displacing a Palestinian and Muslim association with the site.

American Christian fundamentalists, now the backbone of US support for Israel, have a particular vision of the second coming of Christ. It can take place only when the Jews have returned to Israel and created a nation, when Jerusalem is under Jewish control, and the ancient temple is rebuilt. Once the Islamic sites are erased from the international imagination, and the term Temple Mount acquires widespread currency, will the actual erasing of those sites seem so far-fetched? The Temple Mount Faithful are occasionally investigated and arrested for plotting to blow up the Islamic sites. Does language and naming precede and underwrite such an action? In this case, are the words predictive and diagnostic?

The most recent Israeli strategy to maximise the acquisition of Palestinian land, prevent the establishment of a contiguous Palestinian state and impose a policy of economic and social strangulation is the wall Israel has constructed well inside the occupied West Bank. Israelis refer to it as a fence, a 'security fence' or a barrier. Palestinians call it the wall (*al-jidar*) or Apartheid wall. The US media refer to it as a fence, security fence, or occasionally, a security wall. The word 'security' legitimises and deflects questions about the legality of the wall, the intent behind it, its violation of human rights and its highly injurious impact on the local population. Each side of the wall is marked by visuals. On the Israeli side are painted colourful scenes of the countryside—meadows, trees and blue sky. This aestheticises the wall's stark, grey appearance. The Palestinian side bears the marks of colourful, angry graffiti. For example 'Sharon = Nazi', 'Jerusalem is stronger than Apartheid', and 'No Wall'.

## Visions of the future

'Return' and 'refugees' are hotly contested words that reverberate with intense political meaning. Israel has longed claimed that in 1948 Palestinians 'abandoned' their lands and home, as if leaving a place is equivalent to giving up rights to it. Focusing on the construction of moral narratives of Jewish 'precedence of both presence and entitlement', Jayyusi astutely analysed how Israelis frequently deploy the term 'abandoned', with its moral connotations, to describe empty Palestinian villages that could then be renamed and resettled. An abandoned village 'provides a moral ground for entitlement to lay claim to the village land'.[26] And if Palestinians had abandoned their homes, the logic goes, they were not really attached to them. Place and its identity were being constructed through the historical imposition of moral boundaries.

'Refugee' is another freighted term. The international community initially assumed the Palestinian refugees would integrate into neighbouring Arab countries and forget their homeland. The refugee problem was supposed to disappear after a few years of 'rehabilitation' through employment and services provided by the United Nations Relief and Works Agency for Palestinian Refugees (UNRWA). Initially 'Rehabilitation' was in the title, as though refugees were somehow in a pathological state that could be remedied through humanitarian interventions. Israel has insisted that what transpired in 1948 was an 'exchange' of populations. Underlying the claim that Jewish immigrants be classified as refugees is the issue of compensation. Israel contends that it should be absolved of paying compensation to Palestinian refugees or allowing them to return as detailed in UN General Assembly Resolution 194. If Jewish immigrants from Arab countries and Palestinian refugees were part of a population exchange then Palestinian claims to compensation are cancelled by Jewish claims. If Palestinians receive compensation so should Arab Jews.

Israeli law stipulates that Jews from all over the world have the 'right of return'. The right of return for Palestinians is internationally recognised yet denied by Israel. But, in this conflict, there can only be one return, one exile and one victim. Israel thus rejects the notion of Palestinians as victims with the right of return. Palestinians still cling to the notion of return to the homeland but evince a richly reconfigured modernist vision.

In the 1990s when I was working in Palestinian refugee camps in Lebanon, a curious story was being told. A young boy from the Shatila refugee camp has a dream of the long-awaited and fought for return to Palestine. All the refugees board buses and head south for the border. Once in Palestine, the people of the village of Tarshiha return to Tarshiha, the people of the village of al-Bassa return to al-Bassa, and so on. A busload of refugees from Shatila camp chooses not to return to the residents' places of origin. As former Shatila residents, they stay together and build a new village.

The dream story has a genealogy and a political and cultural resonance worth exploring. It was elicited by a Syrian director while filming a documentary on Shatila in the early 1990s. In Lebanese writer Elias Khoury's novel *The Kingdom of Strangers*, Faysal, the 11-year-old boy who had the dream, is later killed by gunfire. Khoury writes: 'he knew he would never return to Palestine—he would go there. No one will return. Return is a fantasy. We return—that is to say we go.'[27] Immediately before relating Faysal's dream, Khoury writes about Emil, an Israeli student in New York city. Emil relates how his father, a Polish Jew, fled the impending Holocaust and ended up in Palestine. '"My father didn't want to return to Palestine," Emil said. "You mean go," I said. "He didn't want to return," he said. "You mean go," I said. Albert Azayev [the father] was not like Faysal.'

Khoury explores the difference between the Polish Jew who is ambivalent about going to Palestine, whose son, 50 years later, dubs it a 'return', and Faysal, who dreams of 'returning to Palestine'. Yet to Khoury, in the present context, Faysal's dream is about 'going' rather than 'returning'. It evokes unmediated linearity on the one hand and on the other points to the ways in which Palestinian exile and the social movements generated in it forged new relationships and shaped identities and ideas of community and polity. I first heard this story in Shatila in 1994 and subsequently among Palestinians in Beirut. In the camp, it was told with both amusement and as a commentary on who the camp residents are and the overwhelming significance of exilic place and identity on their contemporary identity and aspirations. By the time I heard it told by a Palestinian acquaintance in Michigan a couple of years later, I began to realise its potency. A narrative whose currency crosses multiple borders, it locates the refugee camps in a border zone, not just spatially between Palestine, Lebanon and Israel, but as sites where confinement and collective suffering and experiences mediate the seeming linearity of exile between points of departure and points of return/going. The dream encapsulates the refugees' transition from Palestinian village to a more inclusive vision of place, nation and identity. This futuristic narrative of return does not evoke nostalgia for a past that is certainly no longer attainable.

For Palestinian refugees return, or going to, is still imagined within the geographical space of Palestine, but the social relations and the political arrangements such a return entails have been fundamentally and inevitably reconfigured. They are not based on an unmediated, bucolically imagined past organised around kin, village and localised identities; rather, the experience of exile and life in the seemingly narrow spaces of refugee camps has re-created the world, expanding the boundaries of community and lines of inclusion. Exile has forged new social bonds and sentiments and new ways of locating oneself in the world.

As a result of this kind of vision and that of Israelis for a more inclusive state of its citizens, an ideological, as well as geopolitical, third space is identifiable. It is 'Palestine/Israel' which implies recognition of both parties' claims to and presence in the same geographic space. Implicit in the term is the notion of a one-state solution, a state in the space of Palestine/Israel for all its citizens. In other words, a secular, democratic state rather than an exclusivist state where citizenship is based on ethno-religious factors.

## Violence, humanness and human rights

The notion of 'epistemic violence' refers to the process by which colonial thought shaped colonial subjects as inherently different.[28] Over the course of much of the previous century rhetoric and words were selectively deployed, repeated, insisted upon and entered mainstream language to construct Palestinians discursively as beyond the pale of humanity. The moral lexicon deployed by Israelis and the Western media has cast them as irrational, terrorist demons unsuited for membership in the human community; this has become more pronounced in the wake of 11 September and the war on terror which coincided with Israel's increased settlements in the West Bank and Sharon's assumption of power.

From the first decades of the century, when Zionists first encountered Palestinians, to the present period of military occupation and settlement, words used to describe the Palestinians have displayed both consistency and change. This discursive construction of the violent and primitive Palestinian underpins and legitimises his/her continued displacement, political exclusion and occupation. In a broader context, representations of the colonised often fall into a binary opposition between 'inherently violent or innately peaceful'.[29] The paradox between an imputed lack of attachment to place and yet the apparent willingness to fight for it was resolved by classifying Palestinian violence as irrational, without just cause. For example, Zionist discourse referred to the 1936–39 revolt of the Palestinians against both the British Mandate and the growing Zionist movement as 'a series of riots' and those involved as 'a gang of robbers, murderers, and bandits', thus obstructing an understanding of manifestations of Palestinian nationalism and their discontent with colonisation.[30]

Coupled with a violent nature, Palestinians have been classified zoomorphically. Avraham Stern, founder of the Stern Gang or Lehi, precursor to the Likud Party, said: 'The Arabs are not a nation but a mole that grew in the wilderness of the eternal desert. They are nothing but murderers.'[31] In the wake of Israel's 1982 invasion of Lebanon, the then Israeli Chief of Staff, Rafael Eitan, said the Palestinians in the occupied territories would be like 'drugged cockroaches in a bottle'. In reference to the intifada, former Prime Minister Yitzhak Shamir likened Palestinians to 'grasshoppers'. More recently, Labor Party leader Ehud Barak told a *New York Times* correspondent, 'You know, we are still living in a jungle', which he characterises as 'the dark and backward old Middle East'. He explained the difference between the two major political parties in Israel, the Labor and the Likud: 'We're both trying to kill the mosquito...But at the same time we're trying to drain the swamp, while Likud is saying the swamp is ours and we'll never give it up. We believe the only way to overcome terrorism is to solve the source of the problem.' The path chosen is to 'kill the mosquito' by draining the swamp.

In the contemporary occupied West Bank, Hebron is one of the tensest spots. Its 7000 ultra-religious, armed settlers, heavily guarded by the Israeli Army, maintain a presence in the centre of town. In the settler area, where some Palestinians still reside, Palestinians must hold a permit to reside in their own homes. In a lengthy article in *The New Yorker*, on settlers in the occupied territories, writer Jeffrey Goldberg notes that 'what the Jews call King David Street...the Arabs call Marytrdom Street', which speaks to the deadly nature of public space for Palestinians. The Jewish zone is called 'sterile' and only Arabs with passes are allowed to enter. 'Sterile' suggests a medicalised discourse of pathology and disease. As a consequence of this dehumanising characterisation, in a context of occupation where the local population is denied the same civil and political rights as the occupier, its vulnerability to abuse is palpable. For example, in 1994 Baruch Goldstein, a Brooklyn doctor who had immigrated to Israel, entered a mosque in Hebron and gunned down 29 worshipers. He was a hero to many religiously inspired settlers, and bumper stickers read 'Dr Goldstein Cures the Ills of Israel'. Dr Goldstein is not called a terrorist in the US or Israeli media but an 'extremist'. Many settlers immigrate from the USA and bring with them a set of racialised images with deep roots in American culture and history that can then be appended to those existent in Israel, particularly among the most fanatical wing of the settler movement. In reporting on settlers in the West Bank for *The New Yorker*, Jeffrey Goldberg heard Palestinians referred to as 'sand niggers'.[32]

A common Israeli practice is to refer to Palestinians by a generic Arab first name such as 'Ahmed' or 'Fatima'; this is akin to decades of whites in the American South referring to all African American men as 'boys' and calling them 'boy' rather than by their first or last name.[33] The intent was to deny the personal identity and dignity that comes with being afforded recognition as an individual human being.

The philosophy underlying the Universal Declaration of Human Rights, and associated conventions, is that rights devolve by virtue of membership in the human community. By definition, universal human rights implies a community of humans with some common denominator of values. Thus notions of humanity and the concept of human rights are closely interwoven and the distribution of human rights follows the lines of humanity. While universal human rights have been enshrined in international law and accepted by almost every state in the world, human rights violations and torture continue to be widely practised. Aside from issues of sovereignty and lack of mechanisms of enforcement, how do states legitimise and perpetuate the mass violation of human rights? Israel has a well established record of torture of Palestinian detainees. Israel's Landau Commission, which begin its work in 1987 on the alleged use of torture against Palestinian prisoners and detainees, affirmed the right of the state to torture Palestinians by renaming it, euphemistically, 'moderate physical pressure'.[34] Indeed, Israel is the only state to have legitimised torture, so far.

It is commonly accepted that violence against civilians perpetrated by the state is rarely called terrorism. Instead it is couched in the rhetoric of national security, self-defence and legitimate retaliation. International lawyer John Whitbeck is on the mark when he deems terrorism an epithet with 'no intrinsic meaning' and its impact 'thought-deadening'.[35] The term 'terrorist' is often applied to any act of resistance and constructs a subject that is a legitimate target of military intervention and the violation of human rights. Such appellations often implicate whole populations, and then become the rationale for collective punishment. The term has profound implications and is potent, in part, because it locates the 'terrorist' as beyond the pale of civilised society and the reaches of international diplomacy. All encapsulating, with implications of senseless rage, 'evil' and destruction, it requires no further discussion or analysis, nor, most significantly, a context. If one's adversaries are terrorists, the only way to disarm them is not by addressing grievances or causes of discontent and violence, and engaging in dialogue or political negotiations, but by all-out war in which international law can be circumvented. Extrajudicial measures, collective punishment and widely disproportionate military responses to quell acts of resistance can be deployed with a fair degree of impunity. A historical trajectory is identifiable in these terms of reference. For decades, the demon other was the Palestinian male terrorist; now it is the crazed, male, Muslim Palestinian. Secular demons have been replaced by religious ones intersecting with the rise of militant Islam and US declarations of war on terrorism.

McAlister provides an intriguing way of thinking about the US – Israel convergence of rhetoric and action, such as military occupation and the circumvention of international law on human rights. In her seminal book *Epic Encounters*, she tracks the way 'Israel came to provide a political model for thinking about military power and a practical example of effectiveness in the use of that power'. She astutely connects Israeli military power with the assertion of a militant masculinity in the wake of the US defeat in Vietnam. Her analysis points out that Israel was 'both a moral exemplar and an admired military power', a 'combination so potent. . .[that] Israel became a prosthetic for Americans'.[36] The positive image of Israel as waging the good fight made it a model for US military actions. Torture is a recent example of how this kind of moral template has played out in the war in Iraq and the 'war on terror'. Israel preceded the USA in its reconfiguration of what constitutes torture and its willingness to subordinate international conventions on torture to the dictates of the mantra of security.' Revelations of abuse and torture of detainees at Abu Ghraib Prison and Guantanamo have highlighted the extent to which the 'war on terror' had been used to rationalise such illegal behaviour. The *New York Times* (17 October 2004) reported that, 'In March 2002, a team of administration lawyers accepted the Justice Department's view, concluding in a memorandum that President Bush was not bound by either the Convention Against Torture or a federal anti-torture statute because he had the authority to protect the nation from terrorism'.

A set of contrary terms are used by Israelis and Palestinians to refer to violence, death and killings. Palestinian discourse is embedded in an understanding of the conflict as a colonial one where their violence is legitimate resistance to dispossession and occupation by a well armed, well trained and well financed state. The Palestinians, as the non-state actors in the conflict, have light arms and no formal military. Palestinians call those who die in the conflict 'martyrs', a term that has both secular – national and religious meaning. Young people, men and women, who blow themselves up by strapping explosives to their bodies are referred to by Israelis as terrorists, murderers and homicide bombers, but never martyrs. Israeli citizens in the occupied territories, which includes parts of Jerusalem, are often, but not always, considered legitimate targets of violence in Palestinian resistance to occupation.[37] 'Civilian' is commonly understood to mean non-combatant. The Israelis dub all Israeli non-military personnel as civilians and, according to veteran journalist Robert Fisk, have pressured the news media to refer to settlers as simply 'Israelis'. Settling 'civilians' in occupied territory certainly puts up for grabs the meaning of 'civilian' in this context. Are they civilians if they are there by virtue of a military occupation, are heavily armed and protected by the army, and dwell on land expropriated by their government to expand its presence in the occupied territory? Israel has further blurred the meaning of 'civilian' by referring to refugee camps as terrorist hideouts and headquarters. A repertoire of terms refer to the murder of Palestinians by Israeli armed forces. Over the past decade, Israel has engaged in what it calls 'targeted killings' of Palestinian leaders in the name of national security. Fisk reports that the BBC 'ordered its reporters to use the phase "targeted killings" for Israel's assassination of Palestinians'.[38] To Palestinians, they are murders or assassinations.

## Conclusion

The political ideology which calls for Jews to settle in Palestine, for the creation of a Jewish state and for an end to the Jewish diaspora, was for decades described as Zionism by Jews and others. Palestinians referred to adherents of this philosophical and political movement as Zionists. Indeed, they have made a concerted effort not to use the term Jews to refer to those who settled in Palestine and created a Jewish state. This was part of a political stance that emphasised the colonial nature of the conflict and not its religious or ethnic dimensions. In other words, the Palestinian choice to use the term 'Zionism' and 'Zionist' to refer to their adversaries highlighted the modern political nature of the conflict and cleared the way for negotiations, concessions and reconciliation. The early PLO platform of a democratic, secular state in Palestine where Muslims, Christians and Jews would have equal rights and representation was quite opposed to the exclusivism of Zionism.

It has been fairly standard practice to refer to critics of Israel as anti-Semitic or, if they are Jews, as self-haters. Now, in an ironic twist, if one uses the term 'Zionism' or 'Zionist' to emphasise the secular nature of the conflict, one is also called an anti-Semite. The recent turn to claiming that anti-Zionism or criticism of Israel and US foreign policy on the conflict are manifestations of anti-Semitism reflects cracks in the prevalence of an Israeli narrative of the conflict, what Jenny Bourne has called a 'mad scrambling about to regain lost ground'.[39] If one cannot use the term 'Zionist', and refuses to refer to people and this particular movement in religious terms, then there is no legitimate discourse of criticism. The definition and meaning of words are, as Humpty Dumpty reminded us, decided by who is the master.

Words, rhetoric and discourses are more important than ever before. The US and Israeli rhetoric of the 'war on terror' captures the ambiguities and multi-pronged global approach to sustaining US dominance and hegemony in a new global order and to imposing an Israeli map of the Middle East. Words have been drained of meaning and reduced to Orwellian doublespeak. There is no standard definition of terrorism; yet that is precisely why, with all it ambiguity and subjectivity as well, it is a potent word.

## Notes

[1] J Beinin, 'The new American McCarthyism: policing thought about the Middle East', *Race and Class*, 46 (1), 2004, pp 101–115.

[2] S Gasteyer & C Butler Flora, 'Modernizing the savage: colonization and perceptions of landscape and lifescape', *Sociologia Ruralis*, 40 (1), 2002, pp 28–149.

[3] M Martha, M Haritos-Fatouros & P Zimbardo, *Violence Workers. Police Torturers and Murderers Reconstruct Brazilian Atrocities*, Berkeley, CA: University of California Press, 2002, p 27.

[4] See the account of a legal case in which Palestinian memories and narratives of what happened in the village of Tantoura in 1948 were challenged and subjected to a legal process of exclusion and denial of truthfulness. S Esmeir, 'Law, history, and memory', *Social Text*, 21 (2), 2003, pp 25–48.

[5] W Khalidi (ed), *All that Remains: The Palestinian Villages Occupied and Depopulated by Israel in 1948*, Washington, DC: Institute for Palestine Studies, 1992, p 582.

[6] M Trouillet, *Silencing the Past. Power and the Production of History*, Boston, MA: Beacon Press, 1995, pp 113, 114.

[7] J Beinin, 'The Israelization of American Middle East policy discourse', *Social Text*, 21 (2), 2003, pp 124–139.

[8] N Dirks, 'From little king to landlord; colonial discourse and colonial rule', in Dirks (ed), *In Colonialism and Culture* (Comparative Studies in Society and History Book Series), Michigan, MI: University of Michigan Press, 1993, pp 175–208.

[9] D Harvey, 'From space to place and back again: reflections on the condition of post-modernity', in J Bird *et al* (eds), *Mapping the Future. Local Cultures, Global Change*, London: Routledge, 1993, pp 3–29.

[10] J Peteet, *Landscape of Hope and Despair: Place and Identity in Palestinian Refugee Camps*, Philadelphia, PA: University of Pennsylvania Press, 2005 (in press).

[11] E Said, 'Invention, memory, and place', in W Mitchell (ed), *Landscape and Power*, Chicago, IL: University of Chicago Press, 2002, pp 241–259, p 248.

[12] S Schama, *Landscape and Memory*, New York: Knopf, 1995, p 61.

[13] M Benvenisti, *Sacred Landscape: The Buried History of the Holy Land Since 1948*, Berkeley, CA: University of California Press, 2000, p 2. See also S Cohen & N Kliot, 'Place-names in Israel's

ideological struggle over the Administrative Territories', *Annals of the Association of American Geographers*, 82 (4), 1992, pp 653–680.

14  L Jayyusi, 'The grammar of difference; the Palestinian/Israeli conflict as a moral site', in A Moors, T van Teeffelen, S Kanaana & I Abu Ghazaleh (eds), *Discourse and Palestine: Power, Text and Context*, Amsterdam: Het Spinhuis, 1995, p 124.

15  J Bauman, 'A designer heritage. Israeli national parks and the politics of historical representation', *Middle East Report*, 196, September–October 1995, pp 16–19. See also S Slyomovics, *The Object of Memory. Arab and Jew Narrate the Palestinian Village*, Philadelphia, PA: University of Pennsylvania Press, 1998; and Khalidi, *All that Remains*.

16  S Katz '*Adam and Adama*, '*Ird* and *Ard*: en-gendering political conflict and identity in early Jewish and Palestinian nationalisms', in D Kandiyoti (ed), *Gendering the Middle East: Emerging Perspectives*, Syracuse, NY: Syracuse University Press, 1996, pp 85–105.

17  E Shohat, 'Exile, diaspora, and return: the inscription of Palestine in Zionist discourse', in Moors *et al*, *Discourse and Palestine*, p 233.

18  J Goldberg, 'Among the settlers. Will they destroy Israel?', *The New Yorker*, 31 May 2004, pp 48–69.

19  A Shammas, 'A lost voice', *New York Times Magazine*, 28 April 1991, pp 34–35, 48, 78–79.

20  A Shammas, 'Palestinians must now master the art of forgetting', *New York Times Magazine*, 26 December 1993, pp 32–33.

21  Shammas, 'A lost voice'.

22  Peteet, *Landscape of Hope and Despair*.

23  R Fisk, 'CNN caves in to Israel over its references to illegal settlements', 2001, at www.bintjbeil.com/E/occupation/.

24  FAIR, *Media Advisory: Euphemisms for Israeli Settlements Confuse Coverage*, 26 June 2002.

25  R Khalidi, *Palestinian Identity. The Construction of Modern National Consciousness*, New York: Columbia University Press, 1997, p 14.

26  L Jayyusi, 'The grammar of difference'.

27  E Khoury, *The Kingdom of Strangers*, Fayetteville, AR: University of Arkansas Press, 1996, pp 25–27.

28  GC Spivak, 'Can the subaltern speak?', in P Williams & L Chrisman (eds), *Colonial Discourse and Post-Colonial Theory*, New York: Columbia University Press, 1994, p 76.

29  C Nagengast, 'Violence, terror, and the crisis of the state', *Annual Review of Anthropology*, 23, 1994, p 112.

30  T Swedenburg, 'The Palestinian peasant as a national signifier', *Anthropological Quarterly*, 63 (1), 1990, p 13.

31  N Masalha, *Expulsion of the Palestinians. The Concept of Transfer in Zionist Political Thought, 1882–1948*, Washington, DC: Institute for Palestine Studies, 1992, p 30.

32  Goldberg, 'Among the settlers'.

33  *Ibid*, p 48

34  L Hajjar, 'Sovereign bodies, sovereign states and the problem of torture', *Studies in Law, Politics, and Society*, 21, 2000, pp 101–134.

35  J Whitbeck, '"Terrorism": the word itself is dangerous', *Global Dialogue*, 4 (2), 2002, pp 59–65.

36  M McAlister, *Epic Encounters. Culture, Media, and US Interests in the Middle East, 1945–2000*, Berkeley, CA: University of California Press, 2001, pp 157, 187.

37  There is Palestinian debate and disagreement over the political wisdom and legitimacy of attacks on Israelis, which fluctuates with the political–military situation. In general, Fatah does not consider permissible attacks on Israeli civilians inside the Green line, while Hamas fluctuates between accepting this and, at other times, claiming that Israelis, occupying Palestinian land since 1948, can be attacked anywhere.

38  Fisk, 'CNN caves in to Israel over its references to illegal settlements'.

39  J Bourne, 'Anti-Semitism or anti-criticism? A review article', *Race and Class*, 46 (1), 2004, p 135.

# Know thy enemy: Hizbullah, 'terrorism' and the politics of perception

MONA HARB & REINOUD LEENDERS

Caricaturing one's opponent in terms that justify or call for its elimination is as old and common as political conflict itself. Yet few notions have provoked as much disagreement as that of 'terrorism'. While those chastised by their opponents may still take some pride in—and indeed adopt—principally derogatory labels like 'rebel', 'bandit', 'insurgent' and even 'enemy', terrorism has few self-professed practitioners. Therefore, by the rediscovery of the notion in the post-9/11 'war on terrorism', discursive battles have been fought as intensely as military ones, with all contestants and their sympathisers rejecting and placing their mutual characterisations at the core of their disputes. Especially when it comes to the Middle East, the debate tends to concentrate on the (il)legitimacy or (im)morality of applying the terrorism label in individual cases of political agitation and violence or on exact ways of defining 'terrorism'. Yet much less attention has been paid to the epistemological implications of waging a war against an enemy essentialised as terrorist. Evidently, labelling the enemy as such may have direct political advantages, in that it rationalises state-endorsed violence, mobilises support for state policy and communicates a threat to opponents of being treated like its namesakes elsewhere. But for knowing, understanding and predicting the opponent's intentions and actions, the term's merits are far less certain. This should not be a concern only for academics aiming to understand and explain political behaviour *per se*. Regardless of what one thinks of their own agendas, policy makers will have to consider the epistemological implications of how they label their opponents and conceive of the real or perceived threats the latter pose. If doubts are cast over the quality of knowledge their labels may generate, so will these labels question policy makers' ability to influence, transform or neutralise their 'terrorist' adversaries.

The labelling career of the Lebanese armed group and political party Hizbullah is an interesting case in point. Having found itself since its inception in the mid-1980s at the receiving end of mainly US and Israeli policy makers' and analysts' scorn for being an archetypical terrorist organisation, Hizbullah has been surprisingly successful in achieving its stated aims and in enduring the verbal and military onslaught against it. Although it is not the intention here to reduce explanations for Hizbullah's durability to discursive politics, this article suggests that the labelling of Hizbullah both as terrorist and, conversely, as a 'lebanonised' political force about to make a conversion into an unarmed political party, is misleading and incapable of grasping this organisation's complexities. In fact, both labels produced a quality of knowledge inferior to that produced by Hizbullah's own conceptualisation of its enemies. But, most importantly, the debate on Hizbullah's alleged terrorist nature has obscured several of its traits that anyone, including policy makers, should register before passing judgement on the organisation. We argue that the variety of institutions Hizbullah has been carefully elaborating and readapting over the past two decades operates as holistic and integrated networks which produce sets of meanings embedded in an interrelated religious and political framework. These meanings are disseminated on a daily basis through the party's policy networks and serve to mobilise the Shi'a constituency into a 'society of Resistance' in order to consolidate the foundation of an Islamic sphere (*al-*

*hala al-islamiyya*). Accordingly, any prospect of Hizbullah's transformation away from armed 'resistance' should be firmly placed in an analysis of its hegemony among the Shi'a of Lebanon and of the tools it uses to acquire and sustain this status.

## Hizbullah, the 'terrorist' villain

The 11 September attacks on the USA and the world's ensuing preoccupation with stemming the tide of terrorism boosted a consensus about the alleged terrorist nature of Hizbullah. While Israel and the USA had already classified Hizbullah as a terrorist organisation since the late 1980s, several other governments, including Canada (December 2002) and Australia (June 2003), now added the Lebanese organisation to their own lists of terrorist entities.[1] On 3 November 2001 the USA refined its categorisation of Hizbullah by officially labelling it a 'Foreign Terrorist Organization' possessing a 'global reach', thereby authorising the imposition of sanctions against any third party that failed to freeze its assets or extradite its operatives. In addition, three individuals, whom the US considers to be Hizbullah agents, were branded by the FBI as 'Most Wanted Terrorists'. The UK followed suit, albeit by distinguishing between Hizbullah's domestic and political operations within Lebanon and what it considers its 'External Security Organisation', specialising in terrorist attacks abroad. Senior US officials and law makers added their voice to the formal labelling of Hizbullah as 'terrorist' by fiercely denouncing its perceived involvement in global acts of terrorism and hinting that it might be next on the list of US targets. Perhaps most strikingly, Deputy Secretary of State Richard Armitage asserted that 'Hizbollah made the A-team of terrorists [but] maybe al-Qaeda is actually the B-team'.[2] An equally harsh judgement was passed by US Senator Bob Graham, the chairman of the Senate's Intelligence Committee, who described Hizbullah's purported military training camps in the Lebanese Biqa' region as places 'where the next generation of terrorists are being prepared'.[3] In a similar vein former CIA director George Tenet told the US Congress in 2003 that 'Hizbollah, as an organization with capability and worldwide presence, is [al-Qaeda's] equal, if not a far more capable organization. I actually think they're a notch above in many respects.'[4]

The indictment against Hizbullah relies on the organisation's suspected involvement in a series of activities that are deemed terrorist or are terrorism-related. Among the steadily growing number of accusations the following feature.

- Responsibility for the bombings of the US embassy and the US Marine barracks in Beirut in 1983 and the embassy's annex in 1984, and for having kidnapped several US and other Western citizens in Lebanon in the 1980s.[5] Three alleged members of Hizbullah, including Imad Mughniyeh, are held responsible for the hijacking of TWA flight 847 in 1985.[6]

- Orchestrating the attacks on the Israeli embassy in Buenos Aires in 1992 and the bombing of a Jewish community centre in the same city in 1994.[7] In 2002 the organisation was also accused of having recruited Singaporean nationals in a failed plot to attack US and Israeli ships in the Singapore Straits and of having plotted to blow up the Israeli embassy in Thailand.[8]
- Teaming up with al-Qaeda. Hizbullah officials are alleged to have met a group of al-Qaeda members who visited Hizbullah's training camps in south Lebanon, and to have provided shelter to al-Qaeda fugitives in Lebanon.[9] Moreover, Osama Bin Laden purportedly met Imad Mughniyeh in Sudan.[10] Press reports cited unnamed US intelligence sources and a 'senior law enforcer' as having uncovered ties between al-Qaeda and Hizbollah that were 'ad hoc and tactical and [involved] mid- and low-level operatives'.[11]
- Running international criminal networks to finance terrorist activities. These networks allegedly raise funds from the illicit trade in drugs and other goods in the tri-border area of Argentina, Brazil and Paraguay, and from trade in so-called conflict diamonds in the Congo, Liberia and Sierra Leone.[12] Fund-raising activities by Hizbullah members in North Carolina fed speculation about the organisation possessing 'dormant cells' in the USA.[13]
- Providing advice, arms and logistical–financial support to Palestinian groups, including Hamas, the al-Aqsa Brigades and Islamic Jihad, who are equally classified as terrorist organisations.

While referring to undisclosed security sources and citing largely anecdotal or circumstantial evidence, Hizbullah's critics found confirmation of some of their accusations in the party's own public discourse. 'Our slogan is and remains death to America', Hizbullah's secretary-general Hassan Nasrallah told a cheering crowd of supporters in a Beirut suburb in April 2003.[14] Seemingly corroborating suspicions about Hizbullah's support for Palestinian suicide attacks against Israeli civilians, Nasrallah explained in an interview on Arab Al-Jazeera television that he regarded his party as the 'vanguard' (*at-tali'a*) of the Palestinian armed struggle.[15] At the annual 'Day of Jerusalem' commemoration on 14 December 2001, Nasrallah expressed the party's full support for the Palestinian intifada, while justifying suicide attacks against Israeli civilians by pointing out that 'there are no citizens [*madaniyin*] in the Zionist entity [as] all of them are aggressors and participants in the onslaught against the [Palestinian] people'.[16] He later added: 'We will provide the intifada with money, weapons and people'.[17]

In all these assessments Hizbullah emerges as a formidable, if not the most dangerous, exponent of the terrorism that the US State Department believes to constitute 'a fundamental feature of the Middle East political landscape'.[18] Leaving the merits of the individual accusations aside, as a threat the overall classification as a terrorist organisation certainly had a curbing effect on those of Hizbullah's activities that are mostly *not* strictly regarded as 'terrorist' in nature. Although far from being considered legitimate or desirable, Hizbullah's military operations against the Israeli occupation of south Lebanon until May 2000, and its subsequent armed attacks on Israeli troops in the Shab'a farms, have been less frequently portrayed as being terrorist, and when so, mainly by Israeli policy makers and military commanders. Yet the escalated labelling of Hizbullah as a terrorist organisation in the US-led 'war on terror' and hints that it might be Washington's next target clearly helped reduce Hizbullah's actions on the border. In May 2003 a Hizbullah official admitted the party was 'lying low'.[19] Another party official, who is also a member of parliament, described Hizbullah's policy as a 'temporary, tactical retreat'.[20] Ever since, the organisation has shunned any spectacular actions on the border while instigating only minor incidents designed to remind Israel that its front with Hizbullah is still very much alive. Arguably, intimidating Hizbullah via the terrorism label may also have restrained the organisation from becoming active in Iraq by, for example, joining or supporting the Iraqi resistance against US troops—assuming that this intention was there in the first place and that Iraqis would have welcomed Hizbullah's involvement.[21]

From an Israeli and US point of view, labelling Hizbullah as a terrorist organisation had its pay-offs. Yet, in producing a cognitive map, the labelling of Hizbullah as a super-terrorist proved to be much less fruitful. The production of knowledge about and understanding of Hizbullah has suffered as a result. In academia, in journalism and in Western and Israeli intelligence circles, discussing terrorism appears to dispense with even the rudimentary onus of proof that is usually expected in the production of knowledge about virtually any other phenomenon, including those equally abhorred or rejected. For example, highly questionable and unsubstantiated information disseminated by a pro-Israeli website about a high-level '*jihadist*' meeting between operatives of al-Qaeda, Palestinian Islamist groups and Hizbullah in Tehran smoothly found its way via the Israeli media to the mainstream international press.[22] Washington-based think-tanks routinely adopted the information without much questioning and soon the allegation was printed in quasi-scholarly work with more-or-less respectable sourcing.[23] While in other instances an academic work based entirely on evidently biased sources is likely to be laughed off as deeply flawed, a study of Hizbullah's terrorist activities derived from interviews solely among Israeli intelligence officers and with no fieldwork in Lebanon has been widely regarded as an authoritative piece of research on the organisation.[24] Official Israeli guesses on Hizbullah's rocket and missile threat from south Lebanon are routinely mistaken for facts—despite the widely varying numbers suggested and notwithstanding that these estimates go far beyond conceivable possibilities.[25] Similarly testifying to the high degree of misinformation circulating about Hizbullah, one US official agreed to discuss the issue of the organisation's terrorism with the authors by indicating which press reports US intelligence deemed plausible and which it did not.[26]

One could argue that it has simply been Hizbullah's secretive nature that prevented the gathering of accurate knowledge about the organisation. Such is indeed a complicating factor, given Hizbullah's highly effective regime of internal discipline and concealment and given that it has never produced talkative defectors. Judging from the limited successes of Israeli Special Forces in targeting Hizbullah leaders, Israeli intelligence and its allies have for long failed to penetrate the organisation to any threatening degree.[27] Yet, for a convincing explanation for the dismal record of 'terrorism studies' in actually 'knowing' their subject and producing decent analyses of Hizbullah, there seems to be more at play. Rarely have the critics of Hizbullah's 'terrorism' produced thorough analyses of the organisation in its domestic settings or in a historical perspective, not even in an attempt to contextualise their accusations regarding its terrorist agenda.[28] Accordingly, publicly available information is customarily ignored or dismissed as irrelevant at best, resulting in the constant reproduction of factually incorrect assertions, including naming Sayyid Fadlallah as the Spiritual Guide of Hizbullah[29] and firmly dating its foundation to before its actual inception in 1984.[30] The mounting allegations about Hizbullah's internationalist efforts in general—and its ties or similarities with al-Qaeda in particular—systematically do injustice to historical facts and the political stances taken by the organisation, or completely ignore them. For instance, the accusation regarding the supposedly cosy relations between Hizbullah and al-Qaeda conceals the outrage expressed by the party over atrocities jointly committed by the Taliban and its Arab allies in Afghanistan years before the Twin Towers collapsed.[31] Al-Qaeda's second-in-command, Ayman al-Zawahiri, also received vicious condemnation from Hizbullah when in November 1997 his Gama'at al-Islamiyya committed a massacre among civilians in Luxor, Egypt.[32] Hizbullah also blamed the Egyptian Islamists for launching an armed campaign against the Egyptian state without having exhausted the route of dialogue and reconciliation, while diverting resources away from what it sees as the real and legitimate struggle against Israel.[33] Even leaving aside the numerous religious and doctrinal differences between the two organisations,[34] terrorism experts never explained or substantiated their claims that this past of clear animosity has been miraculously overcome, to the extent that the two now perceive their struggle as a unified *Jihad* against a common enemy.

The study of Hizbullah's terrorism not only conveniently ignores historical data; it also lifts events and developments out of their historical contexts anachronistically to serve as proof for its contentions. Al-Qaeda's use of suicide attacks evidently prompted memories of Hizbullah's similar tactics in the 1980s. Yet to subsequently equate the two organisations as being part of one and the same terrorist onslaught against the West ignores and can not account for the fact that Hizbullah has not carried out such suicide attacks since 1985.[35] A similar anachronistic approach underlies the argument that Hizbullah today is essentially a mere tool, or even a derivative, of the Iranian regime. Iranian Revolutionary Guards undoubtedly played an instrumental role in the establishment of Hizbullah in the 1980s. But simply to transpose this historical given in order to account for its subsequent terrorist career and its current status pays no heed to Hizbullah's strenuous and for itself often politically costly efforts to reconcile its Islamist agenda with a form of

174

Lebanese nationalism. It also discards Hizbullah's highly sophisticated catering for the needs of a Lebanese Shi'ite constituency and ignores its growing reliance on donations from the Lebanese diaspora, reinforced by strong indications of dwindling financial support from Iran.[36] Finally, to mention another and related example, assertions that Hizbullah remains committed to establishing an Iranian-style Islamic state in Lebanon and that all its actions are instrumental to this ultimate goal suffer from a similar hiatus in understanding or even registering Hizbullah's evolution. Its 1985 manifesto or 'open letter' did indeed call, *inter alia*, for the establishment of an Islamic state in Lebanon and rejected participation in Lebanon's confessional system.[37] To be sure, the party's leaders still contend that an Islamic state is a goal that deserves to be aspired to when conditions allow and depending on the emergence of a consensus on its desirability. Yet, since the party acknowledges that in pluralist Lebanon this condition can not be fulfilled today or in the near future, it has become a 'legal abstraction'.[38] Accordingly, since Hizbullah's subsequent participation in Lebanon's post-war political system since the early 1990s (see below), it has never mentioned the establishment of an Islamic state in its election programmes, nor have its members in parliament or in elected positions of local government called for an Islamic state or striven towards legislation or policies suggesting an opportunistic strategy towards this presumed goal.[39]

In their ability to know, understand and correctly predict their subject's behaviour, students of terrorism have been seriously hampered by systematically resorting to factual incorrectness regarding what can be known, by skipping relevant historical data, by anachronistic arguing and by relying on philological essentialism. Yet those labelling Hizbullah as a terrorist organisation have had few qualms about these methodological flaws. In this respect the hypothesis should be considered that the inability to know and understand terrorism is inherent to their approach. As one British diplomat said, 'you and I can not know about Hizbullah's terrorist activities because there is no way we can have access to the dossiers about what is going on in its external security wing. But we know for certain it is engaged in terrorism.'[40] This uninformed certainty even produced its own jargon, wherein Hizbullah's 'threat' is said to originate from its 'global reach' and its 'capabilities', as opposed to the organisation's actual operations, political outlook and plans. Indeed, the very terror supposedly spread by Hizbullah is portrayed as so effective exactly because of its unpredictability and the secrecy in which the organisation operates. The labelling exercise consists of imagining Hizbullah as the ultimate alien who *can not be known* or understood. In this sense study of Hizbullah's terrorism appears as the very antipode of both academia and intelligence.

### Hizbullah's reply and perception of its enemies

The barrage of accusations undoubtedly put Hizbullah on the defensive. Especially after the events of 11 September 2001 the organisation made increasing efforts to shrug off the terrorism label applied by its opponents. Its officials and various media outlets responded to the individual charges by strongly denying its involvement in the Argentine bombings and by rejecting responsibility for the US embassy and marine barracks bombings and the kidnappings in the 1980s.[41] Hizbullah also fervently denied any links with Al-Qaeda and repeatedly condemned the bombing of the Twin Towers.[42] Strong denials were also expressed regarding its sending members to Iraq.[43] It refuted allegations that it is running training camps for Palestinian militants.[44] In more general terms the organisation emphasised that its operations are not 'global' but confined to Lebanon and the Israeli–Palestinian conflict, while it denied that it 'at any point of time went to the US to fight them there or in any part of the world'. [45]

Hizbullah's denials indicate that it is acutely aware of the dangers of being implicated by the labelling exercise on terrorism and that it understands that the US 'war on terror' has put it under closer scrutiny. Yet at the same time it has also tried to capitalise on the allegations by deliberately leaving a degree of ambiguity so as to reinforce its opponents' beliefs. This clearly shows from the organisation's response to Israeli accusations over its vast military capability in south Lebanon. Commenting on reports about Hizbullah possessing a large arsenal of long-range missiles, Secretary-General Nasrallah said:

> If we had them, we won't say so because we don't want to reveal our capabilities to the enemy. If we don't have them, we won't say anything either as this would reassure our enemy for free. So we leave them guessing.[46]

Taking this logic a step further, Hizbullah complemented its strong denials of being involved in Iraq with equally strong hints to the contrary. For example, during the US siege of Najaf and its holy shrines in May 2004, Nasrallah told thousands of participants in a protest march in Beirut that Hizbullah's battle against Israeli occupation and Iraqis resisting the US occupation were intrinsically linked and part of a larger battle against US–Israeli designs for the region. In his speech Nasrallah left little doubt that he saw Hizbullah as a major player in this larger battle.[47] Likewise, Hizbullah routinely shrouded its denials of responsibility for the US embassy and barracks bombings in the 1980s by adding praise for the acts and by expressing admiration for their perpetrators.[48] Hence, although it explicitly denied the charges of terrorism, both generally and on a case-by-case basis, Hizbullah skillfully manipulated these same accusations in order to fuel its enemies' suspicions. Consequently, it derived some sort of a deterrence capability from the terrorism label itself; enough to intimidate its opponents and mobilise its own supporters, but within certain bounds to prevent immediate retaliation.[49]

Beside its denials, Hizbullah's positive answer to its critics consisted of a consistent discourse constructed around the notion of 'resistance' (*muqawama*) against occupation. The organisation's mission and identity are rooted in its founders' belief that the Israeli invasion of Lebanese territory in the 1980s ought to be beaten by armed resistance. Even following the low-intensity war in the 1990s and the Israeli withdrawal from south Lebanon in May 2000, the notion of resistance has remained central to Hizbullah's self-proclaimed mission. This is done both by claiming that Lebanese territories (the Shab'a farms and various other 'flashpoints') continue to be occupied and by increasingly intervening in the Israeli–Palestinian conflict.[50] Underlying this 'fixed and invariable dossier'[51] are a complex set of notions and interpretations derived from Shi'a law, Ayatollah Khomeini's theory of the 'rule of the Islamic jurist' (*wilayat al-faqih*), Shi'a history, hagiography and related beliefs that render resistance and holy struggle (*jihad*) essentially a religious duty for the disempowered (*al-mustad'afin*).[52] What is striking is that Hizbullah's broader discourse contains views and characterisations of its enemies that, qualitatively speaking, are poles apart from those offered by the converse discourse on terrorism.

For Hizbullah oppression has been a central element to the experience of the 'Muslim community' (*umma*) with the West. Colonialism and imperialism are singled out as the major constants of how countries like France, Britain and, more recently, the USA have trampled on the Muslim peoples and approached the latter with contempt, double standards and brutal force in order to impose their hegemony. According to the party's ideologists, these battles over subjugation have been reinforced by and interwoven with a major clash between Islamic and Western civilisation. Thus not only is Hizbullah's antagonism against the West phrased in political or ideological terms but by means of a strong rejection of Western culture and its impact on Arab and Muslim society.[53] In this respect Israel stands out as the greatest perpetrator of crimes against the oppressed and the 'greatest evil' (*as-shar al-mutlaq*), to the extent that Hizbullah vows never to reconcile itself with Israel's existence.[54] Recent instability in the Middle East triggered by the US invasion of Iraq and heightened Israeli repression of Palestinian rights only confirmed the party's conviction that its two main enemies—the Israeli state and the US government—are preparing for a showdown against the Muslims of the region. Yet for Hizbullah its antipathy towards Israel remains centre stage in its understanding of and animosity against US policies in the region:

> Today their main aim is Palestine—both before Iraq and after it. When we talk about the occupation of Iraq their aim is Palestine via the gates of Iraq. When Syria, Iran and the Islamic movement are targeted, their aim is Palestine.[55]

What emerges is that, in Hizbullah's view, the latest manifestation of colonialism and imperialism is found in an 'American–Zionist project' that threatens to usurp the entire region, impose its hegemony and complete the destruction of Palestine.[56] Hizbullah's leaders insist that this conspiracy calls for a maximum effort of resistance and *jihad*.

Of course, when taken at face value, nothing in this fierce discourse appears more subtle or sophisticated than the discourse on terrorism. In its views on its enemies, Hizbullah even appears to invite the terrorism label by invoking trepidation and hatred. Yet, despite all its demonising content, Hizbullah's discourse still makes some important distinctions and qualifications, while the terrorism label suffices by presenting a one-dimensional adversary. Saad-Ghorayeb points in this respect to several traits of Hizbullah's discourse that suggest a much more multidimensional perception of its enemies.[57] The organisation may seek the destruction of both Israeli state and society but it conditions the active pursuit of this ultimate aim to its feasibility, as dictated by Israeli military superiority or an eventual peace agreement with Israel by its host Lebanon and its ally Syria. A similar sense of pragmatism is evident in Hizbullah's evolving positions on the US occupation of Iraq. Although it lambasted the invasion and pointed at the excesses of occupation, Hizbullah leaders fine-tuned their discourse to the fluctuating willingness of Iraqi Shi'a leaders to negotiate with the USA.[58] Moreover, even when it expresses animosity towards the West at large, Hizbullah does not aim for the eradication of Western states. It simultaneously expresses admiration for certain aspects of Western culture, including US culture. Neither does it hold a grudge against Western states *per se*, as illustrated by its general approval of France's policies in the region.[59] Hizbullah's leaders also tell both the outside world and their supporters that their conflict is not with the US people but with the US government. In fact, just before the invasion of Iraq, Nasrallah called on fellow Arabs and Muslims to 're-evaluate' their attitude towards Europeans, given widespread anti-war demonstrations in London and other European capitals.[60]

This is not to deny the morally dubious aspects of Hizbullah's views on its enemies or indeed the world at large. The organisation's discourse could be rightly accused of spreading a message of anti-Semitism and racism while evoking violence and hatred, as most of Hizbullah's opponents maintain. Yet, however despicable its views may be, its efforts to conceive, characterise and analyse its enemies show a much greater degree of stratification, diversity and adjustability than the label 'terrorism' is capable of producing. Indeed, Hizbullah's eagerness to know and understand its enemies' history, mentality and plans stands in sharp contrast to the representation of the 'terrorist' as the ultimate alien who can not be known. Examples abound. Hizbullah's media outlets daily broadcast programmes aimed at informing viewers about the nature of Israeli and US societies and politics. Its satellite TV channel, al-Manar, frequently broadcasts footage of Israeli politicians and journalist discussing the latest in Israeli politics. In-house commentators explain the workings of the Knesset in voting for or against Israeli policies *vis-à-vis* the Palestinians. The channel's recent broadcasting of the Syrian-made drama series 'The Diaspora' (*as-Shattat*) may be rightly dismissed as a false and distorted account of the history of Zionism,[61] yet it exemplifies Hizbullah's obsession with the historical evolution of its main enemy. One of its prime time game shows, *al-Muhimma* (The Mission), has for its objective to virtually enter Jerusalem by answering a series of questions dealing with resistance operations, Islamic thought, the Palestinian cause, Western conspiracies, Israeli plots, etc. In this show, the Israeli enemy is challenged through the audiovisual presentation of the merely virtual possibility of conquering Jerusalem, while knowledge about this enemy (and other oppressors) is celebrated and rewarded. This knowledge is also materially re-channelled into promoting the cause of armed resistance since 25% of the monetary award granted to the winning candidate is sent to the Palestinian intifada.

In a similar fashion, the organisation's weekly *Al-Intiqad* (critique) devotes large sections to themes like 'religious aspects of US policies', analyses of Israeli Prime minister Ariel Sharon's intentions and strategies behind his proposed pullout of Gaza and views within the Knesset on the Sharon plan.[62] Hizbullah's websites provide listings of articles in several languages on issues like the influence of Christian fundamentalism on US policies towards Israel, the Jewish lobby in Washington, Israel's evolving notion of national security, Jewish political philosophy, interviews with Israeli academicians and political activists taken from the Israeli press and, indeed, investigations into how the notion of terrorism shapes US foreign policy.[63]

Hizbullah's emphasis on education and research is similarly steered towards knowing the enemy. Anyone visiting its affiliated Consultative Centre for Studies and Documentation in Beirut (see below) will find in its library students reading books and articles by Israeli and US authors about US and Israeli foreign policy, Zionism and Western political science. Thousands of Hizbullah sympathisers have completed their education at the American University in Beirut, often after receiving generous financial support from the organisation. In all these endeavours Hizbullah demonstrates a capability to analyse and predict its adversaries' behaviour and intentions that is far superior to that offered by those insisting on the terrorism label. As a result, both the researcher and the policy maker who is stuck in the paradigm of terrorism finds him or herself in a permanent position of epistemological disadvantage *vis-à-vis* the 'terrorist' he hopes to analyse or, ultimately, to defeat.

## The counter-view: the 'Lebanonisation' of Hizbullah

Several researchers have become discontented with the terrorism label and have sought to analyse Hizbullah differently. Hizbullah's participation in the Lebanese political system prompted a set of studies arguing that the party is becoming 'lebanonised'—a reference to the process of 'normalisation' of its political activities and its gradual transformation into a purely civilian political party accommodated by the Lebanese political system. This process, labelled 'the phase of political *jihad*', substitutes the notion of Islamic revolution with that of political accommodation.[64] Authors agree that Hizbullah has given up its radical agenda and is integrating into national politics with a pragmatic strategy. The 'lebanonisation' of Hizbullah would be a change from the principles of 'rejectionism and violence' towards those of 'domestic courtesy and accommodation'.[65]

This alternative approach to understanding Hizbullah has the merit of producing knowledge about the social base of the party that is largely overlooked by students of terrorism. The 'terrorist' label equates the social base of Hizbullah with poor individuals needing the services provided by the party, and passively dominated by its propaganda activities.[66] The 'lebanonisation' literature introduces a distinction between the armed activities of the party and its social and political action, focusing on the latter and analysing Hizbullah's service delivery success and efficiency among

Lebanese Shi'a. We are told that these activities are organised into formal and less formal institutions, under the jurisdiction of the party's central decision-making structures, and that this 'welfare system' improves 'the daily life of thousands of deprived Shi'a in Lebanon' who have not been getting proper services from the government.[67] Accordingly, Hizbullah is distinguished by two components: the social and political versus the armed branch, suggesting that the latter is bound to be dismantled after the struggle for liberation has been completed.

> The party reveals two complementary aspects. It has committed itself to the militant pursuit of its goals, while working extremely hard to build and sustain a political constituency...In recent years, Hizbullah has been transforming itself, preparing for life after resistance while simultaneously exploiting its commitment to liberate the South in order to gain political support.[68]

The gradual transformation of Hizbullah is explained by a host of factors, including political changes occurring in Iran, and the victory over the conservatives of the Iranian reformers, who encouraged Hizbullah to 'demilitarize its identity and build a broader base in society'.[69] Other external regional strategic factors are also cited as prompting this conversion.[70] In addition, the change is also related to Lebanese domestic politics, which are not in favour of an Islamic revolution, even among Shi'a ranks. The Hizbullah of the post-war era is conceived as being less driven by ideology than by political considerations related to the consolidation of its existence.

The 'lebanonisation' analysis highlights the effectiveness and efficiency of Hizbullah's activities on two levels. First, as a political party managing an array of social services to Shi'a, who have been historically disregarded by the Lebanese state. This perspective looks at Hizbullah from below, and examines its grassroots actions from a political economy perspective. It urges a revision of the party's labelling as a terrorist group, as it introduces evidence of its operation as a typical political party. Thus, implicitly or explicitly, the 'lebanonisation' literature critiques the dismissal of Hizbullah as an extremist or terrorist group by the West.

> While it may be tempting to dismiss Hizbullah as an extremist or terrorist group, this sort of labeling [by the USA] conceals the fact that Hizbullah has managed to build an extremely impressive social base in Lebanon.[71]

Second, the 'lebanonisation' literature reveals how Hizbullah is able to operate successfully as a political party, negotiating its position within the complex arena of Lebanese politics: 'Hizbullah has been transforming itself into a political party [whose decision makers] are little different than the [other Lebanese] leaders [and] have exemplified a sophisticated understanding of Lebanese politics'.[72] This argument fits into the claim made by other authors about the decline of radical Islamism.[73] Like most other Islamic movements, Hizbullah's ideological ambitions are said to be being re-channelled into and somehow neutralised by domestic politics. Hizbullah is not only 'being gradually absorbed by the political system', it has also 'jettisoned its commitment to establishing a system of Islamic rule in the country'.[74] The approach essentially concludes that Hizbullah, as a radical movement, is being caught up in the game of conventional politics: Hizbullah's 'lebanonisation' entails a gradual dismissal of the party's pan-Islamic horizon in favour of what is termed 'Islamic nationalism'.[75]

Hizbullah's participation in the Lebanese political system was indeed the outcome of fierce internal debates in the party. In 1992, before the first Lebanese parliamentary elections after the end of the war and the signing of Taif agreement, Hizbullah's Shura Council was divided into two camps. The first argued against political participation, which was seen as an inevitable compromise with Hizbullah's revolutionary ideals. The second justified this participation by a re-interpretation of the 1989 Taif agreement (which forms the Lebanese post-war constitution); it was argued that participation in the political system would allow the party to change it from within.[76] Eventually, the latter view prevailed, resulting in Hizbullah's participation in the parliamentary elections of 1992, in which it won eight seats (out of 128). Ever since, Hizbullah has participated in both parliamentary and municipal elections, gaining considerable numbers of votes. However, Hizbullah has insisted on qualifying its participation in Lebanon's political institutions while it maintained a certain distance from Lebanese politics in general—thereby allowing its denunciation of the government's practices while ensuring its role as an opposition party. As one of Hizbullah's leaders put it succinctly:

> We distinguish between participation [in the legislative elections of 1992] and our vision of the actual political system that we consider to be the basis of confessional, economic, administrative, and political problems because it is built on a confessional basis and on the basis of *muhassasa* [allotment] that hinders development and impedes people's rights.[77]

Compared to the terrorism approach, the 'lebanonisation' approach certainly has its merits. Yet, by sharply distinguishing between the two sorts of activities of the party—the social and the military—it fails to acknowledge or explain the interactions between them, at least on an ideological level. Harik notes a relationship between Hizbullah's 'success' and its construction of Shi'a 'self-identity', but she does not explain the ramifications or nature of this correlation.[78] In this context Alagha argues that the Islamic state ideology of Hizbullah in the post-Taif era remains 'a political ideology, but *not* a political program'.[79] Saad-Ghorayeb explores how the political evolution of Hizbullah reconciled its core beliefs. She argues that the party is sustained by skillfully negotiating its intellectual and religious commitment to pan-Islamism and its Lebanese sociopolitical role.[80] However, none of these authors explains how these linkages between ideology and programme translate empirically into the party's structures and agency.

Instead of providing clear answers to these questions, the debate about the 'lebanonisation' of Hizbullah is almost entirely focused on the future of the party against the background of its pragmatic transformation. Accordingly,

181

the liberation of the South is viewed as having placed Hizbullah in a 'strategic dilemma'[81] caused by a host of questions: what would its role be after the Israeli withdrawal from the South of Lebanon in May 2000? How would the party sustain its legitimacy as the bearer of the resistance now that there are no Israelis to resist? How would this affect Hizbullah's social and political activities? And how could Hizbullah justify to its constituencies the party's possible further integration into a Lebanese political system it had often lambasted for being corrupt and unworthy?

Hizbullah's own answers are clearly at odds with the 'lebanonisation' thesis.

> The basis of our objectives is related, on one hand, to the national environment governed by the theory of prevention and defense [rade' wa difaa'], and on the other, to the liberation of the occupied Lebanese territories. Thus calling for the demilitarization of Hizbullah is equivalent to calling for the removal of all security measures from Lebanon and for its deadly strategic exposure.[82]

Accordingly, Hizbullah views its military activities as an integral part of its *raison d'être*. Even if the party is not actually engaged in combat, it still reserves the *right* to use armed force for 'prevention and defence'; a right, which, in turn is constantly reiterated and disseminated through the party's social and political activities. This further explains why Hizbullah refuses to participate in the Lebanese government. Indeed, since Hizbullah's military activities remain a key priority, integrating into the government would put the party in a position which would be difficult to sustain internationally:

> If, for example, we take the position of speaker of Parliament [now held by its rival Amal], we would become part of the Lebanese state. As a result, the whole country would be held responsible for our operations against Israel.[83]

Consequently, the literature dealing with the transformation and the accommodation of Hizbullah into Lebanese politics has contributed to presenting it as 'a fixture of Lebanese politics, not simply an armed and violent faction'.[84] This way, it has moved beyond the 'terrorism' label and contributed to producing knowledge about Hizbullah: the 'lebanonisation' literature acknowledged and described the functioning of the party's social activities. However, it has incorrectly situated these social activities as separate from Hizbullah's other functions, whereas Hizbullah leaders conceive resistance as much as a military undertaking as a social and political one. 'A close inspection of the party's internal dynamics reveals that it is virtually impossible to extricate the military from the political or vice versa.'[85] Moreover, the 'lebanonisation' approach has not been able to shed much light on the nature and organisation of the party's social and political activities. More importantly, it has assumed that the reasons behind the mobilisation of thousands of Shi'a individuals by Hizbullah could simply be explained by material interests and the comfort of depending on the party's social network.[86] We believe that other reasons stand behind the process by which large groups of individuals, often not poor at all, *choose* to be mobilised by Hizbullah.

182

## Hizbullah's institutions: a holistic network

A different way of looking at Hizbullah's social and political activities is to consider the possibility that these activities are successful because they operate as an integrated and holistic network. This network produces individual and collective meaning to its beneficiaries, which, in turn, explains how and why Hizbullah is legitimised as a dominant order among Lebanese Shi'a. Our analysis of Hizbullah's actions thus aims to go beyond the two-leg description of the party and hopes to produce more knowledge about its social networks as well as about their political and religious paradigms.

Hizbullah manages a dozen institutions delivering an array of services to Shi'a groups residing in the southern suburb (al-Dahiya) of Beirut, in the South of Lebanon and in the Biqa' area. All these institutions depend administratively on a Social Services Central Unit, located in al-Dahiya. Two categories of institutions can be identified: those providing services related to the armed resistance, and those delivering services to a wider group of users needing social, economic and urban services. These institutions have autonomous boards of administration and have a specific margin of manoeuvre but have to follow a minimal 'political and cultural orientation'—formulated and set by Hizbullah.[87] Before analysing their broader significance in terms of networks, it may be worth looking at the institutions in more detail.

Of the first category of institutions, the associations of the Martyr (al-Shahid, founded in 1982) and of the Wounded (al-Juraha, established in 1990) are two ngos that depend administratively on Hizbullah. Al-Shahid looks after 2500 relatives of martyrs, prisoners and missing individuals. The association manages schools, a hospital, a dispensary and ensures access to a variety of resources through a network of relationships for 'stabilizing the family in its environment'.[88] Al-Juraha takes care of more than 3000 wounded along the same lines.[89]

Of the second category, two Hizbullah ngos propose educational and micro-credit services. The Educational Institute (al-Mu'assasa al-Tarbawiyya, founded in 1991) supervises the education sector and aims at 'redefining the structure of [Shi'a] society' through Islamic learning. It manages nine schools in Lebanon, grouping around 5300 students.[90] The Good Loan (al-Qard al-Hassan, opened in 1984) specialises in providing micro-credit and administers an average of 750 loans per month, at sharply discounted interest rates.[91]

In addition, four other institutions are presented as administratively autonomous from Hizbullah's Central Unit of Social Services, although they are directed either by members or by party cadres, and their employees are affiliated with Hizbullah. Three of these institutions are actually branches of Iranian associations. The Help (al-Imdad, founded in 1987) distributes social services to the poor and the deprived. The Islamic Society for Health (al-Haya'a al-Suhiyya, established in 1984) operates in the medical sector and in public health. It runs 46 medical centres and a hospital, catering for more than 283 000 cases counted in 1995.[92] And the Jihad for Construction (Jihad al-Bina'a, established in 1988) works in the building and management of urban services, especially in the South of Lebanon where needs were and still are particularly high because of the Israeli occupation until 2000. The fourth institution, the Consultative Centre for Studies and Documentation (CCSD, founded in 1988), is a research centre that prepares reports and studies on a variety of social, economic, political, financial, administrative and development topics. It has published more than 300 such reports and conference proceedings; it has organised tens of conferences, and set up a database of more than 500 000 articles.[93] In addition, Hizbullah also operates in the fields of sports and youth, and of women's mobilisation and it owns a number of media institutions: *Al-Intiqad* magazine, the radio station al-Nour (The Light), and al-Manar television, which became available via satellite in 2000.

Hizbullah's institutions manage a diversity of policy sectors: social, educational, medical, urban, economic, cultural and religious. Their organisational structure obeys a strict hierarchy. These institutions operate autonomously but also co-ordinate their actions, exchanging information and expertise, in the aim of strengthening their outputs. The institutions' directors rotate on a regular basis, ensuring a steady administrative turn-over, and building their managerial capacities across policy sectors. They are thus knowledgeable of the whole array of services provided by different institutions, and they capitalise on these resources in defining their plans of action. These plans are subject to the approval of the central party unit, but they conserve a good margin of manoeuvre, as long as they respect the overall sense of Hizbullah mission. Over the years Hizbullah's institutions have worked diligently on improving their policy agendas in the objective of higher efficiency and effectiveness in their service provision. Their actions are driven by concerns over performance, professionalism and progress, which explains their reliance on expertise and scientific know-how. A prime example can be found in the municipal work developed in the suburb of Beirut, which has capitalised on participation and community development paradigms, leading to significant progress in local governance, as illustrated by the UN Best Practices Award given to the Ghobeyri municipality.[94] Another illustration is the research work developed by the CCSD and its scientific contributions to policy literature in Lebanon, as well as to Islamic – European dialogue.[95]

In addition, Hizbullah's institutions are characterised by their holistic approach: they form a network of organisations that provides a compre-hensive set of policies framing diverse components of daily life. This holistic package supplies its beneficiaries with all their material needs, efficiently and with a relatively good quality of service. Thus, it presents an attractive alternative to the unreliable public services, and to the high cost and uncertainty of private services.

Nevertheless, the material and professional characteristics of Hizbullah's networks are not the only explanation of its significant success. Hizbullah's institutions also disseminate codes, norms and values that produce what has been designated by the party as the 'Resistance society' (*mujtama' al-*

*muqawama*). We now turn to the symbolic meanings contained in the services provided by these institutions to further explain the holistic nature of Hizbullah. 'The Islamic party [ie Hizbullah]...carries a methodology of living in its holism [*manhajan li al-hayat bi shumuliyyatiha*] and its mission does not focus on one aspect or the other, even if the priority of *jihad* is apparent.'[96]

## Hizbullah and the production of meaning: *al-Hala al-Islamiyya*

*Resistance as society*

In Hizbullah's view, resistance is a mission and a responsibility for every Shi'a in his or her everyday life. Thus resistance is military, but it is foremost political and social: it is a choice of life, or a 'methodology', as recently emphasised by Nasrallah.[97] The resistance society is the product that Hizbullah's holistic network aims to achieve. This society serves to disseminate the concept of spiritual *jihad*, which is complementary to military *jihad*: 'The prophet told us: combat is a small *jihad*, the biggest *jihad* is the spiritual *jihad*.'[98]

Both forms of *jihad* are essential in building a resistance society unified around specific meanings with which it identifies, revolving around issues of social and moral responsibility, and of commitment to a cause. Hence, resistance goes beyond combat and becomes an individual process, carried out through daily practices related to body, sound, signs and space, transmitting 'religious and community knowledge'.[99] Resistance becomes a priority guiding the individual in his/her choices, more so a 'humanitarian and moral duty'.[100] Moreover, resistance is a religious duty (*fard shar'i*) pious Shi'a are expected to adhere to. Pious Shi'a are expected to emulate a religious leader or reference (*marja'iyya*) who defines the licit and illicit symbolic, social and material practices according to his interpretation of Shi'a rule. The pious Shi'a is said to be a *multazem*, which means literally 'committed'.

According to Hizbullah, the power of resistance is that it is a righteous combat, supported by God, which inevitably leads to victory. The greatest evidence is the liberation of the South of Lebanon in May 2000 and the defeat of the Israeli army by the resistance. Another supporting evidence is the liberation of Lebanese prisoners detained in Israel following long negotiations mediated by Germany about the fate of Israelis captured by the Resistance. Both these pieces of evidence attest to the justness of resistance as a strategy. And both serve Hizbullah in presenting this choice as an honourable option generating a sense of pride, of which Shi'a have been deprived for centuries.[101]

Therefore, the resistance society modifies the perception of the Shi'a individuals as 'disinherited' (*mahrumin*) to one of being 'disempowered' (*mustada'afin*). The nuance is essential, as the latter invokes an opportunity for transformation and change, whereas the former involves stagnation. Through its holistic approach Hizbullah transforms the typical Shi'a victimisation complex into meaningful values of justice, solidarity, community, sacrifice, progress, etc—which, in turn, instigates high self-esteem and a solid sense of pride.

Empirically, the intertwining of the social and military, of the spiritual and the material, are embedded in the policies implemented by Hizbullah's institutions. For instance, the educational policies of the Islamic Institute for Teaching and Education aim at 'redefining the structure of society'[102] (*i'adat siyaghat tarkibat al-mujtama'*) and at erasing the victimisation approach inherent to Shi'a constituencies. Through education the party is able to produce a new 'mentality'—that of a society participating actively in its own reconstruction, in resistance and in economic rebirth.

> The specificity of the Islamic Institute's schools is their particular spirit (*ruhiya khassa*) and their ambiance (*jaww*), which produce mobilization through all the studied topics. We want to disseminate the culture of religious commitment (*iltizam*). We insist on culture, because this is what makes identity. Resistance is not an aim, it is the result of a culture.[103]

The resistance 'identity' and 'culture' are thus essential products of Hizbullah's institutions. Note that their dissemination is carried out by a wide network of less formalised channels than the above-mentioned ngos, divided mainly around women volunteers and local clerics. Through these vehicles Hizbullah has grounded its social action in kinship and family networks. It has also developed a grassroots approach to policy making, based on a participatory methodology: 'making people participate' (*ishrak al-nass*) is a recurrent Islamic rhetoric which has strengthened local community development. Hizbullah institutions have direct contact with the neighbourhoods they service. Two levels of administration actually overlap. One subdivides the territories into quarters administered by 'geographic leaders'; one divides space into zones managed by 'service leaders'. These leaders are informed by networks of volunteers (mostly women who live in the neighbourhood) about potential beneficiaries. Hence, the need is matched with the concerned institution. The dual administrative subdivision—spatial and functional—maximises the outreach efficiency of Hizbullah's networks.[104]

Several other strategies consolidate belonging to the society of resistance on a daily basis: regular commemorations, such as Ashura, and media strategies, as we have seen with al-Manar television, but also a carefully designed iconography. This iconography exhibits in the streets and in public spaces images of martyrs, of religious leaders' images, as well as Palestinian symbols. It depicts physically the core elements of Hizbullah's resistance society: martyrdom, Shi'ism, and the Israeli occupation of Palestine. Hizbullah's Information Unit, which manages the display of this 'popular information', aims to disseminate a message (*rissala*): 'We want to transmit *al-hala* [*al-islamiyya*] that exists in the streets, and that says what is this city, what are its characteristics, and that conveys the identity of this *hala*'.[105]

Hence, through these territorial markings of space, Hizbullah has managed to bring into being an environment, more so a milieu, for the resistance society found in the suburbs of Beirut, which has become referenced as

186

*Dahiyet* Hizbullah—the suburb *of* Hizbullah. In this environment Hizbullah regularly reminds its constituency that it belongs to a *hala islamiyya* and of its mission of resistance. We see how Hizbullah views and carries out its actions through a material lens—the delivery of services and resources, but also through a symbolic lens—inscribing these services in a framework of meanings relating the Shi'a individual to an identity and endowing him/her with a sense of belonging. Consequently, we cannot understand Hizbullah otherwise than through the interplay of both its material and symbolic actions.

### Giving meaning to life: Al-Hala al-Islamiyya

We mentioned before that Hizbullah is the official representative of the *wali al-faqih* (Imam Khamenei) in Lebanon. The *wilayat al-faqih* doctrine was established in an Islamic government with Imam Khomeini in the Islamic Republic of Iran in 1979. We will not discuss this complex political – religious set-up here, but what is important to note is that the association with the Iranian *wilayat al-faqih* endows Hizbullah with a distinct religious identity, which is also translated politically. Hizbullah's leaders strongly believe that the organisation of the daily life of individuals around the system of the *wilayat al-faqih* will assist the establishment of a collective identity conducive to a better society. It is against this background that the organisation of the daily lives of Shi'a by Hizbullah's holistic networks should be viewed. The *wilayat al-faqih* allows Shi'a Islam to exist as a coherent system of government capable of carrying out its actions.

> The *wilayat* is necessary to maintain and apply Islam. It is impossible to realize the great Islamic project with punctual and isolated operations. We need a guiding axis that links the *umma* together. This is what is achieved by the *wilayat* direction and management...[The *wali*] preserves the rules and the system [of Muslims], ensures justice, prevents injustice, and guarantees mechanisms for progress, as well as cultural, political and social evolution, and prosperity.[106]

This *wilayat* is materially translated by the holistic network of Hizbullah. It is also accomplished by the resistance society, in its military and social components. Both the holistic network of Hizbullah and the Resistance society it produces form what is commonly designated in Shi'a circles by *al-hala al-islamiyya*—the Islamic sphere. This *hala* groups the adherents (*multazimin*) to two major religious references (*marja'iyyat*): Fadlallah and Khamenei (or his Lebanese delegate, Nasrallah). We will not dwell here on the existing tensions between both poles.[107]

Adhering to the *hala islamiyya* produces a collective identity generating a strong sense of belonging, which gives meaning to the individual. Indeed, for the *hala islamiyya* to be fully accomplished, each person is responsible for carrying out informed choices based on religious knowledge.[108] The *hala islamiyya* is thus conceived as a collective product, and solidarity as well as volunteering become keys to its development. Hizbullah's institutions make

187

sure to promote the significance of solidarity and community work through a variety of religious narratives and symbolic references.[109] Accordingly, Hizbullah's policy networks not only provide material resources to their beneficiaries, they also give recognition and belonging to a world of meanings. Building on Bourdieu's view of society 'as a mechanism for the generation of meanings for life', we argue here that Hizbullah's *hala islamiyya* has succeeded in giving social importance to Shi'a individuals, and in providing them with reasons for life and death, thus endowing their lives with meaning.[110] Hizbullah's holistic institutions offer a pragmatic and meaningful alternative to Shi'a groups.

By providing Shi'a groups with meaning to their lives, Hizbullah's power is hence strongly and durably entrenched. In short, Hizbullah is a dominant and accepted authority today because it has succeeded in building a solid legitimacy among a majority of Shi'a. The commitment (*iltizam*) to Hizbullah's *hala islamiyya* has become, in many ways, the norm for a majority of the community.

## Conclusion

Labelling Hizbullah a terrorist organisation has seriously hampered the production of knowledge about this organisation. Even when it may have curtailed Hizbullah, as a practitioner of armed operations in the short run, it placed researchers and analysts alike in a permanent position of epistemological disadvantage *vis-à-vis* the 'terrorist' they hoped to analyse or ultimately defeat. Strikingly, Hizbullah itself presented a perception of its enemies that is much more conducive to 'knowing' its opponents. Partly as a result of the shortcomings of the terrorism label, various analysts of Hizbullah developed a counter-view emphasising the organisation's gradual but unavoidable transformation into a conventional political party that will be fully accommodated by the Lebanese political system. Yet, while having the merit of focusing on Hizbullah's grassroots activities, the thesis of the organisation's 'lebanonisation' fails to acknowledge or explain the interactions between the armed and the civilian activities of Hizbullah. We therefore suggested a different approach wherein Hizbullah's social and political activities operate as an integrated and holistic policy network, disseminating the values of resistance while constructing a collective identity derived from the notion of the *hala al-islamaiyya*, or 'Islamic sphere'. In this holistic approach and its large degree of embeddedness in Shi'a Lebanese society, Hizbullah distinguishes itself from many militant Sunni–Islamist organisations. The latter tend to see themselves as a 'vanguard' that is at odds with a society regarded as un-Islamic and hostile to their non-negotiable goal of establishing an Islamic state.[111]

This is not to say that Hizbullah's hegemony and intricate network of institutions, and the values these disseminate have remained unchallenged within Lebanon's Shi'a community.[112] Yet apart from some pockets of dissent, it is against the background of Hizbullah's holistic approach that its popularity and success in mobilising a large and loyal constituency should be understood. Accordingly, any prospect for Hizbullah's transformation away from armed 'resistance' should be firmly placed in an analysis of its hegemony among the Shi'a of Lebanon and the tools it used to acquire this status. In this respect the terrorism approach will have to acknowledge that the 'war against terror' will be a much more difficult endeavour than the simple liquidation of a group of individual militants largely dissociated from their social environment. In fact, in Hizbullah's case, the 'war against terror' would easily escalate into a war against an entire society in which the organisation has immersed itself. In turn, the proponents of the 'lebanonisation' thesis are likely to remain frustrated about Hizbullah's desired transformation into a fully fledged and accommodated political party merely by reinforcing its existing services and local networks. These service-oriented networks, as we have shown, are part and parcel of Hizbullah's notion of resistance and broader notion of the *hala islamiyya*, and cannot be seen in opposition to the organisation's military agenda. Where this leaves the question regarding Hizbullah's future evolution remains uncertain. Yet it is clear that any trigger for the organisation's transformation would have to come from within Lebanon's Shi'a community. This, of course, would require the rise of alternative currents that will have to match Hizbullah's powerful approach based on holistic networks disseminating services and values. For now, the likelihood of such a counter-hegemonic challenge remains remote indeed.

## Notes

[1] The European Union has not listed Hizbullah as a terrorist entity. Yet there is recurring debate in the European Council of Ministers to do so and recent events in Lebanon and UN Security Council Resolution 1559 (*inter alia* calling for the organisation's disarmament) may prompt the EU to classify it as 'terrorist'. Authors' interview with European diplomat in Damascus, 27 October 2004.

[2] Cited by Reuters, 9 September 2002.

[3] Cited in US Council on Foreign Relations, *Collateral Damage: Iraq and the Future of US–Syrian Relations*, New York, 24 April 2003.

[4] Cited in D Byman, 'Should Hezbollah be next?', *Foreign Affairs*, November–December 2003.

[5] See US Department of State, *Patterns of Global Terrorism 2001*, Washington, DC.

[6] These individuals are Imad Mughniyeh, Ali Atwi and Hassan Izzidine.

[7] See Department of State, *Patterns of Global Terrorism 2002*, Washington, DC.

[8] See Byman, 'Should Hezbollah be next?'; and US Council on Foreign Relations, at www.terrorismanswers.org.

[9] See the US Congress Bipartisan Committee on the events of 9/11, findings related to Hizbullah at http://www.insightful.com/products/infact/911/organization/hezbollah/b.html.

[10] See D Benjamin & S Simon, *The Age of Sacred Terror*, New York: Random House, 2002, pp 127–128.

[11] See D Priest & D Farah, *Washington Post*, 30 June 2002. Secretary of State Colin Powell said he was taking the reports 'very seriously'. Cited in *Al-Nahar* (Beirut), 3 July 2002.

[12] See D Farah, *Blood From Stones: The Secret Financial Network of Terror*, New York: Broadway Books, 2004.

[13] US Deputy National Security Advisor Steven Hadley, cited in *The Daily Star* (Beirut), 15 February 2002. Hadley's statement was prompted by the arrest, and later conviction, of 11 Lebanese American sympathisers for cigarette smuggling. See *Christian Science Monitor*, 15 July 2002; and N Blanford, 'Hizballah and Syria's "Lebanese card"', *Middle East Report*, 14 September 2004.

[14] Cited by NewsMax.com, 18 April 2003.

[15] Al-Jazeera transcript of interview with Hassan Nasrallah, 30 November, 10 and 12 December 2000.

[16] Cited in *al-Safir* (Beirut), 15 December 2001.

[17] Statement by Hassan Nasrallah, 30 March 2002, at www.moqawama.tv/arabic/f_report.htm.

[18] Department of State, *Patterns of Global Terrorism 2002*.

19  Authors' interview with Hizbullah members in Beirut, May 2003.
20  Authors' interview with Muhammad Fnaysh in Beirut, 7 July 2003.
21  One UK diplomat said that Hizbullah 'definitely' has sent its operatives to Iraq. Interview with the authors in Beirut, August 2004. Such claims appear to be mainly based on Hizbullah's pro-resistance discourse, combined with historical ties between Islamist militants and members of the *hawza* (Shi'a religious institute) in Najaf with Shi'a in Lebanon. Yet apart from some degree of admiration for Hizbullah among Iraqi Islamists and a remote analogy between Iraqi resistance to occupation and Hizbullah's fight against Israeli occupation, there is little to substantiate these claims. Hizbullah officials gave strong denials. Authors' interview with Hizbullah official in Beirut, May 2003. See also *Al-Nahar*, 31 March 2003.
22  See, respectively, M Kahl, 'Terror meeting in Iran', at http://www.free-lebanon.com/LFPNews/terr/terr.html and *Die Welt*, 28 February 2002.
23  See Michael Rubin, 'No change: Iran remains committed to Israel's destruction', *National Review Online*, 1 July 2002, at http://www.washingtoninstitute.org/media/rubin/rubin070102.htm.
24  See M Ranstorp, *Hizbullah in Lebanon: The Politics of the Western Hostage Crisis*, New York: St Martin Press, 1997.
25  For a discussion, see International Crisis Group (ICG), *Old Games, New Rules: Conflict on the Israel–Lebanon Border*, 18 November 2002, p 16, available online at: www.crisisgroup.org. Pro-Israeli sources even warned that Hizbullah might use biological and chemical weapons against Israel once the USA attacked Iraq. See J Goldberg, 'In the Party of God', *The New Yorker*, 14–21 October 2002.
26  Authors' interview in Beirut, August 2002.
27  An important exception to Israel's inability to penetrate Hizbullah's leadership is the February 1992 assassination of its secretary-general, Sheikh Abbas al-Musawi.
28  The work by Martin Kramer is an important exception. See, for example, M. Kramer, 'Hezbollah: the calculus of jihad', in E Martin, E Marty & R Scott Appleby (eds), *Fundamentalisms and the State: Remaking Polities, Economies and Militance*, Chicago, IL: University of Chicago Press, 1993.
29  On Fadlallah's relations with Hizbullah, see ICG, *Hizbullah: Rebel Without a Cause?*, 30 July 2003, pp 12–14, available online at: www.crisisgroup.org.
30  See A Saad-Ghorayeb, *Hizbullah. Politics and Religion*, London: Pluto Press, 2002, pp 14–15. This is not to deny that Hizbullah's leaders were politically active or indeed involved in acts of violence before establishing the party in 1984.
31  See Nasrallah's statements in *Al-Massira* (Beirut), 24 August 1998, *Al-'Ahd* (Beirut), 6 November 1998, *Al-Anwar* (Beirut), 16 September 1998 and *Al-Mujahid al-Siyyasi* (Beirut), 21 May 2000.
32  See Saad-Ghorayeb, *Hizbullah*, pp 101–102.
33  *Ibid*, pp 23–24.
34  ICG, *Old Games, New Rules*, p 21, n 181.
35  Saad-Ghorayeb, *Hizbullah*, p 133.
36  ICG, *Hizbullah: Rebel Without a Cause?*, p 14.
37  See the Open Letter of Hizbullah (*Nass al-Risala al-Maftuha allati wajahaha Hizbullah ila al-Mustada'fin fi Lubnan wa al-'Alam*) in *al-Safir*, 16 February 1985. For an English translation, see http://www.ict.org.il/Articles/Hiz_letter.htm.
38  Joseph Alagha, 'Hizbullah's gradual integration in the Lebanese public sphere', in *Sharqiyyat*, 13 (1), 2001, p 47. For more details, see Saad-Ghorayeb, *Hizbullah*, p 34ff.
39  Hizbullah's original party flag carried the slogan *at-Thawra al-Islamiyya fi Lubnan* (The Islamic Revolution in Lebanon). Yet recently versions have appeared in Lebanon without it.
40  Authors' interview in Beirut, July 2004.
41  See, respectively, Nasrallah as cited in *Al-Massira*, 24 August 1998, Hizbullah politburo member Shaykh Hassan Ezzedin as cited in *The Daily Star*, 3 October 2002 and Nasrallah on *Al-Jazeera*, 14 February 2002.
42  ICG, *Old Games, New Rules*, p 21.
43  Authors' interview with Hizbullah official in Beirut, May 2003. See also *Al-Nahar*, 31 March 2003 and (Hizbullah MP) Muhammad Raad, cited in *The Daily Star*, 30 September 2003.
44  Interview with Nasrallah in *Al-Watan* (Beirut), 19 March 2002.
45  Respectively, interviews with Nasrallah in *Al-Majalla* (Beirut), 30 March 2002 and *Al-Watan*, 19 March 2002.
46  Interview with Nasrallah on *Al-Jazeera*, 14 February 2002.
47  'Let the entire world hear, in case we are needed in some other arena, that we will not only bear our mantle but we will bear our mantle and our weapons. At your service, oh Husayn!'. Speech by Nasrallah in Beirut, as cited in *Al-Safir*, 22 May 2004.
48  See Saad-Ghorayeb, *Hizbullah*, pp 100–101.
49  In intelligence circles, such tactics of sending back propaganda to the messenger with the aim of confusing or intimidating is known as 'blow-back'.

190

50  For a discussion of Hizbullah's claims regarding Shab'a and other contested territories on the Israeli–Lebanese border or 'Blue Line', see ICG, *Old Games, New Rules*, Appendix B.

51  Cited in Saad-Ghorayeb, *Hizbullah*, p 112.

52  The best exploration of Hizbullah's ideology can be found in *ibid*.

53  On this point see *ibid*, pp 102–111.

54  Cited in *ibid*, p 134.

55  Nasrallah, cited in *Al-Intiqad* (Beirut), 2 May 2003.

56  Speech by Nasrallah in Beirut, as cited in *Al-Safir*, 22 May 2004.

57  Most of the following examples are taken from Saad-Ghorayeb, *Hizbullah*, pp 153–156, 108–109, 140.

58  See ICG, *Hizbullah: Rebel Without a Cause?*, pp 11–12.

59  For example, during a conference held by the movement for francophonie in Beirut in October 2002, Nasrallah hailed what he called 'political francophonie' as a possible 'alternative' to US hegemony in the United Nations. Cited in *The Daily Star*, 15 October 2002.

60  Cited by Robert Fisk in *Dissident Voice*, 18 February 2003.

61  See the commentary by the Middle East Media Research Institute, *Al-Shatat: The Syrian-Produced Ramadan 2003 TV Special*, 12 December 2003.

62  See *Al-Intiqad*, 30 October 2004.

63  See 'Views on Zionism' (*ara'i fi al-sahyuniyya*) and 'About terrorism' (*hawl al-irhab*) at http://www.moqawama.tv/.

64  See N Hamzeh, 'Lebanon's Hizbullah: from Islamic revolution to parliamentary accommodation', *Third World Quarterly*, 14 (2), 1993, pp 321–337.

65  See M Warn, 'Staying the course: the lebanonization of Hizbullah—the integration of an Islamist movement into a pluralist political system', unpublished masters thesis, Department of Political Science, Stockholm University, 1999.

66  See, for instance, Goldberg, 'In the Party of God'.

67  See Hamzeh, 'Lebanon's Hizbullah', p 335.

68  See AR Norton, *Hizballah of Lebanon: Extremist Ideals vs Mundane Politics*, New York: Council on Foreign Relations, 1999, p 2.

69  *Ibid*, pp 34–35; and Hamzeh, 'Lebanon's Hizbullah', pp 323–324.

70  J Harik, *Hizbollah: The Changing Face of Terrorism*, London: IB Tauris, 2004, p 47.

71  Norton, *Hizballah of Lebanon*, p 1.

72  *Ibid*, p 35.

73  G Kepel, *Jihad. Expansion et Déclin de l'Islamisme*, Paris: Gallimard, 2000.

74  Norton, *Hizballah of Lebanon*, p 9.

75  O Roy, 'Le post-Islamisme', *Revue des Mondes Musulmans et de la Méditérannée*, 85–86, 1999, pp 1–2.

76  Saad-Ghorayeb, *Hizbullah*, pp 26–28.

77  Interview with Naim Qassem, cited in *Al-Nahar* (Beirut), 5 July 1996. The term *muhassasa* (literaly 'allotment') in the Lebanese political vocabulary means the division of political powers between the Maronite presidency, the Sunni executive and the Shi'a legislative—also referred to as the 'troika'. The term is stigmatising as it implicitly indicates the corrupt practices that regulate this division of interests between the three political community groups. For more details, see R Leenders, 'Nobody having too much to answer for: 'laissez-faire', networks and post-war reconstruction in Lebanon', in S Heydemann (ed), *Networks of Privilege: The Politics of Economic Reform in the Middle East*, New York: Pelgrave–St Martin's Press, 2004.

78  See Harik 'Between Islam and the system', p 53.

79  See Alagha, 'Hizbullah's gradual integration', p 38 (emphasis added). Alagha shows, through the analysis of Hizbullah's leaders' discourses, how the doctrinal principles of the party have been adapted to its transformation, without compromising ideology.

80  Saad-Ghorayeb, *Hizbullah*.

81  Authors' interview with (Hizbullah MP) Muhammad Fneish, 7 July 2003. See also H Muzahem, 'Hizbullah's future in the wake of the Sep 11 Events', (unpublished), 2003, p 8, who argues that the military role of Hizbullah against the Israeli occupation in the Shab'a farms 'requires an independence of the resistance from the regime while the participation of Hizballah in the government coalition would probably promote some problems for Lebanon at the international level'. Note also that Hizbullah's refusal to participate in the government is also justified by the latter's corrupt practices. The party's vice-secretary emphasises: 'The central authority is known for its confessional system and its corrupt methods that reproduce it…It is natural that we do not participate in this authority because we do not agree with its rationale, its performance and its methodology.' Interview with (Hizbullah Vice-Secretary) Naim Qassem, cited in *Al-Nahar*, 16 August 2004.

82  See Ali Fayyad, 'Mixing between the objective basis and the strategic extension', *al-Safir*, 21 August 2003—this is an excerpt from his reply to the ICG 2003 report. In another reply by Hizbullah's Foreign

Relations Director, Nawaf al-Musawi, the party lists a number of 'causes' Hizballah has still to 'rebel' for, including the plight of the Palestinian refugees in Lebanon, Lebanese prisoners in Israeli jails and Lebanon's access to the Wazzani river's water resources in the south of Lebanon. See N al-Musawi, 'If Hizbullah did not exist...it would have to be created', *al-Safir*, 21 August 2003.

[83] Authors' interview with (Hizballah MP) Muhammad Fneish, 7 July 2003.

[84] See Norton, *Hizballah of Lebanon*, p 10.

[85] See Saad-Ghorayeb, *Hizbullah*, p 116.

[86] See, for example, Harik, *Hizbollah*, pp 93–94.

[87] See (Hizbullah Vice-Secretary) N Qassem, *Hizbullah: The Methodology, the Experience, the Future* (*Hizbullah: an-Nahj, al-Tajruba, al-Mustaqbal*), Beirut: Dar al-Hadi, 2002, p 83.

[88] Authors' interview with *as-Shahid* director, 12 September 1998.

[89] Authors' interview with the public relations director of *al-Juraha*, 4 September 1998.

[90] Authors' interview with *al-Mu'assassa* director, 8 September 1998.

[91] Authors' interview with *al-Qard* director, 2 March 2000.

[92] See *Al-Haya'a al-Suhiyya* brochure, no date.

[93] See CCSD brochure, 2002.

[94] See M Harb, 'Pratiques comparées de participation dans deux municipalités de la banlieue de Beyrouth: Ghobeyri et Bourj Brajneh', in A Favier (ed), *Municipalités et pouvoirs locaux au Liban*, Beirut: CERMOC, 2001, pp 157–177.

[95] In February 2004 the CCSD organised a conference in Beirut entitled 'The Islamic World and Europe: From Dialogue to Understanding'. Various European and regional partners were involved: the University of Birmingham, the German Orient Institut, the Friedrich Ebert Stiftung, as well as the *Confluences* French journal, l'Harmattan French publishing house, and the embassy of Austria. In the conference brochure, we read: 'It is a crucial moment to organize a conference on the theme of dialogue between Europe and the Islamic world. Europe has a dual position with the Islamic world, after September 11. It is important for us to discuss with Europeans who are more open to listen to us.
The conference grouped major scholars and experts, regional and international, and positioned the CCSD as a prominent contributor on the policy and academic research scene in Lebanon.

[96] See Qassem, *Hizbullah*, p 376.

[97] See speech by Nasrallah on the occasion of the liberation of Lebanese prisoners from Israeli jails, 25 January 2004.

[98] Qassem, *Hizbullah*, p 99.

[99] See L Deeb, *An Enchanted Modern: Gender and Public Piety among Islamist Shi'i Muslims in Beirut*, PhD thesis in Anthropology, Emory University, 2003, forthcoming at Princeton University Press, pp 33, 62.

[100] Saad-Ghorayeb, *Hizbullah*, p 126.

[101] The political history of Shi'a is known for having produced representations in which Shi'a are persecuted, marginalised and abused by oppressors. The conspiracy theory still remains in the perceptions of the community and is regularly played out in religious celebrations, notably during the mourning of Ashura. There is always an oppressor who wants to prevent the Shi'a from realising their capacities, from practicing their faith, from claiming their rights: the Sunni imam, the Ottoman emir, the feudal landowner, the political patron, the government, Israel, America, etc. Shi'a enemies willingly maintain Shi'a in a precarious and deprived situation, to prevent them from developing, as they form a potential for rebellion and change that cannot be controlled. These beliefs are common to the members of the resistance society.

[102] Authors' interview with the vice-president of the Islamic Institute, 8 September 1998.

[103] *Ibid.*

[104] Authors' interview with Hizbullah's social services director, 25 August 1998.

[105] Authors' interview with Hizbullah director of the Information Unit, 7 October 2004.

[106] See Qassem, *Hizbullah*, pp 70–71.

[107] It is difficult to document the conflicts between Fadllallah and Nasrallah, or more accurately between Fadlallah and Khamenei. They are related to antagonisms about Shi'a jurisprudence and religious law, which are beyond the scope of this article. See S Mervin, 'La *hawza* à l'épreuve du siècle. La réforme de l'enseignement religieux supérieur chiite de 1909 à nos jours', in M Al-Charif & S al-Kawakibi (eds), *Le courant réformiste musulman et sa réception dans les sociétés arabes*, Damascus: IFPO, pp 69–84.

[108] See Deeb, *An Enchanted Modern*, p 77.

[109] References to solidarity and social work are common across Hizbullah's institutions, where leaders and members mention the importance of volunteering, giving and sharing. The narratives are punctuated by references to Islamic quotes praising social work and participation with the people. During the month of Ramadan these references abound and the concept of '*takaful*' (sponsorship) is widely disseminated, encouraging Muslims to sponsor orphans and needy children.

192

[110] As summarised by G Hage, "'Comes a time we are all enthusiasm': understanding Palestinian suicide bombers in times of exighophobia', *Public Culture*, 15 (1), 2003, pp 65–89, esp p 78.

[111] The writings of Abdul Salam Faraj, an ideologist for the Egyptian Islamic Jihad organisation, are highly illustrative in this respect. See JJG Jansen, *The Neglected Duty: The Creed of Sadat's Assassins and Islamic Resurgence in the Middle East*, New York: Macmillan 1986.

[112] Internal contestations within the Shi'a community against Hizbullah's domination are not exceptional. They are, however, mostly effectively marginalised or co-opted. For example, attempts to use Hizbullah's paradigms (for example, the *wilayat al-faqih* or resistance) for interests that are not operated under the party's tutelage are rapidly brought to a halt. This was the case when a Shi'a entrepreneur began independently from the party to publish a children's magazine propagating the resistance ideology and an understanding of the *wilayat al-faqih*. He was quickly intercepted by Hizbullah's members, who politely informed him that either party members co-partner with him and supervise the publication of the magazine or he would have to put an end to the publication of his magazine—he chose the latter. Also Hizbullah's role in the Elyssar reconstruction project—a state-led effort to redesign and rebuild the southwestern sections of al-Dahiya—has raised serious questions among Shi'a residents. In negotiations with Elyssar, Hizbullah helped facilitate the displacement of residents to allow for the construction of a highway to Beirut airport. Many felt abandoned and let down or expressed doubts about the opaque bargaining done on their behalf by Hizbullah. See M Harb, 'Urban governance in post-war Beirut: resources, negotiations, and contestations in the Elyssar project", in S Shami (ed), *Capital Cities: Ethnographies of Urban Governance in the Middle East*, Toronto: Toronto University Press, 2001, pp 111–133.

# Themes in official discourses on terrorism in Central Asia

STUART HORSMAN

Throughout nearly a decade and a half of independence, the Central Asian states have invested considerable material and intellectual resources in maintaining regime and state security. They have given particular focus to the threats, whether perceived or actual, emanating from Islamist extremism and terrorism. To some extent their concerns have been understandable and justified but there are also concerns that this 'discourse of danger' has been used instrumentally to advance other political objectives including state building and defending a 'gradualist approach' to reform.[1]

The Central Asian regimes have faced the same security dilemmas as many other newly independent states, lacking any prior history of sovereignty and uncertain about their territorial and political integrity.[2] Regime legitimacy, state building and national security have been perceived as parts of a single security dynamic by their governments.[3] Under these circumstances, ideological and physical challenges and threats, whether perceived or actual, have assumed a high profile in the political and security considerations of the Central Asian states.

The local governments and some commentators have portrayed the regional security environment into which these states emerged as dangerous and unstable, with Islamist terrorism being regarded as a key destabilising factor.[4] The collapse of the USSR was marked by sporadic incidents of communal and separatist violence, some with a religious dimension, in Central Asia and further afield. Within a year of independence, the leaders' worst fears about the spectre of 'Islamic Extremism' were realised with the brief existence of an Islamist government in Namangan and the onset of civil war in Tajikistan.[5] (The latter was however simplistically portrayed as an ideological battle between a secular, neo-communist government and Islamists, rather than primarily a conflict between regional groupings.) A number of incidents since then, most notably the actions of the Islamic Movement of Uzbekistan (IMU), have further enhanced the governments' concerns about Islamist-related terrorism. The key terrorist incidents include a string of bombs in Tashkent on 16 February 1999, the IMU's incursions into Kyrgyzstan, and Kyrgyzstan and Uzbekistan in the summers of 1999 and 2000, respectively, explosions at a market in Bishkek in 2002 and a money exchange in Osh in 2003, and further bombing campaigns in March–April and August in Uzbekistan.[6]

This paper will not seek to explore or assess the underlying causes or actual threat level of terrorism in Central Asia. Rather for this study the issue is of 'whether there really is an Islamic threat...is perhaps secondary to the leadership's perception of it.'[7] The focus of the article will be on the official discourses on Islamist terrorism. It will examine how the states perceive, portray and respond to the threat in official statements, policy and the media. There will be a particular reference to the government of Uzbekistan's discourse, as this state has been both the principle target of most terrorist activity in Central Asia and the leading exponent of a terrorism discourse. This form of communication has been a constant and high profile part of regional political life since 1992. Four of the five states, Turkmenistan being the possible exception, have presented their views on terrorism through a range of media including legislation, public statements and the official media, for example. Within these official analyses and portrayals there has been a number of core and constant themes. These, the focus of this article, are:

- an all-encompassing, if not amorphous, definition of the terms *terrorist* and *terrorism*;
- speculative and at times contradictory assessments of the threat;
- the image of the ever-present and well co-ordinated terrorist conspiracy;
- the terrorist as criminal and mercenary;
- the terrorist as lacking in political or religious conviction;
- the pre-eminent role of external ideas and organisations;
- the indigenous terrorist as an aberration of national and regional political and religious traditions, values and realities;
- solidarity between government and society in combating terrorism; and
- implicit throughout, the continuation of Soviet thinking on ideological and physical challenges to the state.

## Defining terrorism

The terms 'terrorism' and 'terrorist' are highly contested concepts, with a multiple range of academic and policy definitions.[8] This paper will use narrow definitions of the terms, which focus upon 'the use or threat [of violence being] designed to influence the government or to intimidate the public or a section of the public...and the use or threat [being] made for the purpose of advancing a political, religious or ideological cause.'[9] Such definitions emphasise the use or intention to use violence by non-state actors to achieve their political goals. Most Central Asian definitions are far broader, if not amorphous. Perhaps the most coherent definition is that of Article 226 of Kyrgyzstan's Criminal Code. This defines terrorism as 'explosion[s], acts of arson or other actions which pose a threat to people and lead to people's death, cause significant damage...or other dangerous consequences...in order to undermine public security, threaten people or exert pressure on the authorities'.[10] Even this definition is open to considerable interpretation. Most other regional definitions are even more nebulous. They contain little demarcation between the use of or the threat of violence and the promotion of non-violent but radical ideas, and between political violence and general criminality. Uzbekistan's 2000 draft Bill on Terrorism, for example, defined terrorism as 'socially dangerous wrong doing' while Article 244 of its Criminal Code draws together in its proscription 'the activities of religious organisa-tions, movements, sects and others which support terrorism, drug trafficking and organised crime'.[11] Likewise Kazakhstan's draft terrorist group proscription list, reportedly based on similar UK, US and Russian legislation, also blurs the debate.[12] Kazakhstani officials have acknowledged that Hizb ut-Tahrir (HT) is likely to be included in the list 'even though there are no real threats or actions of a *terrorist nature*' from HT.[13] A Kyrgyzstani Supreme Court ruling of November 2003 is similarly ambiguous. This ruling outlawed HT along with three other 'terrorist' groups, all of which the republic's security services claimed were 'linked one way or another with terrorist acts committed in the country at different times'.[14] Although Bishkek's legislation sought to emphasise that all the groups were involved in political violence, the evidence it was able to provide on HT and the two Uighur groups has been questioned by many commentators and even undermined by its own officials.[15] A comment by an official from the Kyrgyzstan's Prosecutor General's Office that the ban would allow the government to 'have more opportunities to bring to court those who spread out leaflets calling for the overthrow of the existing authorities' suggests that HT's inclusion in the ruling was a useful tool to silence a political opponent rather than evidence of involvement in terrorism.[16] There is a particular irony in the application of such ambiguous definitions of terrorism given a circular from the Uzbekistani Ministry of Defence, issued after the 30 July 2004 explosions. This stated that the military censor would review all security-related newspaper articles in order to promote 'objective coverage...avoid misunderstandings...and ensure the correct use of military terminology'.[17]

The amorphous definitions and the admissions by government officials of the relative fluidity of the terminology suggest two, not necessarily mutually exclusive, conclusions. First, there is an unwillingness or inability to define terms or apply the relevant legislation precisely. Second, the term 'terrorist' is deliberately broad in focus to include extreme ideological but non-violent threats, as well as, violent threats. These arbitrary and/or amorphous approaches provide political benefits to the governments. The previously mentioned Uzbekistani legislation contains ambiguous and highly subjective concepts such as 'evil' and 'socially dangerous'. In fact these nebulous terms led President Karimov to criticise the 2000 draft bill as 'superficial' and a 'political mistake'.[18] The bill's authors claimed, however, that this loose definition, already existing in Article 155 of the Criminal Code, had been specifically selected as it suited the requirements of the law enforcement agencies and a new, more precise definition would 'complicate their work and the protection of law and order'.[19]

The debate over definitions has been most acute and illustrative in relation to the extremist group, HT. HT has been described as a terrorist organisation by the regional governments for two reasons. First, it is claimed that HT has been involved in terrorist incidents in the region. Second, its ideology and ultimate goal, the establishment of a caliphate throughout the *umma* and not just Central Asia, fall into a wider definition of terrorism, based on intent and rhetoric and not necessarily the advancement of physical violence.

The Central Asian governments claim that HT is a terrorist organisation in the narrow sense of the term, and suggest it has been involved in most of the major terrorist incidents in the region, including the February 1999 explosions, the plot to attack the Coalition airbase at Manas, Kyrgyzstan, in 2003 and the two 2004 bombing campaigns in Uzbekistan.[20] However, in each of these cases HT's involvement has been seriously questioned, and government claims have even been quietly retracted when a subsequent official version of events has been issued.[21] In an off-the-record interview, a senior Uzbekistani law enforcement officer clearly questioned whether HT had been involved in the 2004 attacks.[22] (A then unknown group, the Islamic Jihad of Uzbekistan, claimed responsibility for both incidents.[23]) HT has denied involvement in any of the above attacks and has continued to emphasise its professed adherence to non-violent action.[24] Clearly there is a need to be wary of such statements and there is a debate as to whether HT's adherence to non-violent means is permanent or tactical.[25] However, there is no credible evidence to indicate that HT has been implicated in terrorist acts and Western governments, much to the chagrin of Uzbekistan's Foreign Minister, Sadiq Safayev, do not regard it as a terrorist organisation.[26]

HT is also perceived as terrorist because of its ideas, which are described as anti-constitutional and extremist. Its ideas and recruitment and propaganda activities have resulted in members facing official condemnation, including long-term prison sentences, on a par with actual terrorist groups.[27] This threat from an ideological source reflects the political sensitivity of the new regimes, still seeking to establish national and state identities at a time of political transition. It may also reflect the leaderships' own political education in the ideology-rich Marxist–Leninist tradition.

## Speculation and conspiracies

There is a willingness by the government to offer quick, loose, pre-emptive, if not speculative, assessments on the nature of the terrorist threat, groups and incidents. Such analyses also claim the presence of large-scale conspiratorial networks acting against the state.

One piece of questionable analysis was a 1999 list of extremist groups issued by the Osh Provisional Department of the Ministry of Interior. This list, which continued to be reiterated for the next two years without question by regional officials and media sources, named 10 clandestine groups in addition to the IMU and HT active in Central Asia at the time.[28] However, on closer inspection, there is considerable evidence to question the assessments of the groups' size, objectives and even existence. Most of the groups were probably very small and transient.[29] One name, *Uzun soqol* (Long Beards), was simply a nickname for devout Muslims, while another was a Sufi organisation, the *Nurchilar*, with no connection to terrorism at all.[30] Most tellingly of all, two of the groups, Adolat and Islom lashkarlari, had been closed down by the authorities at least four years before the list was published.[31] The Kyrgyzstanis' claims of continued clandestine activity and threat were probably the result of either poor research or deliberate misinformation. Accusations are quick to be issued and often retracted too. In the immediate aftermath of the February 1999 bombings, Uzbekistan's government initially blamed Hizbollah, although the nature of this organisation changed over time from the well known Middle Eastern group, to a successor movement of the indigenous Adolat and an alleged armed wing of HT.[32] By the time the case came to court, the IMU and the secular politician, Mohammad Solih, had become the chief suspects.

Linked to this analysis is the governments' perception or at least promotion of complex terrorist conspiracies against the state. Clearly terrorism cannot exist without clandestine networks and planning and the IMU's relationship with Al-Qaeda and the Taliban demonstrates that Central Asian terrorists are linked into a broad and complex international network of networks. However the official 'conspiracy discourse' predates this relationship and its claims are far more encompassing than the realties would suggest. As early as 1995 Tashkent had claimed, for example, that Uzbeks were receiving terrorist training abroad.[33] Terrorist plots and incidents are regularly portrayed as the result of well co-ordinated planning involving a number of, often disparate and foreign, individuals and groups. These conspiracies are audacious, if not incredible, in their scale and goals. As noted above, eventual suspicion for the February bombings fell on the IMU and the secular opposition figure in exile and former presidential candidate, Mohammad Solih.[34] Solih was found guilty in absentia. Most independent commentators, however, believed the charges against him were fabricated and politically motivated.[35] In fact, Zainuddin Askarov, who made the claim about Solih's involvement, probably under duress, subsequently retracted his statement.[36] The accusation was nevertheless politically useful as it placed the secular opposition in league with the extremist movement and put both beyond the political pale. This action recalls Montefiore's comments on the 1930s Soviet show trials, which putting 'together such killers from different factions, created an [opposition] of astonishing global, indeed Blofeldian reach'.[37]

The image of an ever-present and co-ordinated threat was revived in 2004 when it was claimed that 'experts concluded that weapons, ammunition and explosives seized at the scene of the crime then [in March 2004] are similar to the ones that were used in the terrorist acts in July of this year and in the 1999 events. This proves that there is an interconnection between them.'[38] However, this contradicts other official statements, including the respective court judgments which found the IMU responsible for the 1999 explosions and HT for the spring 2004 attacks.[39]

### De-legitimising the terrorist: criminality over ideology

There has been a deliberate attempt in official debates to devalue the political, ideological and religious motivation of the terrorist in general, and the IMU and HT in particular. As one Uzbekistani newspaper claimed, for example, extremists 'do not practise any religion [and there are] those among them who do not believe in God at all'.[40] Criminal, mercenary and apolitical motives are emphasised instead. There is some justification in this argument. Terrorism is a crime in itself, terrorist groups often have close relations with organised crime and individual terrorists may be motivated by a number of reasons, including economic gain. The Central Asian experience is probably no exception. It is highly probable that the IMU has been involved in drug trafficking and other criminal activities.[41] Such activities no doubt motivate some members and also provide funds for the organisation. Clearly it is suggested that this vein of criminality runs throughout the movement from its involvement in kidnappings and drug running to petty criminal activities. Two individuals charged in connection with the February 1999 incident were, for example, also accused of stealing clothes and killing a dog.[42] Whatever the provenance of these charges, they may have been publicised to trivialise and devalue the serious and political nature of the principle crime, the then largest terrorist incident in Central Asia.

However, it would be wrong to suggest, as the region's governments and some commentators have claimed, that the IMU's primary *raison d'être* is criminal gain, in particular drugs running, or that 'its leaders resemble little more than a network of militants primarily motivated by economic interest'.[43] Naumkin is keen to dismiss the criminal thesis and argues instead that Adolat and the IMU are underpinned by political and religious objectives. Adolat, the IMU's forerunner, was not, he believes 'merely a gang of murderers and drug dealers...as a number of observers have sought to suggest'.[44] Allegations of drugs trafficking and criminal gain 'hardly allow one to claim they [the IMU] are not terrorists'.[45] Rather its involvement in such activities diverts attention from the fact that it is first and foremost a terrorist organisation. The criminal thesis is arbitrary in its application. While it is used to argue that the IMU is an apolitical criminal movement, various other individuals and organisations, including members of the Russian Border Guard Service, are probably involved in narcotics trafficking too.[46] However, these accusations are not used to suggest that it is their core activity.

HT and its members are also often portrayed in a mercenary and criminal light. In her article, Uzbekistani law professor, Mavjuda Rajabova, stated that all the movements proscribed under the Criminal Code's Article 244, including HT, are 'criminal' groups. Her analysis of HT's organisational structure and its goals was more akin to an examination of an organised crime group. In her assessment she did not acknowledge HT's highly politicised and revolutionary cell-based structure, well known to most other commentators including Uzbekistan's Ambassador to Israel, who offered a far more informed and politically focused analysis of the movement in a newspaper a week before Rajabova's study.[47] It is also often claimed that HT pays individuals up to $100 to join and distribute its leaflets, explicitly suggesting that individuals are attracted by the financial reward, not by political ideas.[48] There is no reliable evidence to support these claims about payment for activities and it seems highly unlikely that many members would find this incentive sufficient compensation for the high risks of involvement with HT.[49]

Another means of attempting to discredit *the terrorist* by the governments has been to suggest that individuals have been tricked or brainwashed into joining the movements. This is seen in official accounts including testimony of re-educated IMU and HT members. For example repentant ex-IMU members have claimed in the official press that they believed they would be attending Islamic education classes rather than joining a terrorist movement.[50]

### External versus national values

Another theme in official discourses has been the emphasis on the external origins and values of terrorism in Central Asia. Indigenous terrorists and their ideas are portrayed as alien and not rooted in Central Asia's national and regional cultural and religious norms, experiences and traditions. They are seen as the antithesis of local values, without 'any nationality'.[51] In fact they are an obstacle to political progress and national consolidation, as highlighted by President Karimov's statement on the February 1999 explosions, which he saw as an attempt to interfere with 'our construction of a new democratic civilized state'.[52]

This argument is further developed to suggest that the government is pursuing, in its counter-terrorism policy, an agenda that reflects national values and aspirations and that these policies are supported by society at large. The governments see themselves as the guardians of an authentic and correct form of Islam, 'which is allegedly incompatible with any other forms of Islam, promoted by unofficial Islamic leaders'.[53] One commentator, reiterating the official line, has claimed that the IMU has 'no patience for official Islam [or] no patience with tradition'.[54] One 'reformed' HT prisoner articulated this view when he stated that Tashkent's battle against radical and independent Islamist groups was not a result of its 'current political interests but [an attempt] to maintain in people's minds the understanding of Islam which has been traditional in Asia throughout the centuries'.[55]

Terrorism's (unsuccessful) challenge to state and society are reflected in Uzbekistani Foreign Minister Safayev's views that the republic was 'not shaken by [the Spring 2004] attacks...Uzbekistan [had] passed this test once again showing that it is an effective country with established civil society institutions...This was an indication that the state and its society are mature.'[56] His comments reflect a core element in the governments' discourses, that the state and society are at one in defeating the terrorist threat, which is an affront to national values, and that it is the patriotic duty of the populace to participate in the counter-terrorism campaign. In Uzbekistan, the *mahalla* (neighbourhood) and other civil structures are called upon or exhorted for their anti-terrorism activism. It is the duty of Uzbekistani citizens to 'protect not only [their] house but also [their] homeland' and those who fail to take an active role are criticised in the media.[57] In one rallying call, the *mahalla* was described as a 'great opportunity for people to close ranks in the fight against any threat'.[58] There may also be an additional objective in this call for popular activism. The articulation of a threat and the need to respond to it may be being used to develop nation and state identities.[59] Safayev in fact referred to the public response to the 2004 attacks as part of a 'social and psychological consolidation' of Uzbek society.[60]

While not wishing to underplay the role of 'the external' in Central Asia's terrorist debate, there is a sense that the regimes are seeking to create a false dichotomy between an authentic, loyal and apolitical domestic Islam, on the one hand, and foreign, extremist and de-stabilising Islamist influences, on the other. In doing so they are presenting monolithic versions of the two and discounting the realities of cross-fertilisation. The probable objective of this demarcation is to undercut the domestic ideological roots of independent and extremist Islamists and underlying grievances that have helped both local (IMU) and external (HT) groups to thrive. This demarcation also does not recognise that Central Asia's 'official Islam' is as much an artificial and contested construct as the IMU's political goals are, being a state-sponsored and manipulated edifice. Rashid's statement about the IMU's lack of 'patience for official Islam...[and] tradition' epitomises the failure to acknowledge that there is more than one form of authentic religious and political tradition in Central Asia.[61] Many Central Asian Muslims, not just members of the IMU, do not therefore regard the officially sanctioned religious bodies as legitimate.[62] An interesting and creative exception to the co-opted nature of official Islam has been the limited rehabilitation (and return from exile) of the respected former Mufti of Uzbekistan, Mohammad Sodiq Mohammad Yusuf.[63] Mohammad Yusuf has been able to offer a critical, relatively independent and well informed critique of HT's and the IMU's manipulations of the tenets of Islam in a way other clerics and officials cannot, although the government has not allowed him to be as active as he could be.[64]

While the IMU has become more integrated into the global *jihadist* networks over time, it did emerge from a particular Uzbekistani, if not Ferghana Valley, context. The IMU is part of the alternative, clandestine and, at times, denied regional tradition. As Naumkin records, there is considerable evidence indicating that the IMU, certainly pre-1999, can be regarded as a product of the region's *parallel Islam* tradition, albeit a radical Salafisti wing of this.[65] The IMU's organisational origins can be seen in Adolat, an Islamist vigilante group that sought to establish *sharia*-based law and order in the city of Namangan in the early post-Soviet period. Adolat was quintessentially Uzbek. Its structure, membership and sense of public activism drew heavily on the Uzbek *mahalla*.[66] It also appears to have won the approval of the city's older, more conservative citizens.[67] Both Adolat and the imus' intellectual origins can be traced to the vibrant but clandestine parallel Islam milieu. Key individuals, such as Tahir Yuldash and Jumabai Khujaev (aka Namangani) were influenced if not schooled by the students of Abdulvali *qori* Mirzayev, who was taught by Muhammadjan Rustamov (aka Hindustani), an axiomatic figure in Central Asia's *parallel Islam* community.[68] Via Mirzayev and his followers, Adolat and the IMU can be regarded as part of the 'local Salafi' tradition, which has existed in the region since at least the 1940s, and possibly as far back as the pre-Tsarist era.[69] If *The Lessons of Jihad* is the key IMU text it is purported to be, then, despite its broadly *jihadist* and Salafi nature, its inclusion of 'themes that are clearly unacceptable to Wahhabi theologians today' also suggests that, intellectually, as well as physically, the IMU was initially isolated from contemporary extremist Islamist debates elsewhere in the *umma*.[70]

The IMU's objectives, although not well publicised, were, at least until its relocation to Afghanistan, also singularly Uzbekistani in focus. Its goals, first publicly articulated in August 1999, have focused on the removal of the Karimov government. At this time, the IMU declared a 'Jihad against the Karimov regime...[with] the aim...[of] creating an Islamic country in Uzbekistan'.[71] In fact, the IMU's national focus was either naively or arrogantly myopic, to the extent that they asked Bishkek 'to leave the mujahedin alone...so they could freely pass [through Kyrgyzstan] on to Uzbekistan, to their homeland', in order to assume their fight with the Uzbekistani authorities.[72] This rather singular focus was still being reiterated as late as 2001, when the chairman of the IMU's Supreme Religious Council, Zubair ibn Abdurahim, refuted that idea that the IMU had changed its name to the Islamic Movement of Turkestan, as suggested by Kyrgyzstani and Russian official and media sources, or had widened its goals to establish a regional caliphate. He stated, perhaps disingenuously by this date, that, 'we have only one enemy—the Tashkent regime. We have no problems with neighboring countries.'[73]

Accusations of external origins and ideas are far more appropriately levelled at HT, given its roots. However, claims that its ideas are 'far removed from the daily pressures and problems of the people and appear to be written from abroad, for global rather than local distribution' are difficult to defend.[74] This alien organisation has had considerable success in recruiting and mobilising sections of Central Asia's community. It has also undergone a process of 'regionalisation'. The initial over-emphasis upon Middle Eastern issues in its Central Asian propaganda has been replaced by literature with an increased focus upon the region's social and political concerns and probably produced in the region.[75] Similarly, despite being an alien organisation, its Uzbekistani members also appear to be aware and possibly respectful of the region's *parallel Islam* traditions.[76] In fact it is possible to argue that its Central Asian experience has re-invigorated HT's global profile and become an integral part of its global campaign, as is evident in its 'Who Killed Farhod Usmanov' web- and leaflet-based media campaign.[77]

## The legacy of the Soviet experience

Many aspects of the present official discourse on terrorism have direct comparisons with Soviet language and practices on terrorism. This can be seen in the ideological and arbitrary definition of terrorism, the 'criminalisation' of the terrorist, the portrayal of vast and usually externally inspired conspiracies against the state and the call for popular mobilisation against the threat. This is probably not surprising given the relative wholesale transition of the political cadres, institutions and political cultures from the Soviet republics to independent states. The evolutionary nature of the transition means that Soviet discourses, experiences and policies have not been entirely jettisoned by the successor regimes. As Whitlock notes, Uzbekistan's fears of large-scale all-encompassing anti-state conspiracies and holding of large public show trials has strong parallels with the Soviet show trials and sensational conspiracies of the 1930s and 1940s.[78] It was alleged at the 1999 trials that after the explosions the accused planned to release sleeping gas and that, while Tashkent citizens were incapacitated, the plotters would kill all ethnic Russians in the city and then seize power.[79] President Karimov's most famous comment on Islamist extremists, that they 'must be shot in the head' and 'if necessary I'll shoot them myself' echoes *Pravda's* headline, 'The Mad Dogs Must Be Shot', issued during the 1936 show trial.[80]

Likewise, the attempt to depoliticise and 'criminalise' the Islamist opposition has echoes of the Soviet campaign against the *basmachi*. The term '*basmachi*' was originally applied to local bandits but was co-opted by the Soviets as a derogatory name for the loose collection of anti-Soviet forces in 1920s–30s Central Asia.[81] According to Whitlock, once the *basmachi* rebellion was physically defeated the process of intellectually destroying it began. This involved the writing of a history in which the *basmachi* were portrayed as feudal, backward and criminal. This propaganda campaign was relatively successful, with the local Muslim population accepting and even reiterating the official version, albeit partly as a result of fear and lack of alternative accounts.[82]

The calls for public counter-terrorist action, even vigilantism, are also reminiscent of an earlier age in which the USSR's citizens were urged to combat anti-Soviet activities and threats, from the *kulaks* and spies of the 1920s to alcohol and other social evils of the 1980s.[83] One contemporary and critical Uzbekistani journalist has gone as far as to say that the present call for vigilante behaviour could take Uzbekistan 'back to the 1930s'.[84]

The fear of externally inspired conspiracies is evident in both periods too. During the trials of those accused of the February 1999 bombings, the defendants were accused of 'making maps and traveling abroad...tainted by contact with foreigners...who wished harm to the homeland'.[85] Similar charges were levelled at the *basmachi* and many other enemies of the Soviet state, including Hindustani, whose KGB persecutors shouted at him, when he was arrested in 1952, that he had "'been to Afghanistan!...[and] Hindustan" as though these things were crimes'.[86] In the 1920s and 1930s the Bolsheviks were concerned about the ideological challenge that pan-Islam and pan-Turkism posed in the region. A united Muslim opposition from within and without, it was feared, would prevent the consolidation process of the USSR, similar to the present fears of the Central Asian regimes.

During the early Soviet period Sufism, which had been active in resisting Russian and Soviet power in the Caucasus and Central Asia, was regarded as the key Islamist threat to the state.[87] However, in the 1980s the threat became increasingly 'externalised', with Moscow suggesting that Wahhabism rather than Sufism was the primary Islamist threat to the USSR. This was an astute political move given Wahhabism's roots in Saudi Arabia and Sufism's strong connections with Central Asia. This elevation of the Wahhabi threat coincides with the global rise of political Islam in this period and the increased sense of threat to the USSR from external Shia and Sunni Islamist ideas from Afghanistan and Iran too.[88] In post-Soviet Central Asia Sufism is now even suggested as a possible indigenous counterbalance to external extremist influences, such as Wahhabism.[89]

## Conclusion

Central Asian governments' discourses have been proactive, aggressive and highly ideological in nature. This is partly a consequence of their genuine sense of insecurity, to some extent itself a result of actual threats, although not necessarily terrorist in nature, from both inside and outside the region. The governments' keen perception of a terrorist threat is also related to the implicit sense of vulnerability that is associated with newly independent states still striving to develop their state- and nationhood. It is also a product of the leaderships' own background in the ideology-saturated Soviet political culture.

There are, however, also instrumentalist dimensions to the governments' discourses on terrorism. As Buzan and Torjesen have both noted, political advantage can be gained by political elites by promoting threats and dangers to state and society. By identifying something as an immediate threat, it becomes a political priority to which resources need to be directed and also diverted from other needs.[90] In Central Asia, the terrorist discourse helps promote a 'stability-first' political culture, which is allegedly necessary 'when a country gains its own statehood, the more so, during a transition period from one system to another [in order] to prevent bloodshed and confrontation and to preserve ethnic and civil accord, peace and stability'.[91]

Given the discourse's suggestion that government and society are unified in their opposition to the actions and ideas of groups such as the IMU and HT, it is also hoped that it will enhance the regimes' legitimacy and develop nation and state identities.

Official Central Asian discourses on terrorism have sought both to emphasise the presence of a significant, ever-present terrorist threat and conversely to downplay, if not negate, it at the same time. To what extent it is possible to maintain the mixed message of a heightened sense of threat and the need for a unified political and social response, on the one hand, and a threat which is apolitical, criminal, alien and unattractive to a Central Asian audience, on the other, is unclear. The discrepancies between these two features of the discourse may prove to be highly problematic and difficult for the regimes to resolve. In the long run they may undermine any effective counter-terrorism policy, which will require an effective, coherent and credible assessment of the nature, roots and extent of the threat.

## Notes

I would like to thank Dr Nick Megoran, Michael Denison and the anonymous reviewers for their collective comments and insights on drafts of this article. The views expressed in this article are the author's own and should not be regarded as a statement of government policy.

[1] For a discussion of the 'discourse of danger', see S Torjesen, 'Distortions in the discourse of danger: the case of small arms proliferation in Kyrgyzstan', in *Central Asia—Perspectives from the Field Conference*, School of Oriental and African Studies, London, 7–8 November 2003, p14. On the 'gradualist approach', see S Horsman, 'Uzbekistan: ten years of gradualism or stagnation?', in S Cummings (ed), *Oil, Transition and Security in Central Asia*, London: Routledge, 2003, pp 47–58.

[2] B Buzan, *People, States and Fear*, Hemel Hempstead: Harvester Wheatsheaf, 1991, p 79.

[3] MJ Gasiorowski, 'Regime legitimacy and national security: the case of Pahlavi Iran', in E Azar & C Moon (eds), *National Security in the Third World: Management of Internal and External Threats*, Aldershot: Edward Elgar, 1988, p 244.

[4] For a critique of this perception of insecurity see S Torjesen, 'Distortions in the discourse of danger', p 14; and for discussion of the politics of Islamophobia in Uzbekistan, see A Bohr, *Uzbekistan: Politics and Foreign Policy*, London: Royal Institute of International Affairs, 1998, pp 25–30.

[5] For an account of events in Namangan, see A Bohr, *Uzbekistan*, pp 26–27; and for an analysis of the political manipulation of the Tajik civil war, see S Horsman, 'Uzbekistan's involvement in the Tajik civil war 1992–7: domestic considerations, *Central Asian Survey*, 18 (1), 1999, pp 37–48.

[6] For more detailed discussion on each of these incidents, see, respectively, M Whitlock, *Beyond the Oxus: The Central Asians*, London: John Murray, 2002, pp 242–264; P Polat, & N Butkevich, *Unravelling the Mystery of the Tashkent Bombing: Theory and Implications*, Eurasian Institute for Economic and Political Research, at http://cas.org/english/Krsten_4_12_00.htm; International Crisis Group (ICG), *Recent Violence in Central Asia: Causes and Consequences*, Brussels, 18 October 2000, pp 3–5; JS Smith, 'The IMU: alive and kicking?', *Central Asian–Caucasus Analyst*, at http://www.cacianalyst.org/view_article.php?articleid = 1761; Institute for War and Peace Reporting (IWPR), *Reporting Central Asia (RCA)*, 244, 7 November 2003; BBC News 'Violent unrest rocks Uzbekistan', at http:news.bbc.co.uk/2/hi/aia-pacific/3581341.stm, 30/03/04; and IWPR, *RCA*, 309, 20 August 2004.

[7] R Kangas, 'The three faces of Islam in Uzbekistan', *Transitions*, 1 (24), 29 December 1995, p 21.

[8] See, for example, '11 September and its aftermath: the geopolitics of terror', *Geopolitics*, 8 (3), Special Edition, Autumn 2003.

[9] The UK Terrorism Act 2000, Chapter 11, Part 1.

[10] Jangy Zaman, Osh, 0000 gmt, 5 December 2003.

[11] Uzbek TV First Channel, 1620 gmt, 15 December 2000; and *Inson va Qonun*, 11 May 2004, pp 1–3. Article 159 also does not distinguish between violent and non-violent anti-constitutional rhetoric and actions, such as calls for the establishment of a caliphate.

[12] Khabar Television, 1500 gmt, 10 November 2003.

[13] *Ibid*, emphasis added.

206

14 The other groups were the IMU/Islamic Movement of Turkestan (IMT); the East Turkestan Liberation Organisation and The East Turkestan Islamic Movement. ITAR-TASS, 0849 gmt, 19 November 2003.

15 See, for example, Jangy Zaman, Osh, 00000 gmt.

16 ITAR-TASS, 0849 gmt, 19 November 2003.

17 Quoted in O Allison, 'Uzbek authorities mobilize mass media to counter Islamic radical threat', at Eurasianet.org, 16 August 2004.

18 Uzbek TV First Channel, 1620 gmt, 15 December 2000.

19 *Ibid.*

20 ICG, 'Radical Islam in Central Asia: responding to Hizb ut-Tahrir,' *Asia Report*, 58, June 2003, p 33; IWPR, *RCA*, 244, 7 November 2003; BBC News, 'Violent unrest rocks Uzbekistan', at http:news.bbc.-co.uk/2/hi/aia-pacific/3581341.stm, 30 March 2004; and IWPR, *RAC*, 309, 20 August 2004.

21 IWPR, *RCA*, 244, 7 November 2003.

22 IWPR, *RCA*, 309, 20 August 2004.

23 See Kavkazcenter.com.

24 See, for example, IWPR, *RCA*, 309, 20 August 2004.

25 For discussion on HT and the use of violence, see ICG, 'Radical Islam in Central Asia', p 25.

26 *Kommersant*, 5 September 2003. Germany has banned HT for its anti-Semitism and incitement to violence under its 1964 Law on Association. DDP news agency, 0753 gmt, 15 January 2003.

27 In 2003 the FCO estimated that there are up to 7000 political and religious prisoners in Uzbekistan. The vast majority of these were accused of belonging to HT. Foreign and Commonwealth Office, *The Foreign and Commonwealth Office Human Rights Annual Report 2003*, at http://www.fco.gov.uk/Files/kfile/FullReport.pdf, p 29. HT members have received sentences in excess of 10 years for simply carrying or distributing leaflets. Those sentenced for involvement in the spring 2004 bombings received sentences ranging from three to 20 years.

28 *Vecherniy Bishkek*, 28 May 1999; *Megapolis*, 4 April 2001, p 9; and ICG Central Asia, 'Islamist mobilisation and regional security', *Asia Report*, 14, 1 March 2001, p 18.

29 Independent and/or substantiated evidence of any activity by these groups is very limited at best, and certainly so after the early 1990s, when there may have been a number of small 'kitchen-table' groups who took advantage of the period's brief spell of political openness. The fact that court cases in Central Asia at present focus on HT, IMU and Wahhabi members also suggests that there may not be any other significant Islamist groups active in the region.

30 M Fredholm, *Uzbekistan and the Threat from Islamic Extremism*, CSRC, K 39, March 2003, p 15.

31 *Ibid*; also see S Horsman, 'Security issues facing the newly independent states of Central Asia', PhD thesis, University of Sheffield, 1999, pp 247–253.

32 See, for example, N Melvin, *Uzbekistan: Transition to Authoritarianism on the Silk Road*, Amsterdam: Harwood Academic, 2000, p 57.

33 *Narodnye Slovo* (Tashkent), 4 February 1995; BBC, *Inside Central Asia*, 211, 16–22 February 1998, p 1. In 1996 Rafik Saifulin, Uzbekistani Institute of Strategic and Regional Studies, blamed Afghanistan, Iran and Pakistan for the perceived rise in 'Islamic fundamentalism' in the Ferghana Valley. R Saifulin, author's interview, Tashkent, 31 October 1996. See also L Usmanov, 'Will the Islamic factor determine the country's future?', *Nezavisimaya gazeta*, 6 January 1994; A Komilov, MENA, 18 October 1998, quoted in Kangas, 'The three faces of Islam in Uzbekistan', p 20.

34 V Naumkin, *Militant Islam in Central Asia: The Case of the Islamic Movement of Uzbekistan*, Berkeley, CA: University of California, 2003, pp 33–34.

35 Amnesty International, *Fear of Forcible Deportation/Fear of Torture*, UA 305/01, 29 January 2001; and Amnesty International, *Uzbekistan: The Rhetoric of Human Rights Protection: Briefing for the United Nations Human Rights Committee*, London, June 2001, p 19. There are serious concerns about the reliability of Askarov's and many other confessions in Uzbekistan. As the FCO has reported, jail sentences often followed unfair trials including the use of torture 'to secure confessions, upon which nearly all prosecution cases rest'. FCO, *Human Rights Annual Report 2003*, p 29.

36 See Harakat website, 29 November 2003.

37 Blofeld is the fictional criminal mastermind in Ian Fleming's James Bond novel. S Montefiore, *Stalin: In the Court of the Red Tsar*, London: Weidenfeld & Nicolson, 2003, p 169.

38 Uzbek TV first channel, 1430 gmt, 19 August 2004 (in Russian).

39 ITAR-TASS, 0623 gmt, 8 October 2004.

40 Adolat, 8 November 2002.

41 See, for example, ICG, 'Central Asia: drugs and conflict', *Asia Report*, 25, 26 November 2001, p 9; and M Fredholm, *Uzbekistan and the Threat from Islamic Extremism*, p 7.

42 Whitlock, *Beyond the Oxus*, p 254.

43 T Makarenko, quoted in Naumkin, *Militant Islam in Central Asia*, p 26.

44 Naumkin, *Militant Islam in Central Asia*, p 48.

45 *Ibid*, p 27.

46 See, for example, O Ruzaliev, 'The Islamic Movement of Uzbekistan: lines to complete the portrait', *Central Asia and the Caucasus*, 3 (27), 2004, p 28.

47 M Rajabova, in *Inson va Qonun*, 11 May 2004, pp 1–3; and O Usmanov, in *Novosti Nedeli*, 6 May 2004, pp 32–33. For a detailed analysis of HT, see S Taji-Farouki, *A Fundamentalist Quest*, London: Grey Seal, 1996.

48 See Fredholm, *Uzbekistan and the Threat from Islamic Extremism*, p 13.

49 As the FCO notes, there have been a number of high profile HT deaths in custody, probably the result of torture. FCO, *Human Rights Annual Report 2003* , p 29; and *Tojikiston*, 27 May 2004, pp 1, 9.

50 See, for example, Keston News Service, 'Central Asia: former Islamic fighter recounts life in training camp', 18 December 2001; and Uzbek Radio First Programme, 1400 gmt, 4 September 2003.

51 President I Karimov, quoted on Uzbek TV First Channel, 1600 gmt, 3 December 2003.

52 Whether Uzbekistan was progressing towards democracy by 1999 is, however, moot. See, for example, Interfax, 'Uzbekistan: OSCE says Uzbekistan presidential elections undemocratic', 14 January 2000. In 2002 Freedom House defined Uzbekistan as a 'Consolidated Autocrac(y) [that] show(ed) no momentum towards meaningful political liberalization'. Freedom House, *Nations in Transit 2002: A Mixed Picture of Change*, p 16, at http://www.freedomhouse.org/research/nitransit/2002/karatnyck-y_essay2002.pdf.

53 G Yemelianova, 'The impact of the post-11 September "war on terrorism" on Central Asia's Umma', paper presented at the CREES Annual Conference, Cumberland Lodge, 13–15 June 2003.

54 A Rashid, quoted in Ruzaliev, 'The Islamic Movement of Uzbekistan', p 25.

55 Quoted in *Zerkalo*, XXI, 30 November 2003.

56 Quoted in 'Uzbek government dismisses link between terrorism and poverty', *Eurasia Insight*, 4 May 2004.

57 O Allison, Eurasianet.org, 8 September 2004; See also Uzbek TV First Channel, 'Ministry of Interior, border guard and villager anti-terror exercise', 1530 gmt, 21 May 2004; and, for a non-Uzbekistani example, see 'Be vigilant or there will be trouble',*Vecherniy Bishkek*, 10 November 2003, p 7;

58 Uzbek TV First Channel, 'Ministry of Interior, border guard and villager anti-terror exercise'.

59 For discussion of the use of another security threat, the Tajik civil war, in Uzbekistan's nation- and state building programmes, see Horsman, 'Uzbekistan's involvement in the Tajik civil war', pp 37–48.

60 Safayev, op cit. There are claims, however, that the public response to the March 2004 bombings was at best apathetic, with mistrust of the official version of events and little sympathy for the police causalities. See IWPR, *RCA*, 275, 6 May 2004.

61 Rashid, quoted in Ruzaliev, 'The Islamic Movement of Uzbekistan', p 25.

62 See, for example, B Dave, 'Inventing Islam—and an Islamic threat—in Kazakhstan', *Transitions*, 1 (24), 29 December 1995, pp 22–25.

63 For more on Mohammad Yusuf's period as Chief Mufti, see M Haghayegni, *Islam and Politics in Central Asia*, Basingstoke: Macmillan, 1995, pp 162–163; and MB Olcott, 'Islam and fundamentalism in independent Central Asia', in Y Ro'i (ed), *Muslim Eurasia: Conflicting Legacies*, Ilford: Frank Cass, 1995. For his current, independent views, see 'Uzbekistan—former chief mufti calls for lifting of restrictions on Islam', *Forum 18*, 1 November 2004.

64 See, for example, Uzbek BBC World Service, 1600 gmt, 11 September 2003; and ICG, 'Radical Islam in Central Asia', p 35.

65 Naumkin, *Militant Islam in Central Asia*, pp 18–20.

66 *Ibid*, p 21.

67 *Ibid*.

68 *Ibid*, p 19.

69 *Ibid*, pp 18–21.

70 *Ibid*, p 53.

71 The IMU's more specific goals were: the freeing of all religious prisoners in Uzbekistan; the removal of President Karimov's government; and the establishment of a *sharia*-based state. IMU statement, 28 August 1999; and ITAR-TASS, 28 October 1999, p 48.

72 IMU statement, 28 August 1999; and Voice of the Islamic Republic of Iran, 1530 gmt, 11 October 1999.

73 Quoted in B Pannier, 'Central Asia: IMU leader says group's goal is return of Islam', *RFE/RL*, 6 June 2001.

74 A Rashid, *Jihad: The Rise of Militant Islam in Central Asia*, London: Yale University Press, 2002, p 13, quoted in Hizb ut-Tahrir, 'The inaccuracies of the book 'Jihad: The Rise of Militant Islam in Central Asia' written by Ahmed Rashid, Yale University Press, ISBN 03093454', at http:www.war-against-terrorism.info/waragiant/article/articles14.htm, accessed 1 September 2002.

75 See, for example, HT, 'The Constitution of Uzbekistan is the law of disbelief and falsehood', 7 December 2001; and *Andijonnoma*, 23 June 2001, p 2.

76 Personal communication with the author.

77 See, for example, one of HT's websites, www.war-against-terrorism.com.

[78] Whitlock, *Beyond the Oxus*, pp 242–264.

[79] *Ibid*, p 246.

[80] Reuters, 2 May 1998, quoted in Bohr, *Uzbekistan*, p 29; and Montefiore, *Stalin*, p 171.

[81] Haghayegni, *Islam and Politics in Central Asia*, p 17.

[82] Whitlock, *Beyond the Oxus*, p 246.

[83] See for example, N Usmanov, 'Useful points of collaboration', *Kommunist uzbekistana*, June 1989, pp 47–48.

[84] Arena, at http://www.freeuz.org, 14 August 2004.

[85] Whitlock, *Beyond the Oxus*, pp 253–254.

[86] *Ibid*, p 96. See also A Vaksberg, *The Prosecutor and the Prey: Vyshinsky and the 1930s Moscow Show Trials*, London: Weidenfeld & Nicolson, 1990, p 139.

[87] J Voll, 'Central Asia as part of the modern Islamic world', in BF Manz (ed), *Central Asia in Historical Perspective*, Boulder, CO: Westview Press, 1994, p 65.

[88] Y Ro'i, *Islam in the CIS: A Threat to Stability?*, London: Royal Institute of International Affairs, 2001, pp 26–27.

[89] The term Wahhabism was used by the Soviets and now by the post-Soviet governments pejoratively for any Islamic group or trend they wished to label as seditious. Z Baran (ed), *Understanding Sufism and its Potential Role in US Policy*, Washington, DC: Nixon Center, 2 May 2004.

[90] See Torjesen, 'Distortions in the discourse of danger', p 14.

[91] I Karimov, interview with *Komsomolskaya pravda*, quoted in ITAR-TASS World Service, 1131 gmt, 12 February 1993, SWB SU 1616, B4 18/2/93.

# Index

For Product Safety Concerns and Information please contact our EU representative GPSR@taylorandfrancis.com Taylor & Francis Verlag GmbH, Kaufingerstraße 24, 80331 München, Germany

Batch number: 08151941

Printed by Printforce, the Netherlands